NO PRICE TOO HIGH

CANADIANS AND THE SECOND WORLD WAR

DND/NATIONAL ARCHIVES OF CANADA

**Funeral for soldiers of the Black Watch,
Ossendrecht, Netherlands.**

Canadian troops outside burning jail, Caen, France, 1944.

NO PRICE TOO HIGH

CANADIANS AND THE SECOND WORLD WAR

TERRY COPP

with
RICHARD NIELSEN

Foreword by
BARNEY DANSON

McGraw-Hill Ryerson Limited
Toronto New York Auckland Bogotá Caracas
Lisbon London Madrid Mexico Milan New Delhi
San Juan Singapore Sydney Tokyo

No Price Too High

McGraw-Hill Ryerson Limited
300 Water Street
Whitby, Ontario LIN 9B6

1 2 3 4 5 6 7 8 9 TRI 4 3 2 1 0 9 8 7 6

Printed and bound in Canada

Canadian Cataloguing in Publication Data

Copp, Terry, 1938–
  No price too high

Includes bibliographical references and index.
ISBN 0-07-552713-8

1. World War, 1939–1945 – Canada. I. Title.

D768.15.C6 1995   940.54′0971   C95-932426-7

PUBLISHER ~ Joan Homewood
DESIGNER AND PROJECT CO-ORDINATOR ~ Robin Brass
PRODUCTION CO-ORDINATOR ~ Sharon Hudson
PAGE MAKEUP ~ Robin Brass Studio
COPY EDITOR ~ Lynn Schellenberg
MAPS ~ Paul Kelly, Gecko Graphics (except p.200, Molly Brass)

H.G. AIKMAN/DND/NATIONAL ARCHIVES OF CANADA/PA108174

Nursing sisters of No. 10 Canadian General Hospital, Royal Canadian Army Medical Corps, Arromanches, France, July 23, 1944.

CONTENTS

Airmen departing from Winnipeg's Canadian Pacific Railway station for overseas service, 1940.

WESTERN CANADA PICTORIAL INDEX/UNIVERSITY OF WINNIPEG

FOREWORD

ANY OF THOSE AMONG US WHO SERVED in the armed forces during the Second World War and lost close friends in battle believe that later generations of Canadians have had little opportunity to learn about this important part of our nation's story. The achievement as well as the sacrifice of Canadians needs to be understood and the events approached in the context of a war that was fought for the noblest of aims.

No Price Too High is written from the perspective of those who actually participated in this monumental struggle. The men and women of the army, navy, air force and merchant navy, their sweethearts and families, as well as those who served on the homefront, are portrayed in their own words, and the narration seeks to place events in the context of the times.

No Price Too High explains the political and military realities that challenged Canadians to participate in a just and necessary war. Their hopes and fears demanded that every military resource available be used to win the war. The very real prospect of defeat, with all its consequences, was particularly threatening in the early years of the conflict and called forth a supreme effort from the Canadian people.

The tragic loss of lives, the disruption of family life, the arbitrary displacement of people and the considerable political tensions of the war years were part of a struggle against the "most monstrous tyranny" known to humanity. The marvel was that this nation of some eleven million people, scattered over a vast land mass, saw almost a million of its sons and daughters voluntarily enlist in defence of their democratic way of life. To transform a small, virtually unequipped military into a powerful army, navy and air force was a remarkable achievement. To accomplish this while developing a powerful industrial sector and expanding food and raw material production was a miracle. Canada's extraordinary war record helped to establish this nation as an important participant in world affairs at the United Nations and elsewhere.

The film series that inspired the book was conceived by Richard Nielsen and Anderson Charters. Their proposal offered the opportunity to tell the story of the war in a way that would allow the voices of veterans to be clearly heard.

I was so taken with their approach that I committed myself to seeing that this series was produced. The first step was to incorporate the No Price Too High Foundation with a distinguished Board of Directors. More than $1.5 million was raised from foundations, corporations, veterans organizations and the many generous private citizens who shared our concern that the story be told while those who participated are still alive.

The Board of Directors was augmented by other distinguished veterans to form an Advisory Committee available to assist the producers, writers and film editors. They read successive versions of the scripts and viewed early "cuts" of the films, providing valuable advice at each stage.

The corvette HMCS *Barrie*, June 1945.

The producers had full authority and control of all aspects of the production, but they benefitted immensely from the opportunity to receive input and reaction from men and women who were participants in the events described.

Anderson Charters organized a nationwide search for letters, photographs and diaries that would allow the voices of ordinary men and women to be heard. The Foundation wishes to express its thanks to all those who responded to our request for assistance. Terry Copp, Professor of History at Wilfrid Laurier University and author of a number of books on Canada's war effort, joined the team as a consultant and "on camera" commentator.

The book version of *No Price Too High* combines the photographs and first-person accounts assembled for the film series with a new and original narrative, written by Terry Copp. Professor Copp has drawn on ideas developed in the film script by Richard Nielsen and James Wallen but the book is intended to complement the films, not reproduce the script.

The Board of Directors of the No Price Too High Foundation believe that this project will provide all Canadian, especially future generations, with an opportunity to understand an important part of our national heritage.

THE HONOURABLE BARNETT J. DANSON, PC
CHAIRMAN, NO PRICE TOO HIGH FOUNDATION

Board of Directors, No Price Too High Foundation

Chairman, Hon. Barnett J. Danson, PC

St. Clair Balfour, OC, DSC, BA, LLD
Col. John H.C. Clarry, MBE, ED, CD, QC
Robert G. Dale, DSO, DFC, CD
Hon. Willard Z. Estey, CC, QC
Hon. Alastair Gillespie, PC
Russell E. Harrison
Hon. Hartland de M. Molson, OC
BGen. W. Denis Whitaker, DSO & BAR, CM, ED, CD
David Wishart, FCA

Advisory Committee
Russell E. Bannock, DSO, DFC
Col. J. Douglas Crashley, CM, CD
Catherine Drinkwater
LCol Thomas Gilday, DSO, ED
Anthony Griffin
Vice-Admiral Ralf Hennessy
Col. George E. Renison, DSO, CD

Secretary, Agnes Vanya

PREFACE

IN THE FIRST DECADE AFTER THE WAR, Canadians had little difficulty understanding the achievements and sacrifices of the men and women of the armed forces; the horrors of the Third Reich were fresh in everyone's mind. No one doubted that Canadians had made a major contribution to the defeat of an enemy that had threatened the survival of civilization.

In the 1960s and '70s, however, a new generation, which knew only the benefits of postwar prosperity and little of the costs, began more and more to question the validity of all wars, perhaps because the war they saw on television in Vietnam seemed to lack legitimacy. Writing and film making about the Second World War more often portrayed Canadian veterans as the victims of unscrupulous politicians or incompetent commanders. The battles fought were at times portrayed as unnecessary and without purpose.

This stirred a deep response among people who remembered the times and the importance of the issues involved. All across the nation, veterans gathered to talk to one another and to seek ways of re-establishing an accurate collective memory of the meaning of the sacrifices of war.

This was the context within which the No Price Too High Foundation was established. The veterans who worked tirelessly to raise the money for the No Price Too High television series were determined that their story should be told.

The book *No Price Too High* was written in the same spirit.

Acknowledgements
Sections of this book are based on my previous work, including *Maple Leaf Route* (5 vols.) written with the late Robert Vogel and my articles for *Legion Magazine*. As with all my other work on the Second World War, Bob Vogel's influence is ever present.

No Price Too High was written under considerable

Ground crew maintaining a Lancaster bomber of No. 6 Group, RCAF.

pressure to meet an early deadline. This would not have been possible without the assistance of Anderson and Susan Charters, Lana Pitkin, Esther Bruce, Lynne Doyle, Michael Bechthold, Allan Thurrott, Linda Copp, Ken Macpherson, Larry Milberry, Carl Christie, Lynn Schellenberg, Paul Kelly, Molly Brass and the production team at McGraw-Hill Ryerson. The following researchers employed by Norflicks Productions assisted with the documentary and photo research: Mary Burnel, Barbara Chernin, Robert C. Dalzell, Serge Durflinger, Louise Elliott, Christopher Gagosz, Christine Hamlin, Barbara Lugtenburg, Susan Rajsic, Dominic Stubbs and Rachel Zolf.

I was a reluctant convert to Richard Nielsen's approach to the scripts of the "No Price Too High" documentary series and it was not until I saw the first "rough cuts" that the conversion was complete. The book version has been strongly influenced by Richard Nielsen's vision and I hope his ideas are fairly represented here. Barney Danson read the manuscript and offered helpful comments on many issues. Joan Homewood, publisher of trade and professional books at McGraw-Hill Ryerson, offered valuable advice throughout the writing period.

Robin Brass selected the letters and photographs and with his outstanding design put the material into a format that captures both the impressionism of the film series and the linear narrative of the text. *No Price Too High* benefits greatly from Robin's creativity.

Errors, omissions and opinions are the sole responsibility of the author.

TERRY COPP
WILFRID LAURIER UNIVERSITY

The destroyer **HMCS** *Ottawa* in 1938, one of the six destroyers in the Royal Canadian Navy at the outbreak of war.

NATIONAL ARCHIVES OF CANDA/PA182833

PART I

FOLLY

British Prime Minister Neville Chamberlain is mobbed by reporters on his arrival from Munich, where he met Hitler and reached the agreement that betrayed Czechoslovakia to win "peace for our time."

THE DECISION TO BUILD A GREAT MEMORIAL on Vimy Ridge, "to commemorate the heroism ... and the victories of the Canadian soldier in the Great War," was finalized in the spring of 1922. The House of Commons offered unanimous support for a motion to create a large memorial park dedicated "to Canada's ideals, to Canada's courage and to Canada's devotion to what the people of this land decreed to be right."

Vimy was to be the site of the largest Canadian memorial but seven others were also to be built. In Newfoundland, then a separate British colony, a similar commitment to remembering the sacrifices and achievements of the Royal Newfoundland Regiment led to the construction of five "Caribou" monuments marking the Regiment's battlefields. The largest, at Beaumont-Hamel, was dedicated in 1922 with Field Marshal Haig as the guest of honour.

Haig, the Commander-in-Chief of the armies of Britain and its Commonwealth-Empire in France, was widely respected as the general who had defeated the Kaiser's armies and saved the world from the menace of German aggression. When Haig visited Canada in 1925 to mediate a dispute among veterans' organizations, he was greeted by large, enthusiastic crowds anxious to applaud the man who had led the Allies to victory.

The eastern face of the Vimy Memorial. The architect, Walter S. Allward, described his concept in these words: "At the base of the strong impregnable wall of defence are the defenders, one group showing the breaking of the sword [lower left], the other the sympathy of the Canadians for the helpless (inset). On the wall stands the heroic figure of Canada brooding over her valiant dead." "The Defenders – The Breaking of the Sword" sculpture was modified to remove "militaristic" imagery.

NATIONAL ARCHIVES OF CANADA/PA183629 (INSET: LCMSDS/WILFRID LAURIER UNIVERSITY)

The idea that the First World War was a heroic and successful struggle to defeat German militarism was shared by the vast majority of people in Britain, France and Canada. There was also broad support for the peace settlement embodied in the Treaty of Versailles. Germany, it was believed, had started the war and would have to pay the price. The destruction of much of Belgium and northern France was to be compensated for by payment of reparations so that homes, factories, churches and schools could be rebuilt.

Germany was also required to restore Alsace-Lorraine to France and to transfer territory to the new state of Poland. Strict limitations were placed on Germany's military, which was forbidden to own tanks, warplanes or large ships. The part of Germany on the west bank of the Rhine was demilitarized to hamper an easy advance into the heart of France. These and other measures, designed to prevent Germany from renewing the campaign to dominate Europe by force, were seen as legitimate ways of preventing another war, while the newly established League of Nations and International Court of Justice worked out the rules for a new international order.

This view of the Great War and the peace settlement was never accepted within Germany and quickly became unfashionable among liberal and left-wing intellectuals in Britain, the United States and Canada. The history of the origins of the war was "revised" to argue that Germany had been drawn into the war reluctantly by her allies. The real causes of the war were said to be rival imperialisms, the naval race, the armaments industry or simply capitalism. If Germany was no more "guilty" than France or Britain, the moral basis for restraining German military power or requiring reparations did not exist.

The development of "revisionist" ideas about the causes of the war was paralleled by a growing disillusionment with the heroic image of the soldiers. The fighting on the western front had killed millions of young men under circumstances which were easily condemned. The very nature of trench warfare, with its battles for a few hundred yards of mud, enraged critics. The generals, or at least the British generals, who ordered attacks like those on the Somme in 1916 were caricatured as "donkeys" or criminals. Haig, the soldier's hero, came in for particularly harsh criticism.

The poets, novelists and journalists who portrayed the Great War as a futile dance of death felt no obligation to explain what they would have done in Haig's place. After 1914 the presence of large German armies on Belgian and French soil created a dilemma for both sides. The Germans had failed to force a French surrender but they had won a major victory. If an armistice was to be negotiated, Germany would dictate the terms. Neither side would discuss the question because both were confident a decisive victory could be won on the battlefield.

The Germans launched the first great offensives of 1915. One was directed at the Ypres salient where the 1st Canadian Infantry Division fought with great valour in the face of repeated attacks using chlorine gas. In 1916 the German army sought to bleed the French army to death by attacking at Verdun. The British agreed to try to take the pressure off their ally by mounting a point offensive along the River Somme. When it was over, a million men had died, with equal losses on both sides.

The year ended with a military stalemate and a

LCMSDS/WILFRID LAURIER UNIVERSITY
The "Caribou" at Beaumont-Hamel, a Newfoundland and now Canadian memorial park in the Somme Valley. Here on July 1, 1916, the Royal Newfoundland Regiment suffered 684 casualties, of which 310 were fatal. The regiment was rebuilt and fought in a number of successful battles which are marked today by smaller versions of the Caribou monument.

13

variety of peace proposals, all of which depended on the willingness of France and Britain to accept at least a partial German victory, something neither parliamentary nor public opinion was willing to support. For 1917 the German plan was to fight defensively in France while starving Britain by waging unrestricted submarine war. This strategy brought the United States into the conflict in April 1917, forcing the German General Staff to plan to end the war before the large numbers of American troops reached Europe.

In 1917 the Allies mounted new offensives using innovative tactics. At Vimy Ridge the well-rehearsed Canadian Corps won a splendid victory, but it went unexploited; the offensive of which it was a part sputtered and died. Elsewhere the stalemate continued. The year 1918 brought the threat of a decisive German breakthrough. The October Revolution had taken Russia out of the war, allowing Germany to transfer troops to the west. The American buildup was very slow and it would be mid-summer before their expeditionary force was ready. When the German offensive faltered, the German army had suffered more than one million casualties. Their generals recognized that the four-year-long struggle to dominate western Europe had failed. After the Al-

lied counter-offensive began at Amiens on August 8, 1918, the Kaiser was warned that his army had "reached the limits of its capacity." This was the "black day" of the German army, but it took another three months of hard fighting to force the surrender on the eleventh hour of the eleventh day of the eleventh month of 1918.

In Canada, as in other countries, the battle over the meaning of the Great War divided reasonable men and women. Veterans and the more conservative and pro-British elements of the population, who were the large majority in English-speaking Canada, clung to their original view of the war. In French Canada there was a broad, if unsophisticated, consensus that it had all been futile and that English-speaking Canadians had supported the war and conscription out of unthinking loyalty to Britain.

The "revisionist" approach to the war found its strongest support among intellectuals with ties to the Protestant churches. In 1914 leaders of all denominations had embraced the Allied cause as a moral crusade. In the postwar years, many church leaders were embarrassed by the zeal they had displayed and sought to restore Christian pacifism to their message. Pacifism was frequently justified on secular rather than religious grounds, drawing on literary and historical sources.

Scenes from the Battle of Vimy Ridge, April 1917: Canadians are seen advancing through German wire entanglements (above) and consolidating their positions in the shellhole-pocked landscape (top right). Stretcher bearers and German prisoners bring in the wounded, and (bottom right) King George V visits the battle site, escorted by the looming figure of General Arthur Currie and, at right, General Sir Henry Horne, commander of First British Army. General Currie, a Vancouver militia officer, succeeded Sir Julian Byng in command of the Canadian Corps in June 1917.

As early as 1926 Agnes McPhail, the first woman to become a member of parliament, articulated this quasi-pacifist position, challenging a reference to the Vimy Memorial as honouring the "nobility" of the sacrifice made by young Canadians.

"Will the honourable member admit," she asked, "that what caused the late war is the cause of all wars? Will he admit that the prime cause was an economic one, and that the protection of women and children was no part of it?" George Nicholson, who had served with the Canadian Corps in France, replied that he would admit to nothing of the kind.

The debate over the causes of the war and the nature of the settlement was a minor theme in Canadian life, particularly after the onset of the Great Depression of the

1930s. Canadians were, after all, rarely involved in the international discussions that dealt with German grievances against Versailles. For Great Britain and France the issues were of vital importance. Generally speaking, the French, fearing a restoration of German military power, which they were sure would be used against them, favoured strict enforcement of the disarmament clauses of the peace treaty. British resolve to prevent another European war was undermined by revisionism, pacifism and depression.

The Great Depression of the 1930s threw thousands out of work in North America and Europe and created fertile conditions for political extremism on the left and right. Shown here are relief camp strikers on their "On to Ottawa Trek" in 1935.

None of this would have mattered very much if Germany had continued to be governed by "normal" nationalist politicians merely seeking to undo Versailles and reclaim full sovereignty for their nation-state. No doubt such leaders would have sought territorial revisions and threatened the European balance of power, but it is unlikely that any of them would have deliberately set out to start a major war of conquest.

Adolf Hitler was not a "normal" political leader. With hindsight it is difficult to understand why this fact was not understood earlier, but even Winston Churchill had declared he had no "prejudices against Hitler" in 1932. The following year, with Hitler now Chancellor of Germany, the students of the Oxford Union, the university's debating society, voted overwhelmingly in favour of the resolution "that this house refuses to fight for King and country." In the House of Commons the British government presented a program calling for parity between the French and German armies.

Hitler's seizure of absolute power and the brutal execution of his rivals in the Nazi movement forced some individuals to reconsider. The systematic anti-semitism embodied in the Nuremberg Laws of 1935 horrified millions worldwide and led to much criticism of the Nazi movement, but few related these developments to the threat of war. When Hitler introduced conscription and announced that Germany had already achieved parity with Britain in air power, France responded by doubling its own term of compulsory military service to two years. The British government preferred renewed efforts to promote arms control, signing a naval agreement with Germany that "limited" the German navy to one-third the strength of the Royal Navy. France was not consulted.

The Italian invasion of Ethiopia launched in October 1935 turned attention away from German developments. For a brief period it appeared as if the League of Nations might act effectively by employing sanctions against Italy. The vital resolution, adding petroleum, iron and steel to the list of embargoed goods, was presented to the League by Canadian delegate Walter Riddell and became known as the "Canadian resolution." The debate coincided with the defeat of the Conservatives under R.B. Bennett and the return to office of Mackenzie King and the Liberal party. King and his Quebec lieutenant, Ernest Lapointe, moved quickly to repudiate Riddell's actions, declaring that he had spoken only for himself. The Canadians did not intend to take any initiative on sanctions.

King's position was sharply criticized in English-speaking Canada, where many had hoped that the crisis would establish the authority of the League of Nations and advance the ideal of collective security. In the end, the Canadian position mattered little, for the British and the French governments had already concocted an agreement that allowed Mussolini to continue his war.

There was more to come. In March 1936, Hitler announced his intention to reoccupy the Rhineland with German troops. As he spoke, thousands of his soldiers streamed across the Rhine. This was no mere violation of Versailles; Germany had freely signed a treaty at Locarno in 1925 agreeing to respect existing territorial boundaries and to maintain the Rhineland as a demilitarized zone. For France the presence of German troops on the west bank of the Rhine was a frightening prospect. With a much smaller population than Germany's, France could raise an army only half the size of Germany's. Britain had no army to speak of and the United States was deeply isolationist. The French government hesitated, while the British urged caution and an appeal to the League of Nations. Resolute action would probably have forced Hitler to back down and might have led to his overthrow, but nothing was done. The Rhineland was fortified and Belgium, convinced that France and Britain lacked resolve, declared its neutrality, undermining France's defensive strategy. The year 1936

The Axis dictators: Benito Mussolini (centre) and Adolf Hitler (right). Mussolini, who had seized power in Italy a decade before Hitler came to power, was nevertheless the junior partner in the Axis. His refusal to declare war until France was on the edge of collapse won him the contempt of German military leaders. At the far left is Hermann Göring, commander-in-chief of the Luftwaffe, who committed suicide in 1946 while on trial at Nuremberg. Rudolf Hess (centre, just behind Hitler) was Hitler's deputy until he flew to Scotland in 1941 on a personal "peace" mission intended to convince the British to accept Nazi control of Europe.

NATIONAL ARCHIVES OF CANADA/PA 11478

was the turning point. France and Britain had abdicated responsibility. Hitler would now determine the fate of Europe.

It was in the summer of 1936 that the Vimy Memorial was finally completed. Tens of thousands of visitors were expected, including Canadian veterans and their families who were to travel together to the national memorial. When news that King Edward VIII would preside over the ceremonies was released, the event became the focus of world attention.

A great deal had happened since the architect, Walter S. Allward of Toronto, had designed the memorial in 1922. He described the original concept in heroic terms, emphasizing the values for which Canadians had fought and died. Historical revisionism and the general revulsion from war led to important modifications. The monument, planned as a tribute to the valour, the heroism and the battlefield victories of the Canadian Corps, was transformed by the decision to inscribe on it the names of the 19,000 Canadian soldiers who had no known grave. The monument was now to be an empty tomb, a place of pilgrimage akin to the war cemeteries. The imagery was also changed. Allward's sculpture "The Defenders – The Breaking of the Sword" had originally included a recognizable German coal-scuttle helmet, crushed under the foot of one of the figures. This detail was seen as "too militaristic" and was dropped from the final design.

The "pilgrimage" of 1936, which took place in the shadow of Mussolini's conquest and Hitler's threat to the

Headlines in the Toronto *Globe* of July 25, 1936, announce a major defeat for General Francisco Franco's Fascist forces early in the Spanish Civil War, which dragged on from 1936 to 1939. With military support from Hitler and Mussolini and no significant opposition from the democracies, Franco ultimately prevailed. Other stories on this page describe the trial of some relief workers who rioted, a polio outbreak during the Manitoba election, and the program of the Vimy Memorial dedication.

peace of Europe, was also shaped by the shifting currents of collective memory. At the dedication ceremony, the main speeches given by the King, the President of France and Marshal Philippe Pétain explored the themes of sacrifice and remembrance and made strong appeals for peace. No one suggested that the lesson of Vimy Ridge was the need for well-trained, well-equipped armies capable of defeating a ruthless enemy.

The pilgrimage, like the Vimy Memorial itself, was full of ambiguities. Was it in celebration of the achievement of the Canadian Corps, or in honour of those killed in a tragic and pointless war? Was it an imperial event solidifying Canada's relationship with its new king, or a statement about an independent Canadian nation? Was the monument to be seen as a remonstrance against war or a warning to aggressors that Canada would again play its part if France and Britain were endangered? In the end, no one could say, because in 1936 Canadians had yet to make up their minds on who they were or what role they wished to play.

HITLER

By the time Adolf Hitler seized control of the German state in the summer of 1934, the racist fantasies that fuelled his manic ambition were ready to be translated into a strategic plan. In *Mein Kampf* he had argued for a world in which war between the races was to be the natural order. The Aryan "master race," of which the German people were the purest manifestation, would dominate Europe, enhancing its vigour in the struggle to crush and enslave inferior groups.

Before Germany could launch the campaign to conquer "living space," *Lebensraum*, in the east and lay the foundations of the "Thousand Year Reich," it was necessary to "purify" German society. Jews and the "Jewish-liberal" and "Jewish-Bolshevik" institutions they had created must be purged. Parliaments, unions, the free press, the rule of law and all other "Jewish" institutions would be destroyed. The Jews themselves must be removed from Germany.

Hitler rejected the restrictions imposed by the Versailles Treaty, instructing the military to develop armed forces strong enough to overwhelm all potential enemies. Austria, Hitler's birthplace, would be incorporated into a greater Reich. Czechoslovakia, a creation of Versailles, with its German-language minority, would also be dealt with by force if necessary.

Hitler had no precise timetable in mind, but he never doubted that once Czechoslovakia was neutralized France would be next. The French army was the only military power capable of thwarting his ambitions and there could be no turn to the east until that threat had been dealt with. Britain was to be kept out of Europe by diplomacy or fear. Hitler had no desire to destroy the British Empire so long as the British did not interfere with his plans. The United States, a "mongrel nation," scarcely entered his thoughts. The Soviet state, made up of "subhumans," *Untermensch*, and ruled by Bolshevik terror, would collapse when confronted with his Aryan legions.

All this was quite clear in Hitler's fevered mind, but in 1936 he knew Germany was far too weak to carry out his

Adolf Hitler (left) spelled out his racial ideas and his plans for rebuilding German power in *Mein Kampf.* What others dismissed as ravings, he meant literally. He came to office constitutionally, but soon all real power was in the hands of his Nazi party. (Above right) Berlin troops swore to serve Hitler with unconditional obedience when he became president after the death of Hindenburg. The stagelike setting for the Nuremberg rally (below) was featured in the film *Triumph of the Will* and other Nazi propaganda material. Such brilliantly staged rallies whipped up mass fervour and demonstrations of loyalty.

Germans marching into the Rhineland, 1936. The Rhineland, which included the part of Germany on the west bank of the Rhine, had been "demilitarized" by the Treaty of Versailles to protect France against a sudden invasion. Germany had agreed to maintain this zone free of troops and fortifications in the Locarno Treaty of 1925. Hitler's decision to violate both treaties placed France in great danger but supporters of appeasement insisted "Hitler was only entering his back yard."

NATIONAL ARCHIVES OF CANADA/C24958

program. After conscription was introduced in 1934, the army expanded rapidly, but shortages of equipment and trained leaders took time to overcome. The same was true for the Luftwaffe. The German air force began the conversion to a new generation of fighters and bombers in 1936. By the summer of 1938, there were 3,000 combat aircraft available, though less than half were operational because aircrews had not completed training. The army reached a total of sixty divisions that summer, but only four were armoured, and they were largely equipped with light tanks of little military value.

Still, Hitler could wait no longer. In March 1938, the threat of a plebiscite, which might solidify anti-Nazi opinion in Austria, prompted an ultimatum and an order to occupy the country. There was no resistance, but the German war machine failed to perform as it had in propaganda films. Most of the tanks broke down and had to be towed away or loaded onto railway cars to reach Vienna. Germany was still not ready for combat with a serious enemy.

Hitler was nevertheless determined to advance his plans in 1938. On May 20, he instructed the army to prepare "Case Green," the conquest of Czechoslovakia. Hitler wanted a real war, one that would bring military glory and strike fear into the hearts of his enemies. He shrugged off protests about the strength of the Czech fortifications and the power of its army, demanding results. The Luftwaffe had practised terror bombing in the Spanish Civil War and the Czech air force was weak. It was, Hitler believed, a matter of will. The threat of French or

Winston Churchill told the British House of Commons that "Europe is confronted with a program of aggression, nicely calculated and timed, unfolding stage by stage, and there is only one choice open ... either to submit like Austria or else take effective measures while time remains...." His warning went unheeded.

British intervention was dismissed. Hitler was convinced that both governments were committed to policies of appeasement, which would give him full freedom to reshape the boundaries of Central Europe.

Neville Chamberlain, the British prime minister, cheated Hitler out of his war by agreeing to his demands for the annexation of the parts of Czechoslovakia occupied by the German-speaking minority. They had been citizens of the old Austro-Hungarian Empire. Their territory Sudetenland had never been part of Germany so Hitler's argument for union could not be related to Versailles; it had to be expressed in racial terms. The Munich Agreement stripped Czechoslovakia of its fortified frontier zone and demoralized its people, who had counted on the protection of their alliance with France.

Six months after Hitler declared that Sudetenland was his "last territorial ambition in Europe," he marched into Prague, seizing the Czech treasury, its armaments industry and the materiel to equip several new armoured divisions with Czech tanks and guns.

Poland was Hitler's next objective. He would have settled, at least temporarily, for territorial concessions and Polish support for his campaigns against France and Russia. The Poles resisted, and Hitler, unwilling to risk war on two fronts, authorized negotiations with his arch-enemy, the Soviet Union. The fact that Britain and France had "guaranteed" Poland, and had promised to declare war on Germany if Poland was attacked, caused him little difficulty. With Russia neutralized by the Soviet-German Non-Aggression Pact (with its secret clauses dividing Poland between the two), the western powers would not dare to challenge Germany. France could wait until the Polish question was resolved, then it too would be crushed.

At dawn on September 1, 1939, the German armies attacked Poland.

APPEASEMENT

The two-year period between Hitler's militarization of the Rhineland and the annexation of Austria witnessed a major shift in the European balance of power. In 1936, France, with its 100-division army, could have easily forced a German withdrawal and humiliated Hitler. By 1938, the fortification of its frontier with France and extensive rearmament meant that Germany was a formidable military power.

France still possessed the larger army, but successive political crises and the economic problems associated with the Depression forced the French military to postpone modernization, particularly in their air force. The French had designed excellent tanks and aircraft, but they were not organized to mass-produce such weapons.

France's most significant handicap was fear. No one could forget the losses suffered in the First World War and planning for another attritional struggle seemed almost suicidal. Belgium's decision to abandon its alliance with France, after Germany's occupation of the Rhineland, further undermined France's defensive strategy, creating new problems which no one knew how to solve.

Germany's borders under the Versailles treaty that ended the First World War. The Munich Agreement transferred the vital border areas of Czechoslovakia, where the country's fortifications were located, to Germany. France had now lost an ally that fielded twenty-one regular and sixteen reserve divisions and possessed the third largest armaments industry in Europe.

Worst of all, the British, who had fought side by side with the French in 1914–1918, had reduced their army to less than two divisions and were not planning any expansion.

Britain had begun to reverse the long process of disarmament in 1934, but the new resources were directed at the air force and navy. British strategists, including the government's sternest critic, Winston Churchill, believed that air power was the key to survival. Bombers would serve as a deterrent to German aggression while fighters would protect England from a "knock-out blow" from the air. Naval rearmament was directed not at anti-U-boat measures but at the construction of battleships, aircraft carriers and cruisers to strengthen the British Empire against the threat posed by the Italian and Japanese navies. These strategic priorities meant that in a conventional land war the French army would be left on its own to do battle with the Germans.

The British government, under both Stanley Baldwin, prime minister until 1937, and Neville Chamberlain, who succeeded him, was determined to prevent such a war from taking place. Almost everyone in Britain had lost a son, brother or nephew in the Great War and there was broad agreement that everything possible must be done to avoid another such conflict.

By 1938, the Chamberlain government believed that a policy they described as "appeasement" of the dictators would save Europe from war. France must be pressured to back away from its alliances in Central Europe, especially its guarantee of Czechoslovakia. Italy was to be appeased by recognizing its conquests in Africa and by avoiding criticism of its role in the Spanish Civil War. The French were more than willing to agree to British demands. They could then avoid the risks of confronting an ever more powerful Germany and blame the aban-

The Führer in "liberated" Sudetenland. Hitler greets local people after crossing the old border.

WILLIAM GALLAGHER, COURTESY UNITED STATES HOLOCAUST MEMORIAL MUSEUM

donment of their allies on Britain.

Both countries reacted to Hitler's annexation of Austria with the mildest of protests. The future of Czechoslovakia was now the crucial issue. The Soviet Union, the target of much of Hitler's abusive propaganda, proposed a conference with Britain and France to discuss the Nazi threat. In hindsight, this appeared to be an important initiative, but in 1938 the Soviet Union was in the midst of Stalin's paranoid assault upon his real and imagined internal enemies. Hundreds of veteran Communist party members were executed, including most of Stalin's rivals for the leadership. The Red Army's officer corps was devastated: 13 out of 15 army commanders, 57 out of 87 corps commanders and 110 out of the 195 divisional commanders were "purged," and most were shot. To Chamberlain, the Soviet Union under Stalin appeared as barbarous as Hitler's Germany. Its purged army was thought to be of little military value.

The British and French rejected Stalin's proposal, preferring a paper agreement with Italy that was supposed to promote Mussolini's good will and to caution Germany. While Hitler prepared for war Chamberlain continued his quest for peace at virtually any price. When the Czech government ordered a partial mobilization of its army, in a mistaken reaction to German military exercises, the international press announced a Nazi retreat in the face of military opposition. Hitler was furious with the Czechs and issued orders for the destruction of the country. Chamberlain was appalled by the possibility of war and warned the French government that Britain would not support France in a war over the Sudetenland. Two months later the French government informed the Czechs that "France like England would not go to war" on their behalf.

The stage was set for Hitler to try to provoke a war by making outrageous demands and for Chamberlain to

Hitler outlines his plans for Czechoslovakia to his generals at the "Hossbach Conference," May 20, 1938.

It is my unalterable decision to smash Czechoslovakia by military action in the near future. It is the business of the political leadership to await or bring about the suitable moment from a political and military point of view....

The following are necessary prerequisites for the intended attack:

a) A convenient apparent excuse and, with it,

b) Adequate political justification,

c) Action not expected by the enemy which will find him in the least possible state of readiness.

Most favourable from a military as well as a political point of view would be lightning action as the result of an incident which would subject Germany to unbearable provocation, and which, in the eyes of at least a part of world opinion, affords the moral justification for military measures....

Neville Chamberlain, on his return from meeting Hitler at Munich, spoke to the House of Commons, October 1, 1938.

I think I should add that before saying farewell to Herr Hitler I had a few words with him in private, which I do not think are without importance. In the first place he repeated to me with great earnestness what he had said at Berchtesgaden, namely, that this was the last of his territorial ambitions in Europe and that he had no wish to include in the Reich people of other races than Germans. In the second place he said, again very earnestly, that he wanted to be friends with England and that if only this Sudeten question could be got out of the way in peace he would gladly resume conversations....

French Foreign Minister Georges Bonnet tells the Czechoslovakian envoy that France will not fight, July 20, 1938.

I read to [Stefan Osusky] again the key passages of the British memorandum of May 22, 1938. The British government was not willing to support France in the Sudeten affair.... It considered moreover that the outcome of a conflict would be "doubtful" at the present time.

The Czechoslovak government must fully understand our position: France will not go to war over the Sudeten affair. Certainly, publicly we will affirm our solidarity, as the Czechoslovak government desires, but this affirmation of solidarity is to allow the Czechoslovak government to reach a peaceful and honourable solution. In no case must the Czechoslovak government think that if war breaks out we will be at her side, especially since in this matter our diplomatic isolation is almost total....

From Winston Churchill's speech in the House of Commons after the Munich Agreement, October 1, 1938.

I think you will find that in a period of time which may be measured by years, but may be measured only in months, Czechoslovakia will be engulfed in the Nazi régime. Perhaps they may join it in despair or in revenge. At any rate, that story is over and told. We cannot consider the abandonment and ruin of Czechoslovakia in the light only of what happened last month. It is the most grievous consequence which we have yet experienced of what we have done and of what we have left undone in the last five years — five years of futile good intention, five years of eager search for the line of least resistance, five years of uninterrupted retreat of British power, five years of neglect of our air defences. Those are the features which I stand here to declare and which marked an improvident stewardship for which Great Britain and France have dearly to pay.

avoid war by giving in to Hitler. The Czechs were not consulted. After the second meeting between the two leaders it appeared as if Hitler would reject any compromise and the Czechs again began to mobilize. As public opinion in the west rallied to the Czech cause and the French began mobilizing, Chamberlain returned to Germany to meet Hitler for the third time at Munich. He had told Hitler that "you can get all the essentials without war and without delay," and once in Munich he accepted all of Hitler's demands in return for a promise of future consultation over "questions that may concern our two countries."

Hitler lost his nerve and accepted the agreement. The Czech government, demoralized by Chamberlain's actions, lost its nerve and bowed to the pressure of her allies. President Eduard Beneš resigned after registering a "protest before the world against a decision in which we had no part." Chamberlain had won. Hitler was furious. The war he had planned would have to wait, but next time, he was resolved, there would be no compromise.

MACKENZIE KING

One of the main arguments Neville Chamberlain used in justifying his policy of appeasement was that public opinion in the Dominions was opposed to participation in a European war. Such opposition, if real, was significant. The Empire had played a large role in the First World War. The Australians and Canadians especially had acquired well-deserved reputations as shock troops, the best the Allies had. If the Dominions were unwilling to help Britain and France stop Hitler, the case for avoiding a continental war was greatly strengthened.

Chamberlain knew little about attitudes in the Commonwealth countries, but in 1937 he met their leading politicians at the coronation of George VI. The Canadian prime minister, Mackenzie King, was an ardent supporter of appeasement and was planning to travel on to

William Lyon Mackenzie King (1874–1950), shown in his office at Laurier House, was prime minister through the war years. His political style favoured conciliation and mediation, rather than forthright leadership, in dealing with Canada's deep regional divisions.

Berlin to meet with Hitler. King proposed to warn Hitler that a direct attack on Britain would mean a Canadian declaration of war, but otherwise his visit was intended to promote "friendly relations" between Nazi Germany and the rest of the world.

Mackenzie King was a man of extraordinary complex-

Mackenzie King meets Hitler

I told him I had been anxious to visit Germany because I was most anxious to see the friendliest of relations existing between the peoples of the different countries.... I spoke then of what I had seen of the constructive work of his regime, and said I hoped that his work might continue. That nothing would be permitted to destroy that work. That it was bound to be followed in other countries to the great advantage of mankind.

Hitler said in order to keep his control over the country he had to have the support of the people; that he was not like Stalin who could shoot his generals and

other members of his government who disagreed with him, but had to have back of him what the people themselves really wished, and the German people did not want war or commitments to possible war in advance. (While he was talking in this way, I confess I felt he was using exactly the same argument as I had used in the Canadian Parliament last session.)

... He smiled very pleasantly and indeed had a sort of appealing and affectionate look in his eyes. My sizing up of the man as I sat and talked with him was that he is really one who truly loves his fellow man....

W.L. Mackenzie King, diary

What's the cheering for?

J.W. Dafoe, the editor of the Winnipeg Free Press *and a frequent thorn in the government's side, spoke for a lot of people when he wrote an editorial on the Munich crisis entitled: "What's the Cheering For?"*

The doctrine that Germany can intervene for racial reasons for the "protection" of Germans on such grounds as she thinks proper in any country in the world which she is in a position to coerce, and without regard to any engagements she has made or guarantees she has given, has now not only been asserted but made good; and it has been approved, sanctioned, certified and validated by the governments of Great Britain and France, who have undertaken in this respect to speak for the democracies of the world.

This is the situation; and those who think it is all right will cheer for it.

Winnipeg Free Press, September 30, 1938

ity. As the grandson of William Lyon Mackenzie, the first leader of the 1837 Rebellion in Upper Canada, he saw himself as an advanced liberal on social issues. As the devoted son of a strong and possessive mother, he had developed a private personality that included a strong belief in spiritualism and the ability to communicate with the spirits of the departed. As a politician, King was a skilful mediator who worked endlessly to promote cooperation between French- and English-speaking Canadians, but there was no doubt in his own mind that Canada would never be neutral in a war that threatened the survival of Britain. King, who had begun his career in labour relations, also held strong views about the value of resolving disputes through "compulsory conciliation." He genuinely believed that conflict could be avoided through mediation.

All of this helps to explain King's behaviour in 1937 when he appeared to be under Hitler's spell. Once removed from the dictator's influence, he returned to the policies he had been advocating since his return to power in 1935. King's main political objective was the preserva-

tion of the alliance between the Quebec Liberal Party and English-speaking Liberals in the rest of Canada. It was important to avoid public discussion of issues that might divide the country.

French-Canadian memories of the First World War had little in common with those of English-speaking Canadians. Outside Quebec Vimy Ridge may have symbolized Canada's coming of age, but within the province 1917 was remembered as the year of conscription. The vast majority of French Canadians believed that Canada had no legitimate interest in what went on in Europe and ought to avoid any involvement. They believed that if *les anglais* would forget their loyalty to Britain and place Canada's interests first, the country could declare its neutrality just as the United States had done.

Mackenzie King knew that English-speaking Canada would never support such a policy any more than he himself would. He chose to avoid debate, hoping that appeasement would work and war would be avoided. After the Munich crisis he joined in the chorus of praise for Chamberlain and deeply resented the criticisms of J.W. Dafoe, but he never doubted that Canada would join Britain if war broke out.

AWAKENING

On October 31, 1938, Neville Chamberlain reminded his cabinet colleagues that Britain's foreign policy "was one of appeasement." They must aim, he continued, "at establishing relations with the Dictator Powers which will lead to a settlement in Europe and to a sense of stability." He went on to criticize the press and public for talking too much about rearmament, "as though one result of the Munich Agreement had been that it would be necessary for us to add to our rearmament programmes." Chamberlain's insistence that Munich was the basis for a settlement with Germany, not a way of buying time for Britain and France to rearm, was endorsed by Mackenzie King. No increases were planned in Canada's meagre defence budget.

For many people in Canada and Britain optimism about cooperation with Nazi Germany ended on November 10, 1938, with the shattered glass of the

Kristallnacht. A month before, the Nazis had cancelled all passports held by German Jews and begun the expulsion of Polish Jews living in Germany. Poland, practising its own variety of anti-semitism, refused to admit thousands of families who were held without food or shelter on the Polish–German border. When a seventeen-year-old student, whose parents were among the hostages, assassinated a German embassy official in Paris, Hitler was enraged. The SA or "Brownshirts," the Nazi thugs who had helped Hitler to power, were encouraged to lead a pogrom against Germany's Jews. Synagogues were burnt, Jewish businesses ransacked and looted. The police stood by or provided assistance to the looters. Thousands of windows were smashed, giving rise to the term "night of broken glass." The next day 20,000 Jews were arrested and taken to the new concentration camps at Dachau

Kristallnacht was a night of particularly widespread and vicious attacks on Jews and Jewish-owned businesses all over Germany. (Top left) Shoppers pass by the smashed window of a Jewish-owned store, and (left) the Hildesheim synagogue burns. Anti-semitic posters were common. The one above reads, "The Jews are as useful to us as mice to the corn silo and the moth to clothes. Therefore, they are unwanted here." The half-million German Jews, less than 1 per cent of the population, included famous scientists, artists and intellectuals. Many German Jews had served with distinction in the First World War, but no one, no matter how great his or her contribution, was exempted from Nazi terror.

Protest in Toronto...

Race, creed and class were forgotten yesterday as Toronto, with one voice, protested the martyrdom of German Jews at Nazi hands.

More than 16,000 persons thronged the Maple Leaf Gardens to attend a memorial service for the victims of persecution and oppression; and thousands more were turned away because of lack of accommodation....

The gathering was one of the most cosmopolitan Toronto has ever witnessed. Seated side by side

**JEWS SOB IN SORROW
20,000 TORONTONIANS
PROTEST PERSECUTION**

on the platform, financier and working man, rabbi, Protestant clergyman and Roman Catholic layman voiced heartfelt sympathy for the hundreds of thousands crushed beneath the swastika....

Although Jews were in the majority in the assembly, the gathering on the platform transcended all lines of race or creed. It included Mayor Day, who spoke on behalf of the city, Sir William Mulock, Sir Robert Falconer, Sir Wyly Grier and a score of others, in addition to the speakers. These included Rt. Rev. Peter Bryce, former moderator of the United Church of Canada; Rev. Crossley Hunter of Hamilton; Rabbi Maurice Eisendrath; Rev. J. E. Ward, representing Most Rev. Derwyn T. Owen, Anglican primate of All Canada; E. A. Conway, president of the Holy Name Society, on behalf of Most Rev. James McGuigan, Roman Catholic archbishop of Toronto; and George Watson, president of Toronto Trades and Labour Council....

Toronto Daily Star, November 21, 1938

and Buchenwald. The Jewish community was collectively fined one billion Reichsmarks and excluded from all economic activity.

This outburst of organized violence and the collective punishment of Germany's Jews provoked outrage among ordinary people. Canadians shared this anger and joined in public demonstrations against the Nazi state. In Toronto a protest rally drew 16,000 people to Maple Leaf Gardens and thousands more filled the streets. Smaller

but equally angry meetings were held in many other towns and cities.

Canadians had long practised or accepted their own forms of anti-semitism. Quotas limiting the access of Jews to universities and the professions and restrictions on club memberships and other overt measures of discrimination were commonplace. Though these and similar prejudices against members of visible minorities were accepted, what Hitler was doing shocked Canadians as nothing else had, and there was strong, though unsuccessful, pressure to reverse the government's immigration policy, which prevented the admission of Jewish refugees to Canada.

Throughout the winter of 1938–39 the pace of German military preparations increased, but the policy of appeasement was not fully reversed until March 1939, when Hitler ordered his troops to occupy Prague. Hitler had claimed the Sudetenland was his last territorial ambition in Europe. Now he had grabbed the ancient Czech provinces of Bohemia and Moravia to which Germany had neither historical nor "racial" claims.

Within days what the historian A.J.P. Taylor has called "an underground explosion of public opinion" rocked the foundations upon which the policy of appeasement was built. Public opinion was well ahead of the politicians in both Britain and Canada, demanding action to prevent Hitler from continuing his expansionist drive. Chamberlain, who had initially tried to downplay the invasion, responded to the new mood by proposing that Britain and France "guarantee" the independence and integrity of Poland against German attack. Canadians, even those who had strongly supported appeasement, joined in the applause.

In the Ontario Legislature the members passed a unanimous resolution calling for "immediate action," while in Ottawa Mackenzie King attacked Hitler for the "wanton and unjustified seizure of Czechoslovakia." The Prime Minister warned that if an aggressor was to attack Britain "with bombs raining death on London, I have no doubt what the decision of the Canadian people would be."

PREPARATION

The 1939 session of the Parliament of Canada began quietly in January with the Governor General's speech from the throne outlining a modest legislative program. When Mackenzie King rose to address the house he surprised everyone with a statement on foreign policy that showed how much things had changed since Munich. "I wish to give," he announced, "a statement of Liberal policy as it

Hurricane production at Canadian Car and Foundry. The RCAF received its first Hawker Hurricane fighters from England early in 1939, and production began at Fort William, Ontario, that year, the first Canadian-built example flying in January 1940. More than 1,400 were produced in Canada and most were shipped to the U.K.

is today and as it will continue to be...." He then read out an extract from Wilfrid Laurier's speech on the Naval Bill of 1910:

> If England is at war, we are at war and liable to attack. I do not say we will always be attacked; neither do I say that we would take part in all the wars of England. That is a matter that must be guided by circumstances upon which the Canadian Parliament will have to pronounce and will have to decide in its own best judgement.

In the context of 1939 this statement was a public rejection of the option of neutrality in an European war

and an affirmation of Canadian commitment to the anti-Nazi coalition. It did not commit Canada to an expeditionary force or any other form of direct participation in a war, but it was clear that the government was aligning itself with public opinion in English-speaking Canada.

The defence estimates for 1939 reflected the policy statement and the new urgency created by Hitler's seizure of Czechoslovakia. Expenditures were to rise from $36 million in 1938 to $65 million in the new fiscal year. Most of the additional money was for an air training scheme to train Canadian and British pilots. The Royal Canadian Air Force was to triple in size to eleven permanent and twelve reserve squadrons. The navy would acquire a new destroyer to be purchased in England. Renamed HMCS *Assiniboine,* it arrived in Canada in October 1939 to serve as flotilla leader in a fleet of six destroyers. The army had to be satisfied with an increase of $4 million for new equipment, including tanks, machine guns and howitzers, none of which would be available when war was declared.

These modest attempts to rebuild the Canadian armed forces could have little impact in the few months remaining before the outbreak of war. A sudden change in attitudes could not make up for years of neglect. In 1939, only the navy's destroyers could be described as modern weapons of war. The RCAF had just acquired its first Hurricane fighters, enough to equip one squadron, while the army could not begin to train soldiers, for lack of equipment. Ironically, as it turned out, the army had plenty of time to prepare for battle, and the RCAF benefited from the priority given to the air force in British rearmament. It was the Royal Canadian Navy which suffered most from inadequacies in equipment and training because the RCN's entry into battle could not be delayed.

THE ROYAL VISIT

The visit of the King and Queen in May 1939 is usually seen as an attempt to bolster Canadian commitment to the British Empire in the months before the outbreak of war. This was no doubt the intention of the British government, but this reality should not be allowed to overshadow the greater truth that King George VI and Queen Elizabeth were greeted all across the nation with "an unceasing tide of affection and applause" that had nothing to do with politics or the threat of war. English-speaking Canadians responded with a warmth and sincerity that demonstrated the strength of their loyalty. French Canadians, less engaged emotionally, were charmed and delighted by the visitors.

They arrived in Quebec City on May 17 to be greeted by large crowds full of curiosity. Four weeks later they sailed from Halifax with a massed choir singing "Will Ye No Come Back Again" and the entire city there to see them off. In between they journeyed across the country

A huge army in Canada...

I'm just a new recruit in the Queen's Own Rifles when we're called upon to put on the Guard of Honour at Union Station in Toronto for the arrival of the King and Queen. Our only full-dress uniforms are left over from 1911. We get them out of mothballs and instead of being nice, dark rifle green they're sort of field grey, almost like the German army's uniforms. And they're moth-eaten, just awful. But we have an officer in the regiment whose family runs Parker's Dye Works and they dye them to the proper colour and sew up the moth holes. Then they have to find people who fit the uniforms, and because I fit one of them, I become a member of the Honour Guard.

So the King and Queen arrive at Union Station with Mackenzie King peeking around their shoulders and we're called to attention and give our best royal salute, and the bands are playing, the crowds cheering, and the King and Queen inspect us and then get into a Lincoln convertible and drive off to Woodbine Racetrack for the King's Plate.

As soon as they're gone, we rush back into Union Station and change into our khaki uniforms, with puttees and everything, and they take us up to University Avenue. We stand there lining the street until the King and Queen drive by and we present arms.

Then we're taken up to Queen's Park and the Governor General's Horse Guard, the Royal Canadian Dragoons, ride up on their horses and we're looking very, very smart and they back their horses' rear ends right in our faces....Then they move us back down University Avenue so when the King and Queen came down again, we present arms again....

Ten days later when they visit St. Catharines, we go there by train. We get paid fifty cents a day to present arms, and then it's off to Niagara Falls....We line the streets by St. George's Church in Niagara Falls while the King and Queen attend a service.

After they're inside, we're taken over to the Rainbow Bridge. And when the Royal Train finally comes along with the King and Queen on board, we present arms one last time and see them off to the United States. By this time, the King and Queen are convinced Canada has no shortage of soldiers. If war was declared, the King would know he had a huge army in Canada.

Rifleman Barney Danson, Queen's Own Rifles

Barney Danson later became Minister of National Defence.

The King and Queen sign the City of Montreal guest book before Mayor Camillien Houde as Mackenzie King looks on. Houde was later interned for speaking against war service.

waving from the back of a train, pausing to greet crowds that had gathered from miles away, or driving in an open car through city streets lined with people three and four deep.

To some observers the excitement with which Canadians greeted the royal visitors was evidence of the country's "colonial" mentality but most Canadians ignored such views. English-speaking Canadians saw themselves as British North Americans who had preserved a vital connection with their mother country. This connection, which saved them from being merely American, was a compound of many things – kinship, with family or friends in the old country, a shared past, which incorporated British history and literature into the Canadian identity, and innumerable institutional ties through churches, universities, labour unions and the military. The royal tour was a celebration of that British North American identity, an identity which made it impossible to stand aside if Britain decided to resist Nazi aggression.

Joseph Stalin agreed to a pact with Hitler in the belief that the Soviet Union and Germany could cooperate and share the spoils in Eastern Europe.

Successes can no longer be won without bloodshed...

From "Minutes of the Conference of May 23, 1939 – The Führer on the Present Situation and Political Objectives."

… The ideological problems have been solved by the mass of 80,000,000 people. The economic problems must also be solved. To create the economic conditions necessary for this is a task no German can disregard. The solution of the problems demands courage. The principle must not prevail that one can accommodate oneself to the circumstances and thus shirk the solution of the problems. The circumstances must rather be adapted to suit the demands. This is not possible without "breaking in" to other countries or attacking other people's possessions.

Living space proportionate to the greatness of the State is fundamental to every Power. One can do without it for a time but sooner or later the problems will have to be solved by hook or by crook. The alternatives are rise or decline.…

The national political unification of the Germans has been achieved bar minor exceptions. Further successes can no longer be won without bloodshed.…

The Pole is not a fresh enemy. Poland will always be on the side of our adversaries. In spite of treaties of friendship Poland has always been bent on exploiting every opportunity against us.

It is not Danzig that is at stake. For us it is a matter of expanding our living space in the East and making food supplies secure and also solving the problem of the Baltic States. Food supplies can only be obtained from thinly populated areas.…

The Polish régime will not stand up to Russian pressure. Poland sees danger in a German victory over the West and will try to deprive us of victory. There is therefore no question of sparing Poland and we are left with the *decision:* *To attack Poland at the first suitable opportunity.*

We cannot expect a repetition of Czechia. There will be war. Our task is to isolate Poland. Success in isolating her will be decisive.

Therefore the Führer must reserve to himself the final order to strike. It must not come in a simultaneous showdown with the West (France and England).…

WAR BEGINS

By the summer of 1939 Hitler was determined to lead his country in a war against Britain and France. The British in particular were emerging as the main obstacle to his plans for conquest in the east and the creation of the "Thousand Year Reich." Hitler's intentions were fixed but his timetable was influenced by two main factors. He feared that no other German leader would take the plunge and risk all-out war. If he did not act while he was still young enough to see the war to its end, Germany might fail to achieve the goals he had set.

Hitler was also aware that his policies had finally provoked a response in Britain and France. The German army would be the most powerful force in Europe for the next several years but rearmament in the west and the Soviet Union would soon destroy that advantage. An immediate war was a necessity if Germany was to be victorious.

Hitler's real objective was the Soviet Union but he believed that its conquest was a relatively simple task to be carried out whenever it suited him. The immediate problem was to secure Germany's eastern flank while preparing to destroy the French army. The crucial step was a non-aggression treaty with the Soviet Union, which included a secret agreement to divide Poland.

The Hitler–Stalin pact was announced on August 23, 1939; the orders to attack Poland were issued on the same day. Hitler hoped to persuade the British and French to abandon their guarantee of Poland by repeating pledges that he had no desire for war in the west. In Paris, London and Ottawa there remained those who believed that Poland was not worth fighting for and that Hitler could still be appeased, but most people knew that an attack

Ontario Liberal premier Mitchell Hepburn (left) was critical of Mackenzie King's policies. When Hitler occupied Prague, the Ontario legislature unanimously passed a resolution demanding "support of any action which it may be necessary for the Imperial government to take." J.S. Woodsworth (right), federal CCF leader, opposed all defence expenditure and voted against the declaration of war, describing it as "the inevitable outcome of the present economic and international system with its injustices, exploitations and class interests."

on Poland meant a European war.

Mackenzie King had responded to news of the Hitler–Stalin pact with the telling phrase "the whole British world will face these difficulties with calm, increased by the determination to maintain complete unity." Parliament, he announced, would be summoned if it "became apparent that all efforts for peace had failed." The next day the Prime Minister addressed appeals to both Germany and Poland urging mediation. At home orders were issued to transfer two destroyers to Halifax, to cancel all military leaves and to complete plans for mobilization.

On September 1, the day Germany invaded Poland, the War Measures Act was proclaimed and members of parliament were recalled to Ottawa to meet on September 7. If the United Kingdom became involved in a war in an effort to resist aggression, Parliament would be asked to authorize "effective cooperation by Canada at the side of Britain."

Most accounts of the debate on the declaration of war describe J.S. Woodsworth's speech advocating neutrality. The leader of the CCF had publicly opposed participation in the First World War and in 1939 he declared that he could not change his convictions. His party no longer agreed with him though a number of ministers of the United Church of Canada issued a statement titled "A Witness Against War," which supported his position. These ideas found little support in the United Church or elsewhere. The majority view was expressed by the Liberal Member of Parliament for Algoma, H.S. Hamilton:

It would be idle for me to take up the time of the house in any effort to review the events that have been taking place in Europe or their significance in Canada. He who has eyes has seen or read, he who has ears has heard, and he who has understanding must realize their deep significance in this Dominion.

I suggest that never in all history have the democratic or liberty-loving countries engaged in a greater and more necessary effort to see to it that government of the people, by the people and for the people shall not perish from the earth.

We are confronted with a philosophy that knows nothing of the individual man but his obligation to obey; that knows nothing of the value of human individuality and human liberty, whose instruments

Neville Chamberlain: "This country is at war."

I am speaking to you [from] the Cabinet Room at 10 Downing Street. This morning, the British ambassador in Berlin handed the German government a final note stating that unless we heard from them by eleven o'clock, that they were prepared at once to withdraw their troops from Poland, a state of war would exist between us. I have to tell you now, that no such undertaking has been received and that consequently, this country is at war with Germany.

Mackenzie King...

On Sunday, September 3rd, as you will recall, His Majesty the King appealed to his people at home and across the sea to make their own the cause of freedom, which, on that day, Britain had taken up. If I were called upon to sacrifice out of my life all save one of the influences of the past or of my present possessions, the one thing I would wish to retain is the influence of the Christian training of my childhood days. The Nazi doctrine of force is the very antithesis of what one finds in the Christian gospel. If it prevails, there will be, as I see it, an end to our Christian civilization.

Our effort will be voluntary. The people of Canada will, I know, face the days of stress and strain which lie ahead with calm and resolute courage. There is no home in Canada, no family and no individual whose fortunes and freedom are not bound up in the present struggle. I appeal to my fellow Canadians to unite in a national effort to save from destruction all that makes life itself worth living and to preserve for future generations those liberties and institutions which others have bequeathed to us.

are ruthless and unscrupulous force and violence, an utter negation of all the things we have been taught to value, of the philosophy, to which we hold, that has regard for human personality and human liberty, within by which philosophy we shall yet achieve the splendid destiny that lies ahead of the Canadian people. Believing this, Mr. Speaker, to me this war is Canada's war. To me the defeat of Britain is the defeat of Canada; the defeat of France is the defeat of Canada. To me the death of every British, French or Polish soldier, sailor or aviator in resisting German force and violence at this time is a life given in the service of Canada.

To my mind the effective defence of Canada consists in the utilization of the organized and united power and strength of this Dominion however, whatever, and whenever it can best be used to defeat Germany's armed forces and to destroy the philosophy on which they are based. If the method of doing it involves primarily the utilization of our industrial and productive resources, then I am for that. If it involves partly the use of such forces and also the use of armed forces, expeditionary or otherwise, I am for that. If a certain type of assistance would be most advantageous now, changing to a different type of assistance later, then I am for that. And if the assistance which can effect that which I believe to be so vital can best be given on the Atlantic, on the North Sea, on the fields of Europe, I am also for that.

Hamilton sat down to thunderous applause. Canada was at war.

THE FRENCH-CANADIAN RESPONSE

The events of the late 1930s, which transformed public opinion in most of Canada, provoked a very different response among French Canadians in Quebec. Their collective memory neither included identification with the British Empire nor affection for republican France. Few French Canadians had volunteered to serve in the First World War and no one would have dreamed of arguing that their Canadian nation had "come of age" at the battle of Vimy Ridge. Remembrance Day, which was an important and solemn event in the rest of the country, was ignored in most of Quebec, where war memorials and Legion branches were usually signs of the presence of an English-speaking minority.

The crucial folk-memory in Quebec was

of conscription, imposed by *les anglais* on a hostile population with no interest in an "imperial" war. Politicians in Quebec were frequently accused of exploiting conscription for electoral purposes but Ernest Lapointe, Mackenzie King's Quebec lieutenant, did his best to play down the issue. By 1939 both the Liberal and Conservative parties were on record as opposing conscription for overseas service and Lapointe insisted that this commitment settled the issue.

French-Canadian nationalist leaders, including many prominent intellectuals, remained opposed to any form of Canadian participation in a European war. Maxime Raymond, their parliamentary spokesman, presented an anti-war petition with thousands of signatures to the House of Commons. "Let us declare neutrality," he urged, arguing that it could be a "friendly neutrality" which would see Canada supplying food and essential materials to Britain, France and Poland.

Ernest Lapointe responded to this challenge in a speech which "evoked the most extraordinary demonstration of enthusiasm ever witnessed in the Canadian House of Commons." Lapointe turned to face his Quebec colleagues, urging them to recognize that neutrality was impossible. "No Canadian government," he insisted, could refuse to declare war when the great majority of its

Ernest Lapointe (left), Minister of Justice and longtime leader of the federal Liberal party in Quebec, led the campaign to defeat Quebec premier Maurice Duplessis (above) in the 1939 provincial election. Lapointe's choice, Adélard Godbout, won the election but Duplessis was returned to office in 1944.

people "wished to fight alongside Britain and France." Lapointe then announced that he and all his Quebec colleagues in the cabinet would resign if conscription to overseas service was introduced. This was their guarantee that there would be no repetition of 1917.

Lapointe's status as Quebec's leader was quickly challenged by the premier of Quebec, Maurice Duplessis, who decided to exploit anti-war sentiment by calling a sudden election. A vote for his party, the Union Nationale, would be a "vote against conscription and participation," he declared. Duplessis had underestimated Lapointe's determination. The Liberal leader described the snap election as "an act of national sabotage" and warned that he and his French-Canadian colleagues would resign from the federal cabinet unless Duplessis was defeated and a Liberal government elected in Quebec.

Duplessis was swept from office. Quebec's heart might not be in the war but for the moment it would accept Lapointe's leadership and protection.

JOINING UP

The debate on Canada's entry into the war ended with just four MPs opposed. The appearance of unity was possible because the Prime Minister was deliberately vague on what exactly Canada would do. O.D. Skelton, the

A "boy" in the militia – Reg Roy

I joined the militia in the spring of 1939. I took a course as a signaller at the barracks in Sydney. I was taught by a regular force sergeant and it lasted for several weeks. All of the equipment dated back to the Great War and some of it (heliographs, for example) to the South African War....

Training was basic – arms and foot drill, various lectures based on lessons learned in 1914–1918, map reading, military organization and law, platoon field manoeuvres, a little weapons training, etc. There were no modern weapons, and no military vehicles at camp whatsoever.... It was little more than a seven-day picnic in uniform.

Mobilization started on September 2 when we heard on the local radio station that we should report to barracks at Victoria Park.... We were issued with white spats, red and white half-socks, a kilt and sporran, a 1918 tunic, 1918 webbing and a Glengarry. The tam-o-shanters came later. We were *not* issued with shoes, socks, underwear, shirt, sweater or anything else at that time....

At first we (in Sydney) lived at home but after a few weeks the army took over the old ... church on George Street which stood next to Central School. Two-tier wooden bunks were constructed for the men though these soon were replaced by the familiar steel bunks with flat springs and mattresses. Prior to that we had bolsters filled with straw....

Training remained very basic. We used the old "fours" drill for months. We had rifles, bayonets, and 1914–18 Lewis machine guns. We had no 2-inch or 3-inch mortars, no anti-tank guns and no vehicles. Anything remotely modern went to the 1st Division regiments which were being mobilized up to strength for dispatch overseas. We had no ranges, no areas for company or battalion exercises, no grenade ranges, etc. As a result training became boring. Quite a few of our people transferred to regiments going overseas (the West Novies, for example)....

Clothing came in slowly. One week we would be issued socks, another week we might get shoes and the next week a shirt. Slowly we got the new webbing, and a few military vehicles came our way. Then battle dress was issued. There were three of us with the rank of boy in the unit and we were the last to get it. The three of us were in No. 1 Platoon, Signals, and the only thing we were excused was sentry duty. In the winter, being on sentry duty with a kilt was no fun, so this is why everyone got a battle dress before Boy Walter Kenny, Boy R.A. MacDonald and myself. I might add that at the boy's daily wage of seventy cents a day, we weren't overpaid. We were all duly promoted to privates when we reached our eighteenth birthday.

As far as our "duties" are concerned, there were very few. For a while there was a detachment living under canvas at the airport. For a while there was another out at the Sydney River bridge. Several RCAF flying boats were anchored nearby.... What we could have done if there was an enemy raid is open to question.... Our CO, 2nd IC and most if not all of our company commanders were Great War veterans, but we didn't even learn how to dig trenches, set out barbed wire or use camouflage. We had no gas masks, nor steel helmets. We did learn how to read military maps, go on route marches, perform platoon tactics, and strip and put together a Lewis machine gun. We never fired it however.

Things improved a bit when we went into barracks at Victoria Park. At last the other companies joined us and even though we were still well under strength, one began to see for the first time several hundred men on battalion parade.... More officers and NCOs were sent on courses to learn a little bit about modern warfare and instruct others. Cooks learned how to cook, we began to get proper PT instruction, the new drill was introduced. At Victoria Park a large coastal defence gun was placed on a gun platform. I remember nothing. The date on the breech-block: 1895! ...

The Blitzkrieg in France in the spring of 1940 was a shocker but it seemed so remote that there was no sense of defeatism in the battalion. We envied the regiments going overseas and we all wanted to go ourselves. ...

Lieutenant Reg Roy, Cape Breton Highlanders

Canadians flocked to join up. (Top) The scene outside an RCAF recruiting station in Winnipeg. (Centre left) A parade on Portage Avenue, Winnipeg, of army recruits still in civilian clothes. (Above) A mother says goodbye to a Winnipeg Grenadier. (Bottom left) A train departs.

35

isolationist Under-secretary of State for External Affairs, had proposed that Canada's main military effort should be in home defence and in the training of men for "air service in Canada and a Canadian air force operating in France." The cabinet did not challenge this statement, perhaps because the army was allowed to proceed with a mobilization plan intended to enlist 100,000 men in a Canadian army corps with two divisions plus ancillary troops. The sinking of the unarmed liner *Athenia* on

The 1st Canadian Division embarking at Halifax, December 18, 1939. This was the first contingent of the Canadian army to go overseas.

September 3 and the swift brutality of the German conquest of Poland led thousands to volunteer before the official declaration of war. By the end of September, 58,000 men had joined the army, their purpose to go overseas and fight. Despite elite opinion in Quebec, French-Canadian regiments quickly filled their ranks.

The Prime Minister protested that the military was preparing for an expeditionary force despite government policy, but it was really public opinion and not the generals driving enlistment. On September 16 the government agreed to send the 1st Division to England as soon as possible, though orders were issued to slow down recruiting. Plans for the expansion of the Royal Canadian

Navy were also cut back on financial grounds, and by the end of 1939 the navy had barely doubled in size to just over 5,000 all ranks.

The direction of Canada's war effort was dramatically altered by a British proposal to build training facilities in Canada for all the air forces of the Commonwealth. The British Commonwealth Air Training Plan was welcomed by the government as Canada's main war effort in the hope that it would mean fewer casualties and less chance of conscription. Negotiations with the British delegation were completed in December 1939, and the organization of a program, which would eventually train tens of thousands of air crew, began immediately.

THE PHONEY WAR

The rapid conquest of Poland, made possible by France's failure to launch a promised attack on Germany's western border and by the Soviet Union's sudden invasion of Poland from the east, stunned the citizens of the democracies. The German army, which could hardly have failed to win so uneven a battle, made good use of its armoured forces, supported by Stuka dive bombers. Though the bulk of the German army marched on foot, assisted by horse-drawn wagons, the victory was publicized as a *Blitzkrieg* or "lightning war" that destroyed Poland in three weeks.

Hitler was jubilant and ordered preparation of a new offensive on the western front. Both the army and the air force protested that an autumn offensive was impossible, and Hitler was persuaded to wait. When an aircraft carrying plans for the invasion crashed in Holland, he ordered his generals to develop a new scheme based on a massive armoured thrust through the hilly and forested Ardennes region where the French would least expect an attack.

As the months passed without a new German offensive the western press, which had invented the word *Blitzkrieg*, coined a new term, *Sitzkrieg*, or "Phoney War." It was not a phoney war at sea when German U-boats, "ghost cruisers" and mines sank scores of Allied merchant ships. One bright light amidst the gloom was the Battle of the River Platte, where three British and Australian cruisers defeated the much more powerful pocket battleship the *Graf Spee*. Shortly afterwards, the *Altmark*, a German supply ship carrying the crews of merchant vessels sunk by the *Graf Spee,* was boarded in neutral Norwegian waters. The three hundred prisoners were freed, though the *Altmark* itself was allowed to continue to Germany.

After the partition of Poland, the Soviet Union began to consolidate its hold over the countries of Eastern Europe allotted to Stalin in the Nazi–Soviet pact. Lithuania and the other Baltic states were forced to accept Soviet troops in their countries while Finland, which had won its independence from Czarist Russia in 1917, was informed that the U.S.S.R. required large territorial concessions and a military base in Finland. Negotiations ended when the Soviets decided to demonstrate their military prowess with a sudden attack.

The Finns under Marshal Mannerheim inflicted heavy casualties on the Russians, who were ill-prepared for a winter war. Stalin could not afford to lose a campaign against such a small country and he sent massive reinforcements to the Finnish front. In March 1940 the Finns agreed to sign a peace treaty ending the winter war but providing Germany with a new ally.

The other Nordic countries tried to preserve their neutrality but in the end only Sweden succeeded in avoiding German occupation. The Germany navy badly wanted bases in Norway. Hitler accepted the navy's proposal, adding his own ideas about incorporating the "Aryan" Norwegians into the Reich. On April 9, 1940, the "Phoney War" ended. Denmark was occupied as a stepping-stone to Norway, which was assaulted from the air and by sea. The swift conquest of Norway was greatly aided by the country's leading fascist, Vidkun Quisling, the minister of war. Quisling arranged the surrender of

the garrison at Narvik, allowing German destroyers to land troops and establish a naval base in the first hours of the operation. Elsewhere, the Norwegians fought as best they could and tried to cooperate with a hastily improvised Allied Expeditionary Force.

The French and British had been preparing to mine Norwegian coastal waters in the hope of stopping shipments of Swedish iron ore. News of a full-scale Nazi invasion prompted efforts to land large numbers of troops in Norway, and the Canadians were asked to provide eight companies of infantry to capture the forts occupied by the Germans at Trondheim. The Canadian force, drawn from the Princess Patricia's Canadian Light Infantry and the Edmonton Regiment, moved to Scotland but the assault on Trondheim was cancelled. Apart from two Norwegian-speaking volunteers, who joined a British battalion as interpreters, the Canadians returned to their base at Aldershot.

The Royal Navy sank all ten of the German destroyers sent to Narvik, but the port was not recaptured. Elsewhere, British and French troops, harassed by the Luftwaffe, made little progress. The invasion of Holland, Belgium and France in May 1940 led to the final withdrawal of Allied troops from Norway in June.

THE FALL OF FRANCE

The revised German plan for the conquest of France took advantage of all of the problems facing General Maurice Gamelin as he prepared to defend his country. By 1940, France, encouraged by the British government,

The Anglo-French armies on the Belgian frontier advanced north to meet the German armies attacking the Low Countries, but the main German thrust through Luxembourg and the Ardennes region split the Allied forces. More than a quarter of a million British and French troops were evacuated from Dunkirk while the remaining French armies tried to defend a new line north of Paris. The route of 1st Canadian Division in Brittany is also illustrated. After the fall of France, the puppet Vichy government administered the area south of the armistice line, while Germany occupied the industrial north and the Atlantic coast.

The Netherlands had been neutral in the First World War but Belgium had fought alongside France, remaining an ally until 1936. The Belgian government, seeking to avoid a second German occupation, played into Hitler's hands by refusing any form of co-operation with the French. Since the Maginot Line stopped at the Belgian border, a decision had to be made about extending the defences to the sea or moving into Belgium at the outbreak of war. If Gamelin chose to wait at the border it would mean sacrificing the Belgian and probably the Dutch army. He decided to try to fight the Germans as far forward as possible, away from the industrial areas of northern France. The "Dyle Plan" called for his most mobile armies, including the eight divisions of the British Expeditionary Force, to advance into Belgium at the outbreak of war. The French Seventh Army, waiting at Dunkirk, was to move through Belgium into Holland if the Germans violated Dutch neutrality.

Historians who use hindsight as their major analytical tool have long criticized Gamelin's decision, but no

had abandoned all of its continental allies in an attempt to appease Hitler. Now France's turn had come and the French army faced a strategic dilemma impossible to re-solve. The army was not trained or equipped to under-take offensive operations and would have to absorb the shock of German blows in the hope of slowing down the advance and establishing a solid defensive perimeter. The Maginot Line of fortifications helped because it allowed a thinning-out of troops in that sector, but the border with Italy had to be defended and a decision made about the Low Countries.

Canadian General Andrew McNaughton (right) with General Gamelin at the Maginot Line.

Hitler made his only visit to Paris shortly after the armistice was signed in the same railway car in which the Germans had surrendered in 1918.

one thought there was a realistic alternative at the time. When it became apparent that the main German attack was through the Ardennes to Sedan and the Somme, the northern Allied armies were caught advancing away from the major German penetration. As the Panzer divisions raced for the Channel coast, attempts were made to cut them off, but neither the British nor the French forces proved capable of coordinating a major counterattack, and the northern armies began their retreat to Dunkirk.

Churchill, who had replaced Chamberlain as prime minister the day France was invaded, tried to rally the badly shaken French government. In an attempt to secure the Dunkirk perimeter, 1st Canadian Division was asked to prepare two brigade groups for action. General Andrew McNaughton and a small party of Canadians crossed to Calais and Dunkirk on the night of May 23 while 1st Brigade (the Royal Canadian Regiment, the Hastings and Prince Edward Regiment and the 48th Highlanders) moved to Dover for embarkation, but when McNaughton returned he recommended that Operation "Angel Move" be cancelled. Two days later the evacuation of the British Expeditionary Force began.

Churchill was determined to encourage France to continue the fight. As the French armies gathered to defend the newly established Weygand Line north of Paris, 1st Canadian and 52nd Lowland divisions were ordered to France as a "Second British Expeditionary Force." By the time the Canadians arrived, the Weygand Line had been broken, Italy had declared war, and the only remaining hope was to withdraw to the Brittany peninsula, retaining a bridgehead on the continent.

First Canadian Brigade reached the port of Brest on June 13 to find a scene of total confusion. The Canadians were ordered to Le Mans well beyond the boundary of the "Breton Redoubt." Fortunately most units had not gone very far when signs of the total collapse of French resistance led to new orders to reverse direction and return to England. The brigade vehicles had to be abandoned but officers of the Royal Canadian Horse Artillery insisted that the regiment's modern 25-pounder guns be brought back with them.

General McNaughton was understandably critical of

It's a war of ideas...

We – a group of friends and I – have taken the decision. To wear the uniform.... My family has no military tradition, no aged photo of a proud uniformed parent in 1914.... Canada has not had to defend its borders for over a hundred years. Her participation in the Boer and First World War smells more like powder made in England than it does of our soil.

As a Franco-Ontarian, I have had to bear official policy against my language. The marks of incomprehension and the majority's condescension towards my ancestors are ingrained in me. Official propaganda exhorts our sacrifice to save England. Yet Eng-lish Canadians care nothing for the national survival of their French-speaking compatriots. Their language is ignored and scorned in government organizations, particularly the armed forces. Nothing is said about the plight of France....

Tradition, patriotism, security, revenge do not move me.... Something is happening over there [in Europe] that has profoundly touched me, my convictions and my principles. It's a reality I can no longer avoid....

Above all, it's a war of ideas ... of freedom, of rights, without discrimination as to origin, age or colour. This relates to what is going on in my own country, in my province; and in Europe it has gone out of control with cruel savagery....

Lieutenant Claude Châtillon,
Royal 22nd Regiment

the confusion of purpose that marked the expedition. The orders to send the Canadians inland instead of concentrating at Brest were evidence that no one was exercising overall command and control. McNaughton's doubts about the direction of the British army were well founded, but in the aftermath of the defeat of France there was little more that could be said. The Canadians were now needed in another role, and McNaughton reported that his men were "squarely set" for the "important task, the defence of these islands."

IMPERIAL WAR MUSEUM

Their equipment a jumble on the deck, British troops take a last look at the French coast as they evacuate Dunkirk.

A second expeditionary force

Elements of the 1st Canadian Division were hastily moved to France in the futile hope that Hitler's armies could still be stopped. John Ellis of the Royal Canadian Horse Artillery took part in this short-lived expedition.

... The Royal Canadian Horse Artillery, of which my 54th Battery became a part, was sent to France. (We were horse artillery in name only as we were fully mechanized.) We left the port of Plymouth, Devon, and were taken to the port of Brest in northwestern France.... [where] we were loaded onto boxcars painted with the words: Huit chevaux quarante hommes.... We travelled 400 kilometres to a site about twenty kilometres from Paris, where we met our drivers with our guns and tractors and we prepared to go into action the next day to stem the German attack on Paris itself. I slept in a ... barn that night and we all washed next morning in the long, large horse-watering trough, much to the anger of the French farmer.... Orders came down ... that the French government had surrendered and we had

about two days to return to Brest. We ... started the long drive pulling our guns behind our tractors, which we called "Quads." The roads were clogged with fleeing refugees. People pushing all their worldly possessions in baby buggies, wheel barrows, bicycles.... The roads were strafed several times by German aircraft Messerschmitt 109s.... We finally made it to Brest where we were instructed to destroy all our brand-new equipment.... We were supposed to blow up our guns but our commanding officer, Major Stanley Nash ... instructed the crane operator to swing those guns aboard. ... Thus we [were] the only Allied regiment to bring our guns out of France. Mind you, this was almost two weeks after the famous retreat at Dunkirk.... Major Nash received the Distinguished Service Order for disobeying the destroy order.

... On the fields overlooking [Plymouth] harbour there were hundreds of people welcoming the heroes back from France. I certainly wasn't any hero, and I never fired a shot and the only Germans I saw were piloting the 109s.... At any rate, we drove back to our old barracks at Aldershot fully convinced we had lost the war.

John Ellis

An ambulance driver at the front

A young ambulance driver with the rank of ensign serving with Ambulance Chirurgicale Légère 279, Betty Scott provides a glimpse through her letters and journal of the relaxed life that prevailed at the front near the Belgian border – and the chaos that ensued as the Germans advanced into France.

March 22, 1940

We had the most frightful gale here about a week ago which blew our hospital as flat as a pancake. It was all under canvas, and commonly known as the circus – all except the operating theatre which is in metal sections. The few invalids there had just been moved a few minutes before the whole thing collapsed....

There seems to be a good deal of activity in the air today but I think they are all our own machines. At night they are always Boche, but they fly very high and we don't take cover unless the nearby anti-aircraft battery lets fly at them. I can also hear big guns in the distance – the wind must be in the right direction....

Women ambulance drivers close to the front lines in France, 1940.

CANADIAN WAR MUSEUM

April 8, 1940

There's been a lot of air activity lately, and the guns go off at some time or other daily. Cecil was at some place yesterday where they had just brought down an enemy plane and she saw the injured pilot in the distance. And ... one of the other drivers was having her hair done the other day in the nearest town at the same time as the New Zealander who brought down two German planes and then landed himself by parachute between the two lines. He was wounded in the leg but fortunately started to crawl in the right direction and a French officer saw him and brought him back to their lines....

We've had quite a gay weekend, as usual. The Théâtre D'Armée came to entertain us again, this time with quite a large orchestra.... Champagne afterwards at the Officers' popotte – this must be a very healthy place, because

I'd *die* in London if I ate and drank the things I do here....

What's the war news at home at the moment? Nobody here knows anything, though there's always a lot of chat about our hospital being sent either to Norway or the Balkans. Whatever happens they are all determined that "Les Anglais" must go too!...

April 30, 1940

We had quite an amusing picnic yesterday but I didn't get back in time to do my packing before dinner.... At about 8:30 p.m. I got a message to say that we were not to leave this morning, as there had been a hitch over our billets and we weren't wanted until tomorrow. At this there was a general rejoicing in the hospital, which developed into an impromptu party which included both officers and men. Such a riot, in fact, that today is a frightful anticlimax....

May 13, 1940, *from her journal*

Refugees coming through the town, in huge numbers. Nearly all the shops are shut and popotière very worried as to how she is to get her supplies of food. No arrangements made as yet by H.O.E. 10 for such an emergency. Most householders have now fled, leaving drivers in sole possession of their billets.

More bombs dropped in the vicinity of the popotte. Very dangerous for drivers to be on the road now as cars are being machine-gunned.

In a later letter, written after her return to England, she continued her account of events in France.

May 14 was a grizzly day for me, with all those air raids, the obvious objectives being the bridge and the railway station about fifty yards from our popotte. The others didn't get nearly such a bad start as they only had one raid that day and that was while they were lunching in the mess at Grand Pré before evacuating the Direction du Service du Santé to Somme Dieu.... Most of the officers tried to get under the table and one was in such a hurry he bumped his nose on one of the legs and made it bleed — so that it was all more funny than frightening. But I spent most of the day in the cellar of our popotte listening to the inferno of noise outside and watching the walls literally tremble and bulge. If only one had heard the sound of an A.A. gun or an Allied chaser plane it wouldn't have been so disheartening, but the Boche just came over in droves and when they'd dropped their bombs they machine-gunned the streets and the remaining refugees....

Our stay in Ancemont was, on the whole, a pleasant one, once we got settled into the Château. Our jobs were always hazardous but we chose our routes with care and had the most uncanny luck in avoiding trouble, sometimes just leaving a town five minutes before it was bombed, or being on an alternative road when the other was getting a dusting....

May 18, 1940, from her journal
Drivers wearing tin hats constantly now as cars are frequently machine-gunned on the roads. The technique is to draw up hastily under the shelter of a tree — if any — and fling oneself into the ditch....

June 10, 1940, from her journal
News very bad this morning and much talk of the hospitals having to retire further back. Drivers ready to leave at a moment's notice....

From a later letter
Our retreat, which started on June 11, would have been fun too, if only it hadn't been such a tragedy.... [Scott's passengers] were all dreadfully gloomy and ashamed of the way things were going — there was certainly no treachery and no pro-Axis sentiment amongst the men we worked with, and before we left they were all agreed that *whatever happened* the French navy must not fall into German hands....

June 13, 1940, from her journal
Monsieur Paul Reynaud's speech at 11:00 p.m. that of a beaten man. Drivers prepared for the worst and ready to leave at a moment's notice.

June 17, 1940, from her journal
Arrived at Macon at 4:30 a.m. and slept for two hours in cars just outside town. Left again at 9:30 a.m. and then sat in main road (choked with convoys and alongside railway) for four hours, waiting for General Causeret to get his orders from the Quartier General. Rumours that Germans were already in Macon made us nervous for his safety....

June 19, 1940, from her journal
Here at 11:30 p.m. we heard the BBC broadcasting in French, repeating General de Gaulle's message to all soldiers who wished to continue the fight to make their way to Toulouse. This indicates that the road to Bordeaux may still be open, and we decided to make a dash for it tomorrow, taking with us a wounded RAF pilot from this hospital who seems strong enough to stand the journey.

June 21, 1940, from her journal
[Arrived at] Bordeaux at 6:30 a.m. Drv. Myer spotted a British destroyer alongside quay in town and asked if they would take our wounded officer on board and look after him. Were told to come back again at 9:00 a.m. for the answer.... [The British Consul] had already left, and the advisability of a dash to Bayonne (petrol permitting) was under discussion when Ensign Miss Scott noticed an RAF car parked in the square and spoke to the driver, who was French. He volunteered the information that the British Air Attaché was still in Bordeaux, and was finally induced to disclose his name and address. Ensign Miss Scott then saw the Attaché, who arranged for the destroyer to take over the wounded pilot and instructed her to go to Arcachon, where Unit would be picked up by British cruiser....

June 22, 1940, from her journal
Came on board HMS *Galates* about 5:00 a.m. after very unpleasant two hours in small boat, and spent day zigzagging up and down coast, waiting for British Ambassador.

June 23, 1940, from her journal
Cruiser left for St. Jean de Luz this morning, and at 2:00 p.m. passengers were trans-shipped to SS *Ettrick* – a P&O liner converted into a troop ship. Accommodation on third mess deck in hammocks.

June 26, 1940, from her journal
Dropped anchor outside breakwater at Plymouth....

Betty Scott, ambulance driver

Corridors of power

William "Pat" Patterson, from Winnipeg, had recently entered Mackenzie King's employment as assistant to his former professor, J. W. Pickersgill.

My dear Mother,

To begin at the hind end first, today I met Mr. King – in fact I saw him – for the first time. I was going along the Privy Council corridor, just as he, with Mr. Heeney, came in for the Cabinet meeting. Heeney introduced me – and the PM beamed and placed me right away.

He said he was glad to hear that I was doing good work here – re-marked on the number of times that he and Grandfather had walked together down this corri-dor to Cabinet meetings.... My share of the conversation consisted of "Yes, sir," etc. inserted in the proper places.

I had prepared some stuff for him to use in connection with a forthcoming broadcast and it was reported that he was very pleased with it. (Incidentally, he is very fussy, and if briefs, memoranda, etc. are not just in the form he de-sires, he refuses to recognize their existence.) So at least I have been able to feel that I have got off to a good start. And now the PM knows me, and has me placed – which may be of use in the future....

Bill

Italy had joined Germany by declaring war on June 10. The mood in Canada and elsewhere throughout the Commonwealth and Empire was not defeatist, but it was sombre, as in this letter to William "Pat" Patterson from Jean Partridge, a nurse in training in Mon-treal, whom he would one day marry:

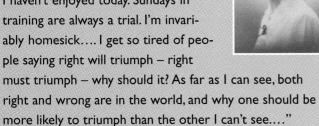

My Dear,

I haven't enjoyed today. Sundays in training are always a trial. I'm invari-ably homesick.... I get so tired of peo-ple saying right will triumph – right must triumph – why should it? As far as I can see, both right and wrong are in the world, and why one should be more likely to triumph than the other I can't see...."

Jean

I was sure my number would come up...

J. Ralph Wood of Moncton flew as navigator/bomb aimer on a remarkable seventy-seven bomber missions over enemy territory

Someone once said, "Everyone has fears, but he who faces fears with dignity, has courage as well."... I knew I had fear of being labelled coward or yellow if I didn't volunteer my services to my country. I knew also that I had fear of losing my life if I did volunteer. There was no contest. All that remained was to choose the service I would join. The Navy? No way! I'd probably be seasick before we left the harbour.... The Army? Well, according to stories of World War I ... this meant mud, trenches, lice, bayo-nets, etc. This was definitely not my cup of tea. Air Force? This was more appealing as it presented a picture of your home base in a civilized part of the country accompanied by real beds with sheets, fairly good food, local pubs with their accompanying social life, with periodic leaves.... Be-ing a fatalist, I was pretty sure my number would come up, and in the air it would be swift and definite.

Ralph Wood

STOP WAITING
GET READY to BEAT HITLER
GO
ENLIST NOW

NATIONAL ARCHIVES OF CANADA/C19281

What should I do now?

G. Hamilton Southam, of the newspaper family, agonizes in letters to his family over what role he should play in the coming events.

November 12, 1939
Although Oxford is quite normal, as I have explained, I am rather dissatisfied nevertheless. I feel that I should be doing some real work; even if there were no war I would feel like that. After all, I *am* 22, which is quite the age to turn away from books and face the world.... Don't think that my ardour is being whipped up by any public excitement here, by the way: the atmosphere in England is much quieter than in Canada, if one judges from the newspapers.

November 30, 1939
My problem has never been what I should do a year or more hence, but what I should do now. And considering who I am, a wealthy and therefore independent younger son, a bachelor and therefore with no dependents, it seemed obvious that I should play the most active role possible in what is being done. Now, if there had been an active part in the Canadian war effort for me to play, I should have been delighted to fill it.

But I felt very deeply, and told you before I left, that if it became clear that there was no place for me with the Canadians, I should join the English. We differed on this point, because you thought that I owed it to Canada to look no farther about me than her national interests necessitated; whereas I have always thought that it was better to consider the wider interests of the whole Commonwealth....

You know, I do not for one single moment think that I shall really see any fighting. I have only discomfort and boredom to look forward to, although some of the work will be interesting; there will be no "glamour" or excitement. The only comfort is that I am sure that it will all be over in a few months.

December 13, 1939, having joined the army
This is an interesting job: the food is good, the barracks appalling, my companions-in-arms a very nice lot – mostly Cambridge lads....

December 24, 1939
I regret that my work leaves me no time for reading – or, to put it another way, as I am a soldier now I no longer do any thinking....

Hamilton Southam saw a good deal of action, serving with the Royal Canadian Artillery in Italy and northwest Europe.

Winston Churchill, speech, May 13, 1940

You ask, What is our policy? I will say: It is to wage war, by sea, land and air, with all our might and with all the strength that God can give us; to wage war against a monstrous tyranny, never surpassed in the dark, lamentable catalogue of human crime. That is our policy. You ask, What is our aim? I can answer in one word: Victory – victory at all costs, victory in spite of all terror; victory however long and hard the road may be; for without victory there is no survival.

PART II

LIFE-LINE

Upper deck of **HMCS** *Pictou* in rough weather, 1942.

H.J. NOTT/DND/NATIONAL ARCHIVES OF CANADA/PA107903

With the fall of France, Britain and the Commonwealth were left alone to face the full weight of Hitler's military machine. Canada, a nation of just over eleven million people, became Britain's principal ally. Australia, New Zealand, South Africa, India and other parts of the Empire-Commonwealth could offer soldiers and food supplies, but only Canada had significant industrial potential. And, as the British military theorist Basil Liddell Hart reminded his readers, Canada possessed fourteen of the twenty basic commodities needed to wage modern war, including nickel and aluminum, not to mention uranium.

As the German armies swarmed over France, it was evident that Canadians understood the new reality they faced. One journalist described Ottawa, previously "the quietest capital in Christendom," as a "cauldron of excitement" shocked out of its complacency by a new and "wholesome fear." Throughout May and June 1940 Mackenzie King met with his war cabinet to find ways of making a useful contribution, "not considering expenditure."

The leisurely pace of rearmament during the Phoney War had left Canada ill-prepared to provide emergency assistance. The one fully-formed fighter squadron available was ordered to England, arriving in time to participate in the Battle of Britain; four RCN destroyers, based in Halifax, were sent to help guard the English coast; and a Canadian brigade was made available to garrison Iceland, relieving British troops. These measures were appreciated in Britain, but Canadians demanded more resolute action and far-reaching commitments from their government.

Mackenzie King, whose Liberal party had been re-elected with a large majority in the spring, responded with the National Resources Mobilization Act, proclaimed into law on June 21, 1940. The NRMA gave the government the power to issue "orders and regulations requiring persons to place themselves, their services and their property at the disposal of His Majesty in the right of Canada." The conscription of men for military service, the primary purpose of the NRMA, was specifically restricted to Canada and its territorial waters, so the government's promise not to impose conscription for service overseas was now expressed in an act of Parliament.

In the summer of 1940 the NRMA was little more than a political gesture. The first men called up did not report until October, and then it was for just thirty days of training. Fortunately, there was no shortage of volunteers. The 3rd Canadian Infantry Division had no difficulty completing recruiting, and when the 4th Division was authorized in May, the ranks were quickly filled. By the end of 1940, 177,000 Canadians had volunteered for army service overseas.

The RCAF was fully occupied with the British Commonwealth Air Training Plan, but the disaster in Europe brought a new urgency to the program. The RAF requested the immediate transfer of fourteen of its own flying schools to Canada and eventually established twenty-six of the 141 BCATP schools. At the same time the British government announced that it could not supply the promised aircraft for training. The small Canadian aircraft industry was quickly transformed with new mass production facilities established in Montreal, Toronto and Fort William. No one could create an air plane engine industry overnight, and the U.S. government agreed to provide engines for Anson trainers built in Canada.

The Royal Canadian Navy had undergone some ex-

> The battle of France is over. I expect that the Battle of Britain is about to begin. Upon this battle depends the survival of Christian civilization. Upon it depends our British life, and the long continuity of our institutions and our Empire. The whole fury and might of the enemy must very soon be turned on us. Hitler knows that he will have to break us in this island or lose the war. Let us therefore brace ourselves, that, if the British Empire and its Commonwealth last for a thousand years, men will say, "This was their finest hour."
>
> Winston Churchill

pansion since the outbreak of the war but attention was focused on acquiring armed merchant cruisers and Tribal-class destroyers, which could be used against German surface raiders. U-boats, which had nearly choked off supplies to Britain in the First World War, were not considered a serious threat, partly because the German navy had so few of them. Fortunately, Canadian shipyards had begun construction of corvettes, modified whalers, to be used for convoy escort in coastal waters. These "cheap and nasties," as Churchill called them, could be built in the small shipyards of the St. Lawrence and Great Lakes as well as British Columbia. Fourteen Canadian-built corvettes were commissioned in 1940, ten into the Royal Navy and four into the RCN. The "Destroyers for Bases" agreement, in which the neutral United States acquired bases in Bermuda and Newfoundland in return for fifty obsolete American destroyers, added six ships to the RCN. In the spring of 1941, twenty-six more corvettes were ready for service if crews could be found.

Admiral Leonard Murray could not have foreseen the collapse of the French army and the threat of U-boat bases in Brittany when he appeared before the Finance and Defence committees in February 1940, but he was determined to lay the foundations for a large Canadian navy. His proposals called for a fourteen-fold increase in expenditures to establish naval training and operational bases, while using every shipyard for construction or repair. After June 1940, naval expenditures increased at a rapid pace and the RCN, which had been scheduled to reach a total of 1,500 officers and 15,000 ratings by 1942, reached that figure in half the time.

The defeat of France had a profound effect upon opinion in French Canada. Despite nearly two centuries of separation, many French Canadians found themselves

Admiral Leonard Murray presents awards to crew members of the St. Croix after the sinking of a U-boat.

deeply moved by the plight of their mother country. When the mayor of Montreal, Camillien Houde, prompted by a newspaper reporter's leading question, urged Montrealers to avoid registering under the NRMA, he was promptly interned. Most Quebeckers joined in condemning Houde's foolishness and there was broad acceptance of the need for the NRMA. By January 1941, more than 50,000 French Canadians were in uniform, mostly in the army, the only service with French-language units.

The new sense of urgency was also reflected in a reorganization of the cabinet. J. L. Ralston, a Nova Scotian who had commanded a battalion in the Great War, left Finance to become Minister of Defence, responsible for the expansion of the army. An Air Minister, Charles "Chubby" Power, and a Minister for Naval Services, Angus Macdonald, were added. Ralston's appointment did much to convince English-speaking Canadians that Mackenzie King truly supported an all-out war effort. Colonel Ralston was widely respected and he played a role for English-speaking Canadians not unlike the one played by Ernest Lapointe in Quebec.

THE BATTLE OF BRITAIN

The "miracle" of Dunkirk meant that more than 300,000 Allied soldiers would be available to fight another day, but they had left most of their equipment behind and there were signs of demoralization. Churchill's speech to Parliament on June 4 with its commitment to "defend our island whatever the cost may be" restored confidence and energized preparations to defend Britain. Much had already been done, as the Luftwaffe would soon discover.

German planning for Operation "Sea Lion," the invasion of Britain, began in mid-July after Hitler issued a directive requiring the German armed forces "to eliminate the British homeland as a base for the further prosecution of the war against Germany, and, if necessary, to occupy it."

Hitler hoped invasion and occupation would not be necessary. On July 19 he announced that he "would see no reason why this war need go on," that Britain should simply accept German domination of Europe. The British government ignored Hitler's so-called peace offer. On July 27 the German army was told to prepare forty-one divisions for the invasion of England. However, the fleet would not sail unless the Luftwaffe had gained air superiority over the Channel and the English coast, so Reichsmarschall Hermann Göring was told to "smash the British air forces in as brief a period of time as possible." The invasion was set for September 16.

On August 13, "Eagle Day," the air battle began. The Luftwaffe deployed 2,422 aircraft against Britain, including 864 Messerschmitt Bf 109 single-engined fighters. Against this force the RAF could counter with 226 Spitfires and 353 Hurricanes. In the hands of good pilots the Spitfire and the Bf 109 were evenly matched, but the slower Hurricane had to rely on its manoeuvrability and opportunities to gain altitude above German formations.

The British had been planning the air defence of their island since 1938. Information from a network of radar stations supplemented by reports from the Observer Corps allowed Fighter Command to get its aircraft aloft and in good position before the bomber stream reached England. The Luftwaffe's mission to "smash the British air force" meant finding ways of winning dogfights, destroying airfields and bombing key factories. German bombers proved highly vulnerable to fighter attack and had to be closely escorted by German fighters. The Junkers Ju 87 "Stuka"

The two best known Canadian squadrons were the RCAF's No. 1 Squadron and the RAF's 242 largely Canadian squadron, led by swashbuckling British ace Douglas Bader, who had lost both legs in a 1931 air crash. Here pilots of 242 Squadron pose before a Hurricane fighter. Douglas Bader is in the centre and William McKnight is on the wing.

It happened by mistake...

One of 242 Squadron's aces was the young and cocky William McKnight, who had already won a DFC over France.

I suppose you have heard about my decoration by now – it all happened by a mistake one day. I got separated from the squadron and was sort of pissing about on my own – you know, boots shaking, knees knocking, etc. – when about fifteen Ju 87s came out of the clouds and started to bomb the fleet. I got four and luckily chased the rest off, but the funny part is that, while I was doing this the rest of the boys got jumped by 109s as usual right above me but on top of the clouds. So while I was having all the fun, they were keeping everything away from me.

William L. McKnight

dive bomber, which had wreaked such havoc against demoralized ground troops, proved too slow for real air combat and had to be withdrawn. The twin-engined Me 110 destroyer-fighter was too sluggish to handle "Hurri" and "Spit." In the first five days of the battle the Germans lost 255 aircraft to the RAF's 184. New fighter production organized by the Canadian expatriate Max Aitken, Lord Beaverbrook, replaced all the RAF losses and increased the number of Spitfires available.

SOUTHAM INC.

Members of No. 1 RCAF Fighter Squadron, commanded by Squadron Leader (later
Group Captain) Ernie McNab. Left to right: Flying Officer W.P. Sprenger, FO O.J.
Peterson, Flight Lieutenant W.R. Pollock, FO P.B. Pitcher, S/L McNab, FO P.W. Lochnan,
F/L E.M. Reyno, FO E.W. Beardmore, FO S.T. Blaiklock and FO R.W. Norris. Most mem-
bers of the squadron were from Montreal.

Bullets seemed to be popping all around...

October 18, 1940
Dear Charlie,
It was the good luck of our squadron to arrive here and
begin action just when things became hottest in the air
over England. We learned more about combat flying in
our first few weeks against the enemy than we could
ever have been taught in months of practice. It has
proved to be a thrilling game, full of scares, spills and
some sorrow – a clean game and one in which you at
least feel that you have a chance to rule your own destiny on your own ability – plus, of course, a lot of luck.
At first we were extremely nervous, as any normal human being would be, but as we put each patrol or encounter behind us we gathered confidence until we
came to think very little of touring the skies searching
out quarry. And there was usually plenty to be found,
particularly during September... when so many German
aircraft were knocked down and I can assure you it is an
awe-inspiring sight to see the sky literally dotted with
hundreds of aircraft – the most shattering feature about
seeing so many planes is not so much the proximity of

great numbers but the initial doubt as to how many are
friendly and how many hostile.
Flying Officer William Sprenger

September 3, 1940
Dear Ruth,
By this time Mother will have received a cable telling
briefly that I was injured last Saturday in bailing out of
an aircraft. I hope the contents of the cable did not
alarm any of you because the incident was really minor...
We were on a patrol looking for an enemy raid when
suddenly from a blind spot several enemy aircraft came
down upon us. One picked me as a target and bullets
seemed to be popping all around the inside of the cockpit – the aircraft started to smoke, so there was no alternative but to get out, which I did at about 15,000
feet. The parachute opened very nicely and everything
was calm and quiet as I floated towards the ground. I
was greeted by some farmers who immediately treated
me to a cup of tea and called a doctor, who tended the
superficial wounds I had received.
Flying Officer William Sprenger

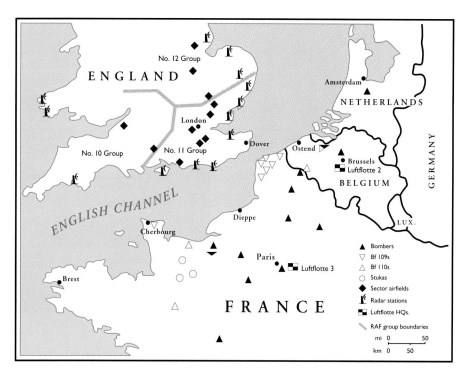

After the defeat of France, the Luftwaffe established airfields in Normandy to attack Southampton, Portsmouth
and Plymouth. Air bases in the Pas de Calais were used to
attack eastern England and London. Fighter Command's
No. 11 Group under Air Vice Marshal Keith Park, a New
Zealander, bore the brunt of the German offensive.

Residents of the south of England became accustomed to a sky full of aircraft
activity. Here a flight of Hurricanes passes overhead. The Hawker Hurricane and the
Supermarine Spitfire accounted for 1,733 enemy aircraft during the Battle of Britain.
(Inset) Max Aitken, Lord Beaverbrook, the Canadian expatriate newspaper baron,
was Minister of Aircraft Production in Churchill's wartime cabinet.

No. 1 RCAF squadron joined the
fray on August 20. Canadian pilots in
RAF 242 "Canadian" squadron had
already won their spurs in combat,
and there were hundreds of other
RCAF air and ground crew involved
in the battle. The climax came on
Sunday, September 15, Battle of Britain Day, when the Luftwaffe staged a
massive effort. German pilots were
told that the British were on their last
legs, but in countless dogfights it was
the Luftwaffe that was on the defensive. More than sixty German aircraft
were shot down, enough to convince
Hitler that air superiority
could not be won in time for
the planned fall invasion.
Operation Sea Lion was
postponed indefinitely. Hitler turned his attention to
Russia; he had lost what
would prove to be one of the
decisive battles of the war.

THE BLITZ

Hitler had specifically forbidden the Luftwaffe to bomb what
he called "open cities." Bombing
Warsaw or Rotterdam was one thing
– the Poles and Dutch could not hit
back – but there was no point in risk-
ing British retaliation against German cities until "Sea Lion" was
launched; then London would be attacked by air to sow confusion and
assist the landings. But on August 23
London was accidentally bombed
and Churchill ordered a reprisal raid
on Berlin. Hitler now demanded retaliation. On September 7, German

A "scramble." Hurricane pilots race to their planes to intercept enemy aircraft.

bombers dropped 330 tons of high explosive on London, more than were dropped during the entire First World War. The "Blitz" had begun and would last fifty-seven consecutive nights before the city won a brief respite.

The Blitz was the first systematic bombing campaign against a civilian population in history. Other cities and towns had been "terror bombed" on a single day or for short periods, but in the fall and winter of 1940–41 Hitler set out to discover if his enemy could be defeated by undermining Britain's industrial power and its will to continue the fight. The neighbourhoods of London, Southampton, Birmingham, Liverpool and Coventry became the front lines in a new kind of war.

Losses were staggering. In the first three weeks 7,000 civilians were killed. By the following summer the toll reached 44,000 dead with another 60,000 seriously injured. Almost a quarter of a million homes were destroyed and three quarters of a million were made homeless. At first London bore the brunt, but by mid-November other industrial and port cities had become the focus of the attack. In Glasgow 1,200 people were killed or injured in a single night. The raid on Coventry, November 14–15, 1940, was particularly deadly. Four hundred and fifty German bombers guided by radio beams dropped 500 tons of high explosive and 900 incendiary bombs. The centre of Coventry was a "sea of fire, clearly visible for many miles." More than a thousand people were killed or seriously wounded, many with horrible burns. The great cathedral was destroyed and twenty-one important war plants badly damaged. No one who knew

the truth about Coventry could doubt the impact that bombing could have on production and morale.

London's worst night was December 29, the last raid of a grim year. It was exceptionally dark with strong winds. Hundreds of incendiaries were dropped in a two-and-a-half-mile circle around St. Paul's Cathedral, and high-

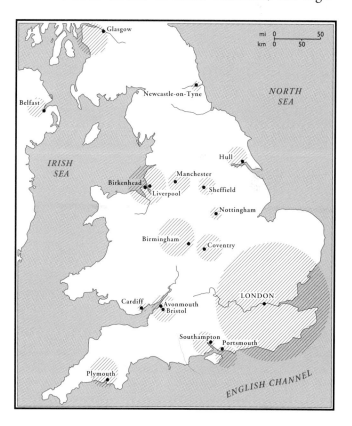

The Blitz, September 1940–May 1941. The shaded circles represent the *weight* of bombing on each city. London was the most frequently attacked of British cities with 18,000 tons of bombs dropped in eight months. Liverpool and Birmingham were next, but Coventry and Plymouth were the most heavily attacked in relation to their size.

Scenes of the Blitz were photographed by King Whyte, an RCAF PR officer in London. Taking refuge at the wail of the sirens became a grinding routine for Londoners. Thousands passed the nights in bomb shelters or in the deep tunnels of the underground rail system. Especially hard hit were the docks and East End since German bomber crews preferred to strike at the part of London closest to their bases in France.

explosive bombs fell throughout the area. Nearly fifteen hundred separate fires burned, many out of control. The two largest fires covered areas of one half and one quarter of a square mile. The financial district, known as the "City," was virtually destroyed.

There was little that could be done to prevent the raids or to defend the cities. Anti-aircraft gunnery was ineffective and night-fighters were almost non-existent. The Blitz of 1940–41 ended when Hitler, satisfied that Britain could not interfere with his plans, transferred the weight of the Luftwaffe to the Balkans and then to the Russian front. The German air force had sown the seeds of the whirlwind; German civilians would reap the harvest.

C.D. Howe is shown at the wheel of the 100,000th military vehicle to be produced in Canada. General Motors, Ford, Chrysler and other companies ceased production of civilian vehicles, using their assembly lines to manufacture trucks, scout cars and Bren gun carriers. By the end of the war Canada had produced 800,000 military vehicles.

ORGANIZING THE ECONOMY

The military crisis of the summer of 1940 changed everyone's assumptions about the war, including the government's plans for the economy. Job growth had occurred in some industries, but by the spring of 1940 there were still 600,000 Canadians on relief with the unemployment rate stuck at 10 per cent. Now, with British war production desperately needed for home defence, Canada had to develop its own arms industries. In the First World War, Canada produced mostly simple munitions; in 1940, airplanes, tanks, trucks, ships, radar and other sophisticated weapons were required, and ways had to be found to produce them.

This responsibility was assigned to C.D. Howe, the Minister of Munitions and Supply, who became the czar of Canadian war industry. An American-born engineer, who had helped design the Lakehead's giant

Thousands of women found work in munitions industries. Here Ethel Mitchell welds a Bren gun magazine.

grain elevators, he had entered politics as a Liberal in 1935 and quickly attracted King's attention. Howe had close contacts with private business and drew on these to bring scores of executives to Ottawa to help run his industrial empire.

Howe responded to the crisis of June 1940 with his customary energy. By the end of June a Wartime Industries Control Board was established. Orders for war equipment were quickly placed and money made available to expand factories and purchase the necessary machine tools. The new production facilities, financed by the taxpayer, were owned by the government.

Parliament had passed the War Measures Act in 1939, granting the cabinet, or privy council in constitutional language, the power to proclaim Privy Council Orders in the place of legislation. Parliament and public were simply informed that new regulations had been issued. The Wartime Prices and Trades Board controlled the supply of key commodities, fixed rents and established food rationing. The sugar ration, one-half pound a week per person, and the tea ration, "one half of the usual purchase," were minor inconveniences which made people feel involved in the war effort while saving shipping space.

The Board acted quickly to control inflation. In the First World War rapid price increases had shocked and destabilized the country, so when the first signs of inflation appeared in 1940, the Board froze prices, requiring an elaborate review before changes could be made. Price control required wage control, and in early 1941 the National War Labour Board, with nine regional boards, was

Loyal citizens
do not hoard,

RATIONED
SUGAR ½ lb. a week PER PERSON
TEA ½ of the usual PURCHASE
COFFEE ¾ of the usual PURCHASE

NATIONAL ARCHIVES OF CANADA/PA108300

NFB/NATIONAL ARCHIVES OF CANADA/C79525

Ration coupons became part of daily life for Canadian families, with tea, coffee, butter and meat subject to rationing. At 2½ pounds of meat per person per week, there was little to complain about. Gas rationing was more serious for those with cars as only 120 gallons a year was allowed. Liquor and beer rationing varied across the country. In Nova Scotia an adult was allowed one bottle of whiskey or rum or two cases of beer a month.

Women at work in a railway roundhouse. Most such jobs were lost to women when the men returned at the end of the war.

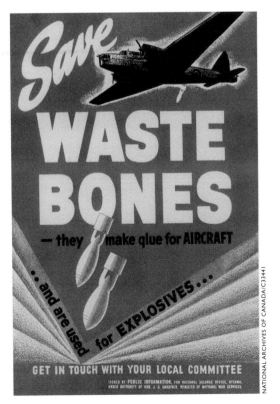

Save WASTE BONES
— they make glue for AIRCRAFT
...and are used for EXPLOSIVES...

GET IN TOUCH WITH YOUR LOCAL COMMITTEE

ISSUED BY PUBLIC INFORMATION, FOR NATIONAL SALVAGE OFFICE, OTTAWA, UNDER AUTHORITY OF HON. J. G. GARDINER, MINISTER OF NATIONAL WAR SERVICES.

NATIONAL ARCHIVES OF CANADA/C33441

created to enforce regulations limiting wage increases to a small cost-of-living bonus.

Hourly workers weren't the only ones to share the burden. All salaries were frozen, with a cost-of-living bonus available to those earning under $3,000 a year. Promotions were subject to close scrutiny and rarely authorized.

These measures, combined with strong demand for workers of all kinds, produced one of the most efficient war-economies in the world. There were jobs for everyone, including married women, who entered the labour force in large numbers. Ordinary Canadians had rarely been able to get steady work even before the Depression. Most of Canada's industries were seasonal, and regular layoffs in mining, forestry, the fishery, transportation and manufacturing were normal. Now there was full employment fifty-two weeks a year, and even if wage rates were frozen, good money could be made through overtime and everyone in the family could contribute. The number of fourteen- and fifteen-year-olds in the work force increased steadily during the war.

RAF Ferry Command

Getting the thousands of aircraft produced in North American factories to Britain forced rapid advances in transatlantic flying. Hitherto, the North Atlantic had been braved by pioneers, but most flights had followed the more southerly routes. Historian Carl Christie describes the work of Ferry Command.

Airpower was one of the keys to victory in the Second World War. We tend to ignore, however, the very planes that made this success possible. Many came from British factories, but many more – even before Pearl Harbor – were built in the United States, and some in Canada. Initially all aircraft from North America reached Britain in the holds of ships, running the gauntlet of the U-boat-infested North Atlantic.

In the summer of 1940, Lord Beaverbrook, Winston Churchill's Canadian-born Minister of Aircraft Production, sponsored a scheme to fly multi-engine aircraft under their own power from American factories to Britain. Despite naysayers at the Air Ministry who said it could not be done (pointing out that the North Atlantic had only been flown by the bravest and most experienced of aviators and then only in the summer months), arrangements were made for volunteers from the Commonwealth and the United States to ferry Lockheed Hudsons across the Atlantic. The Canadian Pacific Railway provided the administrative apparatus. The first seven Hudsons made the flight the night of November 10/11, 1940. By the end of the year twenty-five

had reached Britain successfully and the experiment was judged a success.

Soon, the civilian Atlantic Ferry Organization (or ATFERO), as it was called by its staff, was ferrying aircraft across the Pacific to Australia and southeast Asia, and along the coast of South America and across the South Atlantic to the trans-Africa airway and on to Cairo, Iraq, India and southeast Asia. Canada constructed a new airfield at Goose Bay, Labrador, to take the pressure off Gander as the jumping-off point for transatlantic flights and soon aircraft of shorter range flew to Britain via Greenland and Iceland.

In July 1941 ATFERO was taken over by the RAF as Ferry Command, but throughout the war retained its basically civilian character. Although a British command, it had its headquarters in Montreal, as the first occupant of the new Dorval airport, and relied upon hundreds of Canadian staff in every aspect of the operation. The RCAF, the Department of Transport and Trans-Canada Air Lines helped in a variety of unsung ways.

Though the crews of Ferry Command did not face the dangers of flying against the enemy, theirs was not an easy task. In the course of delivering almost 10,000 aircraft around the world, over 500 military and civilian airmen – more than 200 of them Canadians – lost their lives with Ferry Command. In the process they helped win the war and laid the foundation for postwar commercial aviation.

Carl Christie

Flying in Ferry Command was not without peril. Here a Hudson bomber burns at Dorval. The flight line and other planes awaiting delivery can be seen in the background.

CANAV. COL.

THE U-BOAT THREAT

In September 1939 the German navy was in the middle of a construction program designed to produce a large surface fleet by 1943. The U-boat arm, which had almost defeated Britain in 1917, was not a priority, and only twenty-five of the fifty-seven available U-boats were ocean-going. Most German navy officers shared the British belief that convoys escorted by warships would be safe from submarine attack. The invention of an ultrasonic detector, which located underwater objects from the echoes of pulses generated by an asdic set (now called sonar), seemed to further limit the chances of a successful U-boat attack.

These assumptions changed slowly after the war broke out. The German surface fleet was too small to challenge the Royal Navy and could only seek to tie down British battleships in a blockade. The losses of the *Graf Spee* and the ten destroyers at Narvik, and damage inflicted on other ships, contrasted sharply with the relative success of a handful of U-boats, which sank a battleship, an aircraft carrier and scores of merchant ships. But it was the prospect of U-boat bases in France that transformed German strategic planning for the war at sea. If the long voyage from the Baltic could be avoided, U-boats could operate well out into the Atlantic for much longer periods. Admiral Karl Dönitz, who had long argued the case for the submarine as the decisive weapon against Britain, moved his headquarters to France and began to implement the "wolf-pack" tactics he had devised before the war.

The key to Dönitz's scheme was the use of high-powered radio transmitters to maintain contact be-

A convoy, photographed in 1940 from the deck of an RCN destroyer. The convoy system made it possible for destroyers and corvettes to give some protection to large numbers of slow-moving freighters. Fast liners such as the *Queen Mary*, which was converted into a troopship, usually travelled alone, relying on speed to outwit the U-boats.

This remarkable sequence of photos of a U-boat encounter in the North Atlantic was taken from the Sunderland flying boat that sank it. Frank Cauley of Gloucester, Ontario, was navigator. The sub was surprised on the surface and decided to fight it out. The Sunderland took several hits from gunfire. Emergency leak stoppers patched the large hole, but to patch the smaller shrapnel holes in the hull before they could land, the crew had to chew wads of chewing gum. The Wrigley company later rewarded them with gift packs of Spearmint.

tween his headquarters and each U-boat. The "pack" would spread out in search of a convoy, report its location, and then wait until the "wolves" had gathered to attack. The other innovation, also practised before the war, was to attack at night on the surface, avoiding the problems of slow underwater speed and the danger of being picked up by sonar. Dönitz's plans were greatly helped by radio-direction finding stations which could pinpoint signals from Allied convoys and by British carelessness with codes that were quickly deciphered.

The significance of the new offensive was immediately apparent. In the first half of 1940 the U-boat threat had all but disappeared; but in July thirty-eight ships were sunk, in August, fifty-six, and in October, sixty-three went down. This turnaround was not due to an increase in the number of submarines; German construction yards barely kept up with losses of twenty-eight U-boats sunk by the Allies. Success was won by half a dozen small wolf-packs attacking weakly defended convoys.

The achievements of the period the German navy called the

"happy time" led to a steady increase in U-boat construction. Dönitz claimed that with 300 U-boats he could force Britain out of the war. By the end of 1941 he was close to his goal.

The initial Allied response to the renewed submarine threat was to increase the number of escorts and equip them with radar capable of detecting surfaced U-boats. The Royal Navy was able to take advantage of the cancellation of "Sea Lion," shifting destroyers to the Atlantic, but corvettes, originally intended for coastal patrol, were also pressed into service as mid-ocean escorts. Even with corvettes in action, the Royal Navy was hard pressed to find enough escorts to protect trans-Atlantic convoys. In the winter of 1940–41 the Royal Canadian Navy was asked to build a new base in St. John's and to develop a Newfoundland Escort Force capable of an "end-to-end," St. John's to Londonderry, role.

Properly equipped corvettes could perform effectively as defensive escorts committed to "the safe and timely arrival of the convoy." Unfortunately, RCN corvettes were poorly equipped

Unnatural and unhealthy...

Life in a U-boat is unnatural and unhealthy. There is no sharp distinction between night and day, or even the seasons.... The fog on board gets on your nerves. The perpetual din, the movement of the boat. The effects of drinking strong coffee and too much smoking are bad for the stomach and nerves. I have seen lads of twenty-three, after two years of it, become unfit for seagoing service.

Wolfgang Luth

and too often chased U-boats instead of protecting shipping. The RCN tried to improve the seaworthiness and internal design of the notoriously wet corvette, but there were no modern gyroscopic compasses available, existing sonar sets were obsolete, and new Canadian-built radar sets proved incapable of locating the small target of a U-boat's conning tower. It soon became apparent that only chance could bring a corvette into contact with a U-boat, and then the only useful weapon available was the ship itself, used as a ram.

Fortunately the Battle of the Atlantic did not depend only on the quality of British or Canadian escorts in 1941. Dönitz's need to stay in radio communication with his fleet proved to be his Achilles heel. The German military based the security of their wireless signals on an invention called Enigma. This device, which resembled a typewriter, was an electro-mechanical, wired enciphering machine with a series of wheels that allowed for an infinite number of settings. Pressing typewriter key A would produce C or Z or T depending on

Ice could make a corvette stagger in the North Atlantic swells and made life miserable for the crew. The *Shawinigan* (above) is tied up at St. John's with ice damage that required repairs in the dockyards at Halifax (Below) The *Collingwood*, photographed in 1942.

The loss of HMS Nerissa

On April 30, 1941, HMS Nerissa was sunk in the North Atlantic by submarine attack. Eighty-four Canadian servicemen and nine civilians were among the 207 passengers and crew lost. Private J.H. Mara, an RCMP officer serving with the military police, described the attack in a letter home.

There was a terrific explosion as the torpedo hit the starboard side and all the lights went out. I was thrown against the steel partition of the washroom and was dazed a bit. I had to light a match to find my way out. Water was already in the corridor and the men were rushing past my cabin so that I could not get in there to get my lifejacket. There was absolutely no panic and we got to our boat stations, mine being on the port side. Luckily there was not enough of a list to prevent the launching of the boat. All did not go well and down went the stern first with me in the stern and I got my first sea bath. Luckily I was holding tight as I had a hunch something like that would happen. Eventually the bow came down but the boat was swamped. Some of the boys got out and swam for it, two of them being RCMP lads, and they found a raft. The remainder of us, nineteen in all, stayed put as the airtight drums in the bow and stern kept us afloat. Had we had many more in the boat it would not have held us.

The sub came around to our side of the ship and passed within fifty feet of us, and the second torpedo went under our boat and hit the stern of the ship just outside our cabin. The third hit just before the boilers exploded and the whole middle portion of the ship exploded, leaving the stern and the bow afloat for a few

seconds...There was absolutely no suction when the ship went down as I came across a negro the next day who had been swimming and he said that the bow just missed him.... The sub came to the surface about half a mile away and had all its lights on. I am glad to say we did not drift near it....

We only had two of the ship's crew with us, one a steward who went mad and died within an hour, the other the ship's doc, who did not say anything all night, in fact I did not know he was with us until the next morning. Apparently he did not know much or anything about the lifeboats. They carry a lot of equipment but we did not know where anything was and, being awash, the floorboards were loose and made it difficult to find things. Also the plug in the boat was out and we could not find it so we had to stand with water up to our waists till we were picked up eight and a half hours later. We bailed the water out with our hands all the time and managed to keep about two inches of the side of the boat in view most of the time. It did not do much good but it kept us warm and the big waves only came to our chest instead of going over us. It rained most of the night but there was only a little wind. After a few hours, some of the men started to go and by the time we were picked up we lost seven of the nineteen. Our feet got so stiff that we could hardly move and only managed to get two overboard. The rest were floating about in the boat. The chaps on the destroyer said it wasn't a pleasant sight.... I have never seen such a welcome sight as that destroyer....

Private J.H. Mara

the setting. So long as both parties knew the day's selection, communication was instantaneous and apparently totally secure.

In fact, Polish mathematicians had begun cracking Enigma transmissions well before the war began. Polish-French collaboration led to further refinements and after 1940 work was continued at Bletchley Park in Britain, where the Government Code and Cypher School employed hundreds of men and women decoding and deciphering Germany's most secret messages.

Dönitz's signal traffic was a high priority, and by May 1941 most of the German naval Enigma keys were broken and it became possible to reroute convoys around the wolf-packs. Consequently, despite the steady increase in the number of U-boats, shipping losses declined in the last six months of 1941. By December the Battle of the Atlantic appeared to be under control and "Ultra," as the intelligence based on deciphering German signals was called, seemed to provide a guarantee for the future.

HALIFAX AND ST. JOHN'S

By 1941 Halifax was one of the most important ports in the world. It was the headquarters and nerve centre for Canadian naval operations, the gathering place for North Atlantic convoys, a coastal fortress, a naval training establishment and the location of a 3,500-man RCAF base for air defence and anti-submarine reconnaissance. Around the harbour, repair facilities for Allied ships employed thousands of men and woman. The city was ill-prepared to cope with all these activities. Housing was in short supply and Halifax lacked the restaurants, hotels, bars and other amenities that sailors hoped to find in a port.

Frederic Edwards, a writer for *Maclean's,* described the streets of Halifax in 1941 as filled "with a cross section of the Empire. You may hear," he wrote, "within the space of one block Cockney, Yorkshire, Lancashire and Scottish accents … Egyptian, Malaysian and Hindu seamen wait in line before theatre box offices with airmen from Australia and New Zealand, Canadian soldiers and sailors of Allied countries: Free French, Norwegians, Dutchmen, Poles. After nightfall a civilian on Barrington, the main street, looks as if he doesn't belong."

St. John's, the capital of Newfoundland, was much smaller and even less ready to take on its new role as the main base for anti-submarine operations in the eastern Atlantic. Marc Milner, the naval historian, has compared St. John's to Hvalfjordhur, a makeshift port in Iceland:

Convoy in Bedford Basin, Halifax, April 1942. Halifax was the gathering place for HX "fast" convoys eastbound for Britain, which travelled at minimum speed of 9 knots. SC convoys, which grouped slower ships, sailed from Sydney, Cape Breton.

DND/NATIONAL ARCHIVES OF CANADA/PA112993

It may seem unkind to compare the capital of Britain's oldest colony to a bleak Icelandic fiord, but for warships in need the two ports were equally barren. Facilities necessary for the support of a large fleet of escorts were almost totally lacking.... The lone drydock was fully employed with repairs to merchant men and lacked both equipment and manpower to do work to naval standards. It was, in any event, the only drydock for hundreds of miles. Priority was given to emergency repairs....

The Royal Navy tried to make up for this neglect by sending auxiliary fleet oilers, supply ships and a destroyer-tender to serve as a floating base, but "Newfyjohn," as the sailors called the city, was not brought up to standard as a naval base until 1944. The RCN would have to make do during the two most crucial years of the war at sea.

These problems were evident to all in May 1941 when the first RCN escorts arrived in St. John's. Seven corvettes, *Agassiz, Alberni, Chambly, Cobalt, Collingwood, Orillia* and *Wetaskiwin*, the latter known to all as the "wet-ass-Queen," sailed in early June on their first "North Atlantic run." There was much to learn and too little time available.

OPERATION "BARBAROSSA"

Hitler had always intended to attack the Soviet Union, destroy its armed forces and establish German control of a large part of its territory. His dreams of a "Thousand Year Reich" were based on the "living space" to be acquired in the east where German soldiers, like mediaeval knights, would garrison cities, exploiting the "subhuman" Slavic population as serfs.

The timing of the invasion was influenced by Hitler's frustration at Britain's failure to acknowledge defeat. Russia, he told his worried generals, was Churchill's last hope for continuing the war. A sudden attack, he insisted, with all available resources, would destroy the Soviet Union in a matter of months, certainly before winter.

A detailed plan was ready by December 1940 and German units began to assemble in occupied Poland shortly thereafter. Despite warnings from the British government, which followed the German buildup through Ultra, and reports from a Soviet spy, Richard Sorge in Tokyo, Stalin was convinced that Hitler would not attack. The Soviet Union had been a faithful ally to Germany since signing the Non-Aggression Pact, and Stalin interpreted all warnings as British attempts to provoke war.

Hitler's campaign in the Balkans, which began with the invasion of Yugoslavia in early April, convinced Sta-

It was not the "Hun" but the Red Army that suffered big losses, with 300,000 men taken prisoner in the first week on the central front alone.

lin that he was right. The German army and much of the Luftwaffe would surely be drawn into a prolonged battle against the British and their allies. By the end of the month Yugoslavia and Greece had fallen and British and New Zealand forces had retreated to Crete. Four weeks later Crete fell to a costly and high-risk airborne assault. Hitler had not needed to commit any of the forces preparing for the invasion of the Soviet Union. Barbarossa began on June 22, the earliest date ground and weather conditions would permit.

The Soviet army, slowly recovering from the purges of the late thirties, was beginning a vast re-equipment program, but in June 1941 few of the new T-34 tanks or other new equipment had been delivered. The German army achieved strategic, operational and tactical surprise, overwhelming the Soviet forces. Three large army groups struck deep into the country, one north to Leningrad, one in the centre towards Moscow, and one to the south to capture Kiev and occupy the Ukraine.

Within hours of the invasion Winston Churchill told a worldwide radio audience that "any man or state who fights on against Nazidom will have our aid … we shall give whatever help we can to Russia and the Russian people." There had not been time to consult Canada or the other Dominions but Churchill said he believed the decision was one "in which the great Dominions will in due course concur."

The Canadian government accepted Churchill's initial statement but did not follow the British lead in establishing a formal alliance with Russia. There were no diplomatic relations with the U.S.S.R., and Canadian Communists, who had actively opposed the war effort prior to the invasion of Russia, remained in prison. In 1941, the Soviet Union seemed likely to join the long list of nations under German control, and Canadians still saw themselves as Britain's principal ally.

A poster urging Canadians to do their bit includes headgear of the three women's branches of the services: the Women's Division of the RCAF, the Canadian Women's Army Corps and the Women's Royal Canadian Naval Service.

ENLISTING WOMEN

Great Britain had begun recruiting women for the armed services in 1938 but the Canadian government saw no need to follow this example. When the RAF proposed to send members of the Women's Auxiliary Air Force, the WAAFs, to Canada to work at air training schools, the Canadian cabinet acted quickly to avoid embarrassment.

The Women's Division of the RCAF was authorized in July 1941 and quickly enlisted thousands of young women, 17,000 by 1945. In August the Canadian Women's Army Corps was announced and training bases were established at St. Anne de Bellevue, Quebec; Kitchener, Ontario; and Vermillion, Alberta. More than 21,000 served in the "CWACs." The "Wrens," or Women's Royal Canadian Naval Service, did not begin recruiting until 1942 and grew more slowly. Training establishments at Galt, Ontario, and St. Hyacinthe, Quebec, enrolled 6,718 recruits. All the women who served were volunteers and many sought to play an active role in the "real" war.

CANADIAN WAR MUSEUM 95-00501

Nano Pennefather embarks for England

A cheer of welcome greeted our small flight of forty members of the Royal Canadian Air Force, Women's Division, as we marched up the gangway of the troopship SS *Strathmore*. Along with a group of French-Canadian nursing sisters from Montreal, we joined 4,000 men of the army and air force.

After depositing our kit bags in our cabins, some of us couldn't wait to go back on deck. The soldiers on board were as new to all this as we were.

Some were leaning over the railing getting their last glimpse of Canada; others were sitting in a corner sharing a bottle. A group surrounded a very young-looking private playing a harmonica. Another played an accordion and a third was keeping time with a pair of spoons. As soon as they spotted us someone yelled, "Now we can dance!"

We danced with one soldier then another then another... we danced as I've never danced before. The last partner to cut in was an air force blue and just as I noticed his red armband marked SP – Service Police – he leaned close and whispered, "Go back to your cabin – that's an order."

"Spoil-sport," I grumbled under my breath. I did not share in his concern that there were only about ten women among a few hundred men in the darkened quarters of the lower deck. Some of our wiser sisters took a dim view of our evening's adventure, but for those who were there it was a glorious celebration of our first night at sea.

Nano Pennefather

On the boat to England: Nano Pennfather is on the right.

RCAF Women's Division photographers head out for some flying. Left to right, Flight Sergeant A.D. Lang, M. Dudlyke, M. Clayborne and Jeanne Farris.

Some women did go overseas to serve at Canadian Headquarters in the United Kingdom but most stayed in Canada, where they worked in traditional women's jobs as secretaries, clerks, cooks and laundresses. Others had the chance to learn new skills as electricians, mechanics, and radar technicians, but there was no suggestion that women should be employed in combat roles. Doctors and nursing sisters were the only group to work close to the front lines.

THE BRITISH COMMONWEALTH AIR TRAINING PLAN

The idea of training Commonwealth airmen in Canada had been under discussion since 1938 but the first Initial Training School did not open until April 1940. No. 1 ITS was located at a hunt club in suburban Toronto. Here 164 volunteers joined fifty-seven RCAF pilot officers in the first BCATP course. Most of them progressed to No. 1 Elementary Flying Training School at Malton, but before the end of 1940 there were twelve other EFTSs and eight advanced Service Flying Training Schools.

The BCATP was designed to produce the entire range of aircrew, not just pilots. Specialized air navigation courses began at Trenton, Ontario, while bombing and gunnery schools opened in Ontario, Manitoba, Alberta and Saskatchewan. Wireless, flight engineering, radar and other specialist schools were created, including one for aviation medicine and a school of cookery.

DND/PL20839

Training accidents were common, but seldom as odd as this one, involving two Ansons, one of which landed on top of the other. The Avro Anson was produced under licence in Canada and widely used as a trainer and light transport aircraft.

COMMONWEALTH AIR TRAINING PLAN MUSEUM/BRANDON, MAN.

Washed out

Howie was definitely washed out. I feel sorry for him because I know how bad I'd feel if I were grounded. A lot of fellows here are washed-out pilots. The thing is, they just

couldn't be taught to fly in the short time the Air Force has to spend. There's no disgrace attached to it at all. If you're a born pilot, you'll get your wings, but if you're slow to learn, they just won't spend the time on you. A few of the fellows who washed out as pilots still feel pretty bad about it. This is their last chance as air crew, and they don't seem to have the confidence in themselves that they should.

Leading Aircraftman Wilson Duff, Chatham, N.B.

Trinity to Wellington in a year

I never cease to marvel at the fact that I was writing my final examinations of my first year at Trinity College, University of Toronto, in April 1940, and had been trained as a navigator and on my way overseas by December.

We were flying operations by April 1941, less than a year after I enlisted. Only four of the twenty-two of us from my class would survive our first tour of operations.

Squadron Leader Bob Dale, DSO, DFC, CD

(Left) Bob Dale's class at No. 1 Air Observer School poses in front of an Anson, July 1940. Dale is seated front row left.

(Above) Dale's Wellington crew of 150 Squadron, RAF Bomber Command, May 1941. Dale stands second from left, holding the dog.

65

BCATP scenes

Canada was ideal for training aircrew – usually-clear weather, open spaces, well away from the battle lines, and a flying tradition providing a core of personnel to build on. All across the country, but especially on the prairies, communities became accustomed to the drone of aircraft and the coming and going of classes of recruits. The large photo shows an impressive array of Tiger Moths on the flight line at the Elementary Flying Training School at Oshawa, as student pilots and instructors head out for some flying. The de Havilland Tiger Moth and the Fleet Finch were the chief primary trainers. The other photos, clockwise from the top: a Canadian-made Hurricane at the Canadian National Exhibition, Toronto, in 1941, as part of the recruiting effort; a class in radio operations at Virden, Manitoba, 1944; an Avro Anson, mainly used as an advanced trainer for pilots and navigators; Harvards practising formation flying; Fairchild Cornell II elementary trainers on the prairie at No. 19 EFTS, Virden; and a student gunner in a dummy power-operated turret at Jarvis, Ontario, 1941.

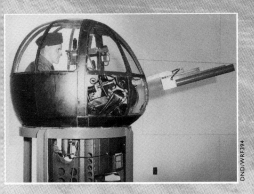

By war's end the BCATP had produced close to 50,000 pilots and 25,000 navigators as part of a grand total of 131,553 aircrew graduates. Eighty per cent of these were Canadians. Canada's "billion-dollar university of the air" was an enormous contribution to Allied war effort. As historian and Wing Commander Fred H. Hitchens put it, "If the Battle of Waterloo was won on the playing fields of Eton ... the air battle of Europe was won on the fields of the BCATP."

WAR WITH JAPAN

Conflict between Japan and the western powers developed out of Japan's aggressive drive to reduce China to the status of a colony. Formosa was seized in 1894, and in 1910 the long bitter struggle to conquer Korea and subdue its inhabitants began. The Chinese revolution of 1911, which gave birth to the Republic under Sun Yat-sen and his successor, Chiang Kai-shek, spurred the Japanese to issue the infamous "Twenty-one Demands" of 1915, requiring the Chinese Republic to accept Japanese hegemony.

Japan was then closely allied with Great Britain, and Britain joined the United States in persuading the Japanese to withdraw their ultimatum. At Versailles, Japan was rewarded with mandates over the German island colonies in the Pacific and the extraterritorial rights in China formerly held by Germany. Japan also established economic control of Manchuria and much of northern China.

Public and congressional opinion in the United States of America was sympathetic to the Republic of China and increasingly hostile towards Japan. U.S. economic interests, Christian churches committed to large-scale missionary activities in China, and the U.S. military, concerned about the size of the Japanese navy, combined to press for the Washington Naval Treaty of 1922. This agreement, accepted reluctantly by Japan, imposed a limit to naval armaments for all the great powers and forced Japan to "affirm" the principle of Chinese sovereignty and equal access to its markets. The British government, pressured by Canada and more importantly the United States, did not renew the Anglo-Japanese Treaty, thus severing an important Japanese tie with the West.

Liberal groups in Japan were prepared to accept a new world order in which Japan could avoid the costs of an arms race and concentrate on economic development in the large areas of Asia already under Japanese control. By the early 1930s liberal politicians had been displaced by militarists and the Japanese army had conquered Manchuria, annexing it to Japan as the province of Manchukuo. Protests against this aggression led Japan to leave the League of Nations, which took no action beyond filing a report.

Japanese troops arriving in China, 1932. After the conquest of Manchuria, the Japanese military forced its will upon Japan, assassinating Prime Minister Inugai and other politicians. The army was determined to militarize Japanese society and conquer China, and the bombing of Shanghai in February 1932 showed just how determined the army was.

The Great Depression struck trading nations like Japan with particular severity, and by 1934 Japan was fully committed to a policy of empire-building with the goal of autarchy, or economic self-sufficiency. The Washington Naval Treaty was renounced and a major naval construction program started. The army grew rapidly, transforming Japan into a militaristic state that devoted most of its national budget to preparations for war. Then, in 1936, Japan joined Hitler's Anti-Comintern Pact, gaining a powerful ally before launching a campaign to conquer much of China.

This undeclared war was fought with incredible savagery. The world watched with horror as the Chinese nationalists in Shanghai were overwhelmed, losing a quarter of a million men. The capture of Nanjing was accompanied by rape, torture and murder on an unprecedented

Chiang Kai-shek (1887–1975), in the front centre of this group, president of the Republic of China, was appointed Supreme Commander of the China Theatre by Churchill and Roosevelt in 1941.

scale – 200,000 Chinese were massacred after the city had fallen. Still Chiang Kai-shek refused to surrender, so the Japanese established a new Chinese state under "the Last Emperor," a puppet ruler firmly under their control.

Western governments protested Japanese actions but no one was prepared to provide more than token assistance to China on the grounds that Japanese expansion did not threaten their national security. This inaction in the face of naked aggression should not be confused with moral neutrality; by 1940 Japan was regarded as a dangerous and barbaric aggressor-nation guilty of serious crimes against humanity.

After the defeat of France, Japan occupied the northern part of French Indo-China (Vietnam), agreed to a military alliance with Hitler and Mussolini, and demanded that Britain close the Burma road, Chiang Kai-shek's only land-link with the west. Churchill accepted a temporary closure; Italy's declaration of war threatened British control of the Mediterranean and the last thing the Royal Navy needed was a third enemy with a fleet as large as Japan's.

General Hideki Tojo, seen here with Stalin in 1940, became prime minister of Japan on October 18, 1941. Tojo was the "embodiment of hard line militarism" and his appointment marked the end of serious peace efforts on the part of Japan.

The United States took a different view. The U.S. Navy had war-gamed conflict with Japan and was confident that while Japan could easily overcome American garrisons in the Philippines in the early weeks of conflict, Japan could not possibly win a protracted war. Japan's economy was one seventh the size of America's and lacked oil as well as most other essential commodities. The Japanese were well aware of this disparity and their strategists had reached identical conclusions.

After Franklin Delano Roosevelt, "FDR" as the press called him, was re-elected in November 1940, he ordered measures designed to rearm the U.S. and warned Japan that further aggression would bring American retaliation. FDR placed an embargo on shipments of war materiel to Japan, instituted the draft, creating a large conscript army, and ordered the U.S. Pacific Fleet with its battleships and aircraft carriers to move from San Diego to a new base in the Hawaiian islands – Pearl Harbor. These moves, combined with publicity about the expansion of the U.S. Navy and the new B-17 Flying Fortress bombers, were intended as evidence that even a neutral America carried a "big stick."

Japan persisted in its suicidal policies, occupying southern Indo-China in July 1941. News of the occupation of Saigon led Washington to announce a new embargo blocking the export of oil to Japan and freezing Japanese overseas assets. Britain, Holland and the Commonwealth countries, including Canada, followed suit.

The oil embargo forced Japan to choose between war and peace because without access to oil the economy and the Japanese war machine would be shut down. If Japan had chosen peace it would have lost very little and gained a great deal. After lengthy negotiations, the American position came down to requiring Japanese withdrawal from China and Indo-China. In return Japan would receive from the Americans "most-favoured-nation treatment and reduction of trade barriers," including the free entry of Japan's main export, raw silk. The Japanese chose to prepare for war while continuing to discuss peace. A decision one way or the other was to be made by November 30, 1941. By then the naval task force that was to attack the American fleet at Pearl Harbor was at sea, and war was inevitable.

HONG KONG

Future relations with Japan had been one of the main topics at the first wartime meeting between Roosevelt and Churchill. The talks, in August 1941 aboard the battleship HMS *Prince of Wales* in Placentia Bay, Newfoundland, are

The Globe and Mail

Metropolitan
Edition

TORONTO, MONDAY, DECEMBER 8, 1941.

JAPAN ATTACKS HAWAII

Tokyo Declares War on U.S. and Britain

IMPERIALS OPEN 'BIG PUSH' IN LIBYA

VON ROMMEL
IS HIT HARD
BY BRITISH

Singapore Raided; Japs Land in North Malaya;
Report Americans Bag 4 Subs, 6 Planes, Carrier

BULLETINS

The U.S. battle-ship *Arizona* afire and listing badly after the Japanese surprise attack on the U.S. naval base at Pearl Harbor, December 7, 1941. Mackenzie King commented: "This is the most crucial moment in all the world's history. The result will be, in the end, to shorten the war."

SOUTHAM INC.

best remembered for the declaration of principles known as "The Atlantic Charter," but they also produced agreement on joint action in the Pacific. Japan was to be warned that "any further encroachment in the southwest Pacific" would "compel U.S. countermeasures," meaning war might follow from attacks on British or Dutch colonies.

On Churchill's return to England he asked the Admiralty to send the *Prince of Wales* and the *Repulse* with an aircraft carrier to Singapore "in the hope of steadying the Japanese political situation." At the same time, General George C. Marshall, the U.S. Chief of Staff, approved plans to send 2,250 additional troops to the Philippines, a move he acknowledged was "a reversal of the long standing policy" against sending reinforcements to an is-

land that could not be defended in an all-out war. Marshall also authorized the transfer of the small number of available B-17 bombers to Clark Field in the Philippines.

The British chiefs of staff had built up army strength in Malaya from nine to thirty-two battalions and proposed the reinforcement of Hong Kong, arguing "Japan has latterly shown a certain weakness in her attitude.... It would have a great moral effect in the whole Far East and would show Chiang Kai-shek that we really intend to fight it out in Hong Kong." The Canadian government was asked to supply "a small reinforcement ... one or two battalions ... in view of Canada's special position in the North Pacific."

The Canadian cabinet considered this request on September 23, seeking ex-

> ### "Not the slightest chance of holding Hong Kong..."
>
> *In January 1941, Churchill, as was his nature, made his view on the matter of defending Hong Kong quite clear. His view was later to change.*
>
> If Japan goes to war there is not the slightest chance of holding Hong Kong or relieving it. It is most unwise to increase the loss we shall suffer there. Japan will think long before declaring war on the British Empire, and whether there are two or six battalions at Hong Kong will make no difference to her choice.
>
> Winston Churchill

A small reinforcement...

This request came by telegram from General C.H. Ismay, Chief of the Imperial General Staff. It was approved by Churchill and dated September 19, 1941.

In the event of war in the Far East accepted policy has been that Hong Kong should be considered as an outpost and held as long as possible. We have thought hitherto that it would not serve any ultimate useful purpose to increase the existing army garrison which consists of four battalions of infantry and represents bare minimum required for its assigned task.

Situation in the Orient however has now altered. There have been signs of a certain weakening in attitude of Japan towards United States and ourselves. ... our view is that a small reinforcement (e.g. one or two more battalions) of Hong Kong garrison would be very fully justified. It would reassure Chiang Kai-shek as to genuineness of our intention to hold the colony and in addition would have a very great moral effect throughout the Far East....

We should be most grateful if Government of Canada would give consideration to providing for this purpose one or two Canadian battalions....Your Government will be well aware of difficulties now being experienced by us in providing the forces demanded by the situation in various parts of the world, despite the very great assistance which Dominions are furnishing. We consider that Canadian Government in view of Canada's special position in the North Pacific would wish in any case to be informed of the need as seen by us for the reinforcement of Hong Kong and the special value of such a measure at present time, even though on very limited scale.

On September 30, General Crerar recommended the Royal Rifles and Winnipeg Grenadiers be sent.

These units returned not long ago from duty in Newfoundland and Jamaica respectively. The duties which they there carried out were not in many respects unlike the task which awaits the units to be sent to Hong Kong.... Both are units of proven efficiency.

... I would be very reluctant to allot them indefinitely to a home defence role as the effect on their morale, following a period of "semi-overseas" responsibilities, would be bound to be adverse. The selection represents Eastern and Western Canada. In the case of the Royal Rifles, there is also the fact that this battalion, while nominally English-speaking, is actually drawn from a region overwhelmingly French-speaking in character and contains an important proportion of Canadians of French descent.

Colonel J.L. Ralston, Minister of Defence, approved Crerar's recommendation October 9, 1941. He later reviewed his reasoning.

It seemed to me ... that above all things we needed time, and I had very definitely in my mind, rightly or wrongly, that if Japan did come into the war the United States would be in too; and I had it definitely in my mind that the United States were none too ready to come in, and anything which would either defer or deter Japan from coming in would be highly desirable from our point of view.... It seemed to me that we had an opportunity to make a contribution, perhaps not large in numbers but certainly effective in its results which we should not disregard.

pert advice from Lieutenant-General Harry Crerar, Chief of the General Staff. Crerar had studied the problem of Hong Kong while attending the Imperial Defence College in 1934 and had written a comprehensive review of both the strategic and operational aspects of a Japanese assault on the colony. Like all other professional students of the question, he concluded that the garrison would be quickly overcome in the event of a major attack. The real issue was how to avert such a battle, and Crerar argued that if an alliance was forged between Britain and the United States, Japan would be deterred from starting a war that it was certain to lose.

Crerar recommended that Canada send a force of two battalions, the Royal Rifles of Canada and the Winnipeg Grenadiers, to Hong Kong. The cabinet agreed and "Force C," under Brigadier J.K. Lawson, left Vancouver in late October, arriving in the colony on November 16. Much has been made of the limited training of these battalions, but both units had been mobilized in 1940 and completed basic training while on garrison duty in Newfoundland and Jamaica. Everyone assumed that there would be adequate time to complete advanced training in the Far East with the new weapons and vehicles assembled for the expedition.

Personnel of the Royal Rifles of Canada (above) en route to Hong Kong, October 23, 1941. (Right) Members of the Winnipeg Grenadiers on the ship for Hong Kong.

Brigadier Lawson, an outstanding Permanent Force officer, noted that both units "contain excellent material and a number of good instructors." After his arrival in Hong Kong he recommended that Canada send a third battalion with an artillery regiment and other troops to create a brigade group. The British chiefs of staff, who still believed that any new Japanese aggression would be directed north against Russia or south to Thailand, agreed, and a formal request was on its way to Canada when the Japanese attack began.

The only hope of saving Hong Kong was through the intervention of Chiang Kai-shek, who had talked of sending ten divisions to assist the colony. Whatever his original intentions, the news from Pearl Harbor and the broad scope of the Japanese offensive ended all thoughts of a Chinese advance to the coast. The garrison was on its own.

The battle lasted until Christmas day and much blood was spilled in a fruitless attempt to stem the advance of an experienced Japanese infantry division supported by artillery and air power. The British commander, General Maltby, was sharply critical of the Canadians, blaming their lack of equipment and training for many of his difficulties. It is true that the trucks, universal carriers and

On December 8, 1941, only hours after the attack on Pearl Harbor, Japan's 38th Infantry Division attacked Hong Kong. Japanese aircraft quickly destroyed the six military planes in the colony. The garrison commander, General Maltby, had placed his British and Indian battalions along the "Gin Drinker's Line" to shorten the front. The two Canadian battalions were positioned to defend against amphibious attacks on Hong Kong Island. The Japanese quickly penetrated the mainland defences and Maltby withdrew to the island. British and Indian troops were unable to prevent landings and the Canadians were employed in a series of costly counterattacks. Hong King surrendered on December 26, 1941.

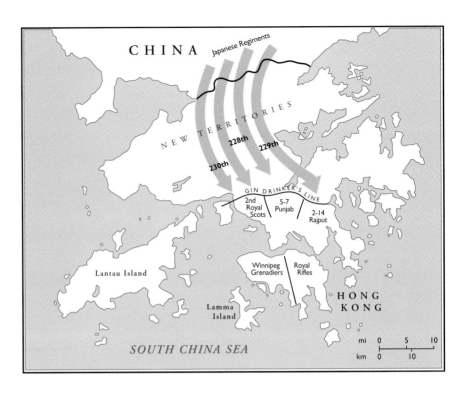

motorcycles sent from Canada never arrived, severely hampering Canadian mobility, but it was British and Indian troops who lost control of the forward defences in the first seventy-two hours, not Canadians.

Once the Japanese had landed on Hong Kong Island it was simply a matter of time. Churchill insisted that the garrison fight to the end and for a time General Maltby seemed to agree. Canadian officers found the attitude incomprehensible. When Brigadier Lawson's headquarters was surrounded, he had gone "outside to fight it out" and been killed. Lieutenant-Colonel Home of the Royal Rifles, now the senior Canadian officer, argued that further resistance was pointless and would only result in a waste of lives. Maltby disagreed and the hopeless struggle continued for several more days.

Canadian losses were heavy; 300 were killed or died of wounds, and 493 others were wounded. During the long years of brutal treatment and near-starvation in prisoner

DND/NATIONAL ARCHIVES OF CANADA/PA116460

Brigadier J.K. Lawson, a permanent force officer serving as Director of Military Training, was appointed to command "C" Force. He was killed in hand-to-hand combat with Japanese troops.

of war camps, another 257 died. Of the 1,975 Canadians who sailed from Vancouver, just over 1,400 made the voyage home in 1945. The attempt to deter war in the Pacific was a costly failure, though at the time it appeared to be a valuable contribution to the Allied cause.

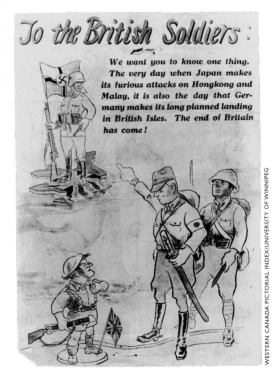

A Japanese propaganda leaflet directed to soldiers defending Hong Kong.

I feel like I'm going mad...

October 29, 1941
We've been at sea for two days. The ship shakes badly, we are all seasick. There are a number of long faces, sudden dashes to the washroom and disgusting accidents in the dining hall....

Yesterday afternoon, the lieutenant gave us a little lecture saying that ninety-nine percent of the population where we are going has syphilis. An interesting perspective for a young man who would like to have an intimate relation with a native. Well, there's always the consolation of free treatment from the army.

December 5, 1941
China is a curious country. What is striking is to see women work. Everywhere you see them carrying massive loads, walking miles as well. These women work at all ages, it's almost unbelievable because they are so frail, yet certainly not lazy.... In some areas – the taverns, hotels and clubs – it is necessary to fend off the young girls at the door.... Some of the guys have bought women for $60 a month. She does everything that a wife would do and is very loyal; that's more than one can say about Canadian spouses.

December 15, 1941
We are being continually bombarded. What monotonous music all the same. This morning's sky was as pure as your eyes, Charlotte. Eleven dive-bombers came to give us a different show.

The bombing is incredible! The earth has been trembling for an hour. It's been the most intense fireworks I've witnessed.... The building is being shaken to its foundations. If one hits the cabin we'll be finished....

The Japanese are now facing us, about a mile away. The water separates us....

All the "anglais" soldiers with whom I was and am in contact are really friendly and impressive. They destroy a little bit of the bad impression that I had of "English"

people. They are not able to understand our nonchalance; it is without a doubt a "canadien" trait that is very useful in war. For example, the other day I was writing my journal as the eggs fell from the sky. "Come on down, Blacky. The raid is on," they yelled from the back. "Just this sentence to finish and I'll be right there," I said. I heard them laughing. Their sense of humour is different from ours.

Georges "Blackie" Verreault (centre) with a couple of friends during training.

December 19, 1941
The situation is getting worse. Yesterday, enemy troops moved closer to the frontier. It seems that they're not far because their machine guns spit mortal venom. Oh, the misery! The noise! ... We're trapped like rats without any hope of escape.... Is it possible that I should die so stupidly, oh Charlotte, will you never see me again?

December 20, 1941
If I ever come back from this Hell, it seems that I will always have a big chip against the Japs. Sharp, Fairley, Orvais were just found dead. All newlyweds. Three more young widows in Canada.

December 22, 1941
Quite an original way to spend Christmas. I've just met my captain. He's not dead, after all.... During the dangerous moments we no longer see him. He practises the art of camouflage. It disgusts me.

December 24, 1941
Tomorrow is Christmas. Tonight, at home, we would have midnight Mass. Here, it's a mass of bombs.

December 26, 1941
Four in the afternoon on Christmas Day, we capitulated, surrendered. We've been beaten by these damn miniature men. How embarrassing! What shame! We ran out of ammunition. So much life sacrificed for this result. It's atrocious that my comrades died for nothing. I am unable to describe what I feel in my heart. I feel like I'm going mad.

Georges "Blackie" Verreault, Signaller, Brigade HQ

All the good men we lost...

It's hard to put into words our feelings when we heard the governor of the colony had surrendered to the enemy. I saw some men break down and cry like children, "What, surrender now?" they sobbed. "After all the good men we lost?"... I never dreamed it could happen, up to the last moment until Lieutenant Corrigan ordered us to lay down arms.

Private Tom Forsyth

"Never dreaming of the disaster that awaited us in Hong Kong" – Tom Forsyth in Jamaica.

Forsyth, of the Winnipeg Grenadiers, survived the rest of the war in a Japanese prison of war camp.

A little boy piloting bombers...

Jean Partridge to William "Pat" Patterson
Dear Bill,
All the girls almost as fast as they graduate are having medicals prior to overseas service. I'll worry about that when the time comes. I still have ten months here. I wouldn't like that work – I know I'd loathe it – but then, it's not a matter of liking, is it?...

Jean

Disillusioned with his job in the Prime Minister's office, "Pat" Patterson joined William Stevenson, the man called "Intrepid," in New York for work he hoped would be closer to the war effort.

Dear Pat,
I should write Harry [her brother] tonight. He'll get his wings the end of this month and then where to? I hope he comes through Montreal. He's almost twenty-two and I can never realize he's grown up. It's hard to think that a little boy who never used to be able to pronounce elevator without a "b" for a "v" is piloting bombers.

Jean

New York
Dear Jean,
While I'm not at liberty to talk much about my work, I can say that I have been disillusioned and disappointed with what I've seen....

Pat

Jean Partridge and Bill Patterson in New York

Children's Memorial Hospital, August 24, 1941
Dearest Pat,
... I'm sorry you aren't satisfied with your work in the U.S.A., but don't talk about finding peace of mind in one of the forces. It's not because I love you and don't want you in the forces that I say that. If I thought you would find real peace of mind there, that is where I should like you to be – not "like you to be," I would loathe it – but want you to be....

Yours as ever, Jean

New York, July 28, 1941, Patterson to Harry Ferns
Dear Harry,
I think that now is really the time for the United States to assert itself.... What a curious position they are in. As a nation they are incredibly rich and strong, but it seems in many ways like a giant's body with the brain of a child or an imbecile.... They have the strength but lack the apparatus of power. With the British, the situation is somewhat reversed. But when our friends here acquire some savvy and ... work up the appropriate national outlook, then I think there will be an imperialism such as the world has not yet seen. If the Russians fulfill your expectations, the world will be centred around two poles. Hurry, hurry, hurry, get in on the ground floor now....

Pat

New York, October 22, 1941, Patterson to Harry Ferns
... Canada has been receiving a good deal of notice here since the announcement of price control.....The thing has possibilities ... interviews with gold star mothers, saying, "I didn't raise my boy to be a statistician." ... where in God's name are they going to put all the newly-born bureaucracy that will be necessary?...

Pat

PART III

THE END OF THE BEGINNING

Halifax bombers, in which many RCAF aircrew flew, were used from 1941 to the end of the war and logged more than 75,000 sorties over enemy territory.

DND/PL40182

To most people the events of the winter of 1941–42 seemed to be a long string of calamities. Images of the American fleet sunk at Pearl Harbor, the heroic but futile defence of Hong Kong, the sinking of the *Prince of Wales* and *Repulse,* and the crushing Japanese victories in the Philippines and Singapore filled the newsreel theatres and newspaper headlines. The initial success of the Red Army's winter offensive in front of Moscow was briefly encouraging, but by January the counterattack had slowed, and the Germans gradually recovered ground.

In reality, December 1941 was the turning point of the war. The surprise attack on Pearl Harbor was a disaster not for the Americans but for the Japanese. The losses at Pearl Harbor were not nearly as serious as they seemed: the vital aircraft carriers were safe at sea and neither the oil storage nor the dockyard facilities were seriously damaged. America still held its major Pacific base and would soon mount the first attacks on Japan's empire.

The biggest problem for Roosevelt and his military advisors was what to do about Germany. Japan, they believed, could readily be defeated, but a German victory on the eastern front threatened Britain and ultimately the United States. Fortunately, Hitler resolved their dilemma by declaring war on the United States five days after Pearl Harbor. The U.S. Congress, left to its own devices, would have focused all energies upon Japan; now Roosevelt and General George C. Marshall, U.S. Chief of Staff, who had reached agreement with the British on a "Europe First" policy, were free to plan the war that really mattered.

The Soviet counter-offensive was another sign that the war was changing. Hitler's entire strategy in the east was based on the belief that the Soviet Union, like France, would sue for peace once

its armies had been defeated. By late November 1941 Hitler could argue that he was close to victory, but the winter campaign, which cost the German army a quarter of a million men, raised new doubts about German invincibility. If the Soviets could survive another summer of German attacks, their industrial potential, combined with that of the United States, would surely turn the tide. This was certainly the view held by Winston Churchill, who telegraphed to Roosevelt on December 12 that "he was enormously relieved at the turn world events have taken." To his foreign secretary, Anthony Eden, he wrote, "The accession of the United States makes amends for all, and with time and patience will give certain victory."

Churchill also had a clear plan of action for 1942, which he presented on his first visit to Washington in December 1941. The grand strategy that he proposed was based on the idea of gradually "wearing down" the German military machine. Russia was to be supplied with as much lend-lease aid as possible, while North Africa was to be cleared of the enemy by attacks from Egypt and new Anglo-American landings in French North Africa. RAF Bomber Command, aided by the United States Army Air Force, would "affect German production and morale by ever more severe bombing of their cities and

Winston Churchill addresses the Canadian House of Commons, December 1941.

harbours." Only limited operations would be attempted in the Pacific.

The U.S. chiefs of staff were not pleased with Churchill's proposals. The United States Navy wanted greater resources for the Pacific and General Marshall was strongly opposed to a diversion of resources into the Mediterranean. In the end, Churchill had his way; 1942 was a year in which the British Commonwealth and the United States gambled that the Soviet Union would survive until they were ready to assume a larger share of the war effort.

Churchill spent Christmas at the White House and then travelled north to Ottawa to meet with King's war cabinet and address the House of Commons. The atmosphere in the House was electric, for most Canadians revered Churchill as their heroic war leader. This was the speech in which Churchill reminded the members and the world that after the fall of France it had been suggested that "in three weeks England would have her neck wrung like a chicken." With studied dramatic pauses he intoned, "Some chicken. Some neck."

Churchill's visit reassured Canadians, but the country could not escape the grip of partisan politics, and much energy was diverted to an unnecessary debate over conscription for overseas service. Before that divisive issue was out of the way, the government's decision to relocate Japanese Canadians from coastal regions of British Columbia to internment camps in the interior was implemented.

The summer of 1942 brought no relief from an overwhelming sea of troubles. The raid on Dieppe produced casualties to an extent that deeply shocked Canadians, and the news from the eastern front was of one calamity after another. In the skies over Europe and on the seas, the toll of Allied casualties mounted. Rumours of U-boats sinking ships in the St. Lawrence River spread like wildfire, and a secret session of Parliament was held to confirm the rumours and describe countermeasures.

In retrospect, 1942 was, in Churchill's phrase, "the end of the beginning," but to those who lived through the year, it was a time of disappointment and frustration.

THE JAPANESE CANADIANS

In 1941, there were 23,224 persons of Japanese origin living in Canada, 22,000 of them in British Columbia. More than half were Canadian citizens, the rest permanent residents. They were largely employed as fishermen, lumber and sawmill workers, and market gardeners. Most lived in tightly knit communities preserving the Japanese language and culture and maintaining close ties with their mother country.

The Japanese in Canada were subject to serious restrictions on their civil liberties as a consequence of deeply ingrained prejudices against Asians. Neither those born in Canada nor those who became Canadian citizens were permitted to vote, and they were legally barred from certain occupations. Other forms of discrimination in jobs, housing and social relations reinforced their isolation from the rest of British Columbian society.

Public attitudes towards the Japanese community were also influenced by news of atrocities committed by Japanese troops in China and by the overall international situation. After Japan aligned itself with Germany in September 1940, the federal government appointed a "special Committee on Orientals in British Columbia," which reported that "not a single accusation of subversive acts on the part of the Japanese had been substantiated." The greatest danger to public order, the Committee reported, was not Japanese disloyalty but "the animosity of white Canadians against the Japanese in general." The report suggested measures designed to reassure the majority. Japanese Canadians were not to be accepted for military service, and a voluntary registration of the entire community, under RCMP supervision, was ordered. This registration, which included fingerprinting and photographs for identification cards, revealed that 1,500 children of Canadian residents were at school in Japan, a fact press and politicians used to support generalized accusations of disloyalty against the Japanese community.

After December 7, 1941, the government moved quickly to intern thirty-eight individuals alleged to be dangerous to national security, impounded Japanese fishing vessels, and closed Japanese-language schools and newspapers. These prudent actions, similar to measures taken against the German and Italian communities, did not calm the public in British Columbia. The media, particularly influential newspapers like the *Vancouver Sun* and *Victoria Times*, led a campaign, supported by most municipal, provincial and federal politicians in B.C., for the removal of the Japanese population "east of the Rockies."

King's government was in a quandary. The Royal Canadian Mounted Police and the military authorities were satisfied that no further action was required. The leaders of the Japanese community were cooperating fully and the Department of Labour recommended that nothing be done to interfere with their economic contribution to the war effort. This assessment enraged the spokesmen from British Columbia, who insisted that "they did not trust persons of Japanese racial origin," who were "a menace to public safety." Further, they claimed there was an immediate danger "that anti-Japanese riots may break out and it will be necessary to call out troops to defend Japanese residents from attack by other Canadians."

The federal government capitulated and on January 14, 1942, ordered that all enemy aliens (German, Italian and Japanese) be moved out of "protected areas" on the Pacific Coast. This order-in-council, which did not apply to the 12,500 Canadian citizens of Japanese origins, was sharply criticized in British Columbia, and in February the government bowed to public pressure and "every person of Japanese race" was removed from the coastal region. Most of the internees were settled in renovated ghost towns in the Kootenay and Slocan valleys; others were sent to road camps and the sugar-beet fields of Alberta. During the war their property was sold off without proper compensation, and a policy for postwar deportation of large numbers of innocent Canadians was approved. The Canadian government lacked the courage and political will to resist public

Prudent precautions

Feelings ran high after Pearl Harbor and the Canadian declaration of war on Japan. Initial official reaction was to take prudent emergency measures and forestall civic unrest.

Quick action to prevent sabotage by Japanese nationals and to forestall anti-Japanese actions by the civilian population of Vancouver has been taken by RCMP officials here. Safety measures include: 1) Internment of all "undesirable" Japanese; 2) Tying up every Japanese-owned fishing boat in B.C.; 3) Closing of all Japanese language schools; 4) Newspapers printed in Japanese forbidden to publish....

The interned Japanese will be treated the same as the Germans, Italians and others who have been held under the Defence of Canada regulations. Nationals who are not interned will still be allowed to carry on their business and earn their living....

Sergeant Barnes stated that every precaution has been taken to see that there will be no acts of terrorism against local Japanese. Leaders of the Japanese community have been contacted and asked to see that nothing is done that will give an opportunity for violence or vandalism....

Vancouver Sun, December 1941

Anti-Japanese hysteria soon took over, with newspapers and local politicians leading the campaign...

Start now to plan for Jap exclusion

Mayor Cornett will have enthusiastic support from most citizens in his campaign to keep the Japanese out of Vancouver – forever....

The *Sun* believes the best bet, and the most logical stand, is for Vancouver to lead a campaign that will ensure the return of all persons of Japanese origin to Japan after the war....

After the war ends, present regulations will not prevent Canadian-born Japanese ... moving from one part of British Columbia to another – that is, from the interior back to the coast.

So the only effective answer is to place them aboard ships and escort them to Kiska and points west.

Editorial, *Vancouver Sun*, August 31, 1942

Scenes from the relocation of Japanese-Canadians to the British Columbia interior: A train arrives at Slocan City; a community kitchen at Greenwood from which food was taken to each apartment; and youngsters wait for their train in April 1942.

When a people gets panicky...

Muriel Kitagawa was a twenty-nine-year-old mother of two in 1941. Her brother Wes, twenty-one, had just begun medical studies at the University of Toronto.

Dear Wes,

So far as the new war affected us, I really haven't much to say. It is too early to estimate the effects.... We have been tempered for prejudice these long years. Only in the West End has it intensified into overt acts of unthinking hoodlumism like throwing flaming torches into rooming houses and bricks through plate glass. We've had blackouts the first few nights but they have been lifted. All three Japanese papers have been closed down. We never needed so many anyway.... All Japanese schools have been closed too, and are the kids glad! We're getting immune to the hitherto unused term "Japs" on the radio and on the headlines of the papers....

There have been the usual anti-letters-to-the-editor in the papers. Some of them are rank nonsense, and some of the writers think like that anyhow, without the provocation of war. The majority of the people are decent and fair-minded and they say so. The RCMP is our friend too, for they, more than anyone else, know how blameless and helpless we are. When a people gets panicky, democracy and humanity and Christian principles go by the board....

Strange how these protesters are much more vehement against the Canadian-born Japanese than they are against German-born Germans, who might have a real loyalty to *their* land of birth, as we have for Canada. I guess it is just because we look different. Anyway, it all boils down to racial antagonism which the democracies are fighting against.

Mur

March 3, 1942

Dear Wes,

This is just to warn you: Don't you *dare* come back to B.C., no matter what happens, what reports you read in the papers, whatever details I tell you in letters. You stay out of this province. B.C. is hell.

Rather than have you come back here, we'll come to Toronto if we can.

I'll keep you posted by letters, but I repeat, there is nothing for you here. Even if you quit school, stay in Toronto — anywhere East of the Rockies.

Yoshi Higashi went to Camp last night with 7 hours notice.

Eddie will be about the last to go anywhere, whether to another branch bank or elsewhere. If I really need you I'll come to Toronto. *Remember!*

For the love of God, don't come here. Not you, a single male. You'll be more help to me and to the others if you stay where you are — free — even if starving.

Love, Mur

81

An anti-conscription rally in Montreal and (right) posters from the Ligue pour la défense du Canada.

opinion in British Columbia and chose the path of least resistance.

In 1988, the Japanese community received an official apology on behalf of the nation. This was not an attempt to rewrite history; it was an acknowledgement that a democratic state has an obligation to treat all its citizens and residents justly even in times of great peril and high emotion.

THE PLEBISCITE

Throughout the summer of 1940 and well into 1941, Canadians were remarkably united in support of the war. In Quebec, the radio broadcasts of Louis Francœur brought news of the conflict and its meaning to homes across the province. Francœur was to Quebec what Edward R. Murrow was to still-neutral Americans – a voice challenging listeners to confront reality. His program was so popular that the texts of his broadcasts, "La Situation, Ce Soir," were printed and sold at newsstands. French Canadians enlisted in record numbers throughout 1940 and 1941 and support for Canada's war effort was widespread.

This fragile unity collapsed in the fall of 1941 with the revival of the conscription issue. The series of dramatic Allied reverses at sea, in the western desert, in Russia and then at Pearl Harbor, Hong Kong and Singapore, led many English-speaking Canadians to demand that Canada do more. Some newspapers began to editorialize about conscription for overseas service and the Conservative party turned to Arthur Meighen, the architect of

Death of Ernest Lapointe

Ernest Lapointe (1876-1941) served continuously in Parliament from 1904 until his death. After the death of Wilfrid Laurier he became the chief spokesman for French Canada in national politics. Lapointe was ill for almost a year before his death. He was deeply moved by the defeat of France and troubled by his own role in supporting appeasement.

His death struck the popular imagination, which conjured up stories of plots and assassinations. Wasn't it a sign that the rampart was beginning to crumble? He had been chief spokesman for Quebec in the cabinet and before the bar of Anglo-Canadian opinion. It was thanks to him that the French-Canadian delegation had accepted participation. He had overthrown Duplessis in October 1939. He was also the man of the pact, the guarantor of the compromise – "participation without conscription." I doubt that at this stage he could himself have quelled the crisis, either by persuading Anglo-Canadians to moderate their demands or by once again drawing French Canadians into the wake of the King government, but this remains pure conjecture. What is certain is that his disappearance from the political scene weakened the cause of national unity.

Then, two weeks later, the United States was catapulted into the war. American isolationism disappeared overnight. Until then we had been the only American country at war. Now the most powerful democracy in the world had entered and was to throw all its energies into the war effort and mobilize all its human and natural resources. At the same time its entry on the scene was marked by disaster. Immediately the war took on a more tragic complexion. A feeling of duty and urgency swept over English Canada.

From A. Laurendeau, *The Conscription Crisis*

A nation divided

As I looked at the returns I thought of Durham's report on the state of Quebec after the Rebellion of 1837 and '38. He said he found two nations warring in the bosom of a single state. That would be the case in Canada… unless the whole question of conscription from now on be approached with the utmost care.

William Lyon Mackenzie King, diary

Take off your glasses…

Donald C. Macdonald was a reporter for the Montreal Gazette until 1942 when he joined the RCNVR.

Donald Macdonald, future Ontario NDP leader, campaigned for the "yes" side in the plebiscite.

Last Sunday, Donald unexpectedly came to Montreal. Reason, St. Hyacinthe's "NO" plebiscite voters were holding a mass meeting. Fearing the soldiers would start brawls on the issue, the authorities ordered all of them out of town. They were only too glad to conform. But I suspect there will be some brawls before the plebiscite is over. I've urged Donald to be careful and to be sure to take off his glasses if he feels a fight coming on.

Dorothy Seiveright
Macdonald College, Ste-Anne de Bellevue

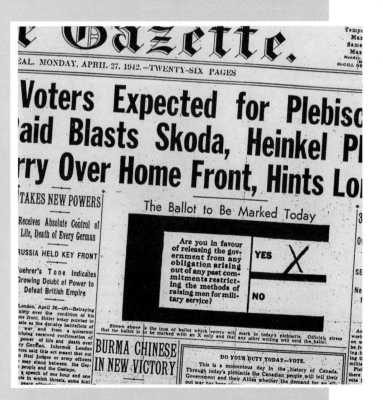

The Montreal *Gazette* reproduced the plebiscite ballot on the morning of April 27, 1942, voting day. In Montreal, as elsewhere, voters split along linguistic lines."

conscription in World War I, as their new leader. Meighen, never a man for compromise or conciliation, immediately issued a proclamation calling for a "National Government" and compulsion for service overseas.

King, who feared and hated Meighen, was in a state of panic and was further stunned by the death of his Quebec lieutenant, Ernest Lapointe. The prime minister had always relied on Lapointe to guide him on matters related to French Canada. King was now on his own, isolated, uncertain and irrational. To combat Meighen and the conscriptionist press he decided to introduce a plebiscite. In January 1942, Canadians were told that they would be asked to release the government from its pledge not to impose conscription for overseas service. Voting was to take place in late April, so there was ample time for extremists on both sides to inflame public opinion. In his account of the campaign for a "no" vote in Quebec, André Laurendeau recalled how the nationalist cause in Quebec was dormant until the plebiscite was announced. Suddenly there was an issue that could be used to rally French Canadians against the government and the war effort. The plebiscite split Canada along linguistic lines. In Ontario more than 80 per cent voted "yes," while in Quebec 73 per cent (85 per cent of French Canadians) voted "no." Partisan politics had dealt a deadly blow to Canadian unity.

THE AIR WAR: 1942

Churchill's strategy for 1942 required the navy and the air force to carry the burden of the Commonwealth war effort. In 1940 he had advocated priority for the strategic bombing of Germany, arguing that "the navy can lose us the war but only the air force can win it…. The fighters are our salvation but the bombers alone provide the means of victory."

By the end of 1941 he was much less confident that air power alone could be decisive. Bomber Command had begun a new offensive in July 1942 aimed at "dislocating

Air Chief Marshal Sir Arthur Harris, who developed RAF Bomber Command into the Commonwealth's principal offensive contribution to the war effort in 1942-43.

IMPERIAL WAR MUSEUM

the German transportation system and destroying the morale of the civil population as a whole and of the industrial workers in particular." This meant attacks on targets in the Ruhr industrial zone when moonlight permitted, and the bombing of cities on the Rhine when darkness required an easier method of identification. Other German cities were also listed as prospective targets.

Despite a sustained effort, which cost Bomber Command heavy casualties, little was accomplished by the offensive. Reports from Germany, including those of neutral observers, cast doubt on RAF damage claims, and the British Air Staff's own investigation, the Butt Report, demonstrated that just one aircraft in five got within five miles of its target. Over the Ruhr only one in ten dropped bombs "within the 75 square miles surrounding the target." The problem was not target identification but navigation to the general area where the objective was located.

Churchill expressed great reservations, informing Air Marshal Charles Portal that it was a mistake to claim too much for bombing. Exaggerated estimates of the effects of air attack had "depressed the statesmen responsible for pre-war policy and played a definite part in the desertion of Czechoslovakia…." There was, Churchill insisted, "no certain method of winning the war," they could only "persevere."

After a disastrous raid on Berlin in November when thirty-seven bombers were lost in severe weather, the Prime Minister insisted on a change in strategy. "There is no point at this time," he wrote, "in bombing Berlin…. Losses which are acceptable in battle or for some decisive military objective ought not to be incurred merely as a matter of routine." The RAF was to pause and "re-gather their strength for the spring."

Halifax bomber and crew

Last-minute check

A little soccer before take-off

A flying 25-ton bomb just looking for an excuse to blow up...

Op No. 20, Essen, June 5, 1942
Tonight we completed my twentieth op and took part in the third 1,000-bomber raid. It was a hot one and they were ready for us. The damn flak was like lightning flashing in daylight all about us as the searchlights grabbed us over the target. The shell bursts made a squeaky, gritty noise. The smell of cordite was strong and you had the feeling that someone was underneath kicking your undercarriage, keeping time with the bursts. We were glad to get back without too much damage....

Op No. 21, Essen, June 8, 1942
Essen again. You begin wondering how much more it can take. Our crew consists of two Englishmen, a Scotsman, an Irishman, a Welshman and myself as the Canadian ... and all nervous as hell. It must be remembered that each bomber was really a flying 25-ton bomb just looking for an excuse to blow up. The five tons or so of high-explosives and magnesium flares, plus another three or four tons of high-octane fuel, provided the ideal mixture for a violent explosion when hit in the right place by an explosive bullet or shell. We were losing too many of our friends. It was not very pleasant, when you awoke in the morning to see them gathering up the personal effects of those who failed to return from last night's raid. The normal crew of a Hallybag being seven, three aircraft missing meant twenty-one wouldn't be around any more. New replacements would soon arrive and fill those empty beds. And so the war goes on!

Flight Lieutenant Ralph Wood
Bomber Command, RAF

With the future role of Bomber Command in doubt, both the army and the navy pressed claims for new priorities. General Alan Brooke, the Chief of the Imperial General Staff, sought an expansion of the Army Co-operation role, while the Royal Navy pressed the claims of the Fleet Air Arm and Coastal Command. The ensuing intense debate was not resolved until July 1941 when Churchill, his eyes on the new German offensive in Russia and his forthcoming visit to Moscow, supported an expansion of Bomber Command from thirty-two to fifty squadrons.

The RAF would employ these additional bombers in a new strategy devised in the winter of 1941–42. The Air Staff had concluded that, even with the aid of new navigation devices, night-bombers could only locate target areas such as large towns and cities. A list of forty-three German industrial centres, with a combined population of fifteen million, was drawn up with aiming points in city centres, not railyards or factories. Bomber Command was to hit what it could find when it could find it.

In February 1942, the RAF found the right man to implement the strategy. Air Marshal Arthur Harris had played no role in the formulation of the policy, but he enthusiastically supported it. His problem was that Bomber Command did not have the numbers or types of aircraft available to carry out the "area-bombing" directive. On March 1, 1942, 167 four-engined bombers were operational, but only 20 Halifaxes and 4 Lancasters were available.

Harris proceeded carefully, husbanding his resources and experimenting with tactics. "Gee," a navigational device which permitted pilots to fix their position from a radio-pulse receiver, had enough range for the Ruhr or North Sea ports. Gee allowed bombers to reach the approximate area of the target even in poor weather and helped Harris to organize "bomber streams," which concentrated aircraft, re-

ducing the chances of night-fighter interception and the time-over-target for bombing.

Harris staged a series of spectacular raids designed to demonstrate what could be done. The first, against the Renault truck plant west of Paris, was brilliantly executed, destroying 40 per cent of the factory. Next was Lübeck, a German port on the Baltic Coast, which was attacked with incendiary bombs. There was little war industry in Lübeck; the aim was to lower German morale and demonstrate that there were costs involved in attempts to conquer Europe. Cologne, on the Rhine, was selected for the first "Thousand Bomber Raid," and all those who had endured three years of unchecked Nazi aggression applauded this bold stroke.

The Royal Canadian Air Force officially joined the battle in April 1941 when No. 405 Squadron was formed. Hundreds of RCAF aircrew were serving in RAF squadrons; now a separate Canadian air force was to be created. By the time of the Cologne raid five RCAF squadrons, including No. 425 "Alouette" squadron, a well-publicized French-Canadian unit, flew missions over Germany. These and other Canadian squadrons were equipped with the twin-engined Wel-

Bombing up a Halifax.

IMPERIAL WAR MUSEUM

Preparing for a sortie

Pilot Officer Jerrold Morris describes a typical bombing mission in 1941. Wing Commander J.F. Fulton, known as "Moose," was killed in action and 419 Squadron honoured his memory, becoming 419 (Moose) Squadron.

Moose would take the stand and call for silence while the roll was called; then the briefing began. First he would give us general facts about the raid, such as the number of aircraft detailed and the concentration; then the Intelligence officer would outline the nature of the target and reasons for the attack. The Met man took over to give us an estimate of weather conditions likely to be encountered, and finally Moose would run over tactics to be employed, and give advice generally. He usually ended up by saying, "Enemy fighters – I don't think you'll have any trouble with them. Good luck!"

When I got to the hangar, navigators were working around a large table with their topographical maps and plotting charts…. Navigators made their own calculations, and then compared results with others. When we had finished we went to the locker room…. Dressing up was a long process for the gunners; it was a cold ride in the turrets and they wore as much clothing as they could from woollen underwear to electrically heated suits. On top of this went a Mae West buoyancy jacket and parachute harness.

Outside the hangars we stood around and chatted, waiting for transport. The last rays of the sun spread over the flat landscape and there was a chill in the air. The padre handed out flying rations, and the doctor offered caffeine pills to anyone inclined to be sleepy. We scrambled into vans, packed in tight, the navigators hugging their bags of equipment; at each dispersal a crew dropped off and farewells were shouted.

There was work to be done around the machines in the hour before take-off. Gas cocks to check, photoflashes to fuse and mount, detonators to load in the secret equipment [Gee] for emergency destruction and, more often than not, propaganda leaflets to stow near the flare-chute…. When we were through we could lie down under the kite and smoke and chat with the ground crew.

You went through all the motions, the briefing room,

Photos of insouciant bomber crews capture the camaraderie but not the stress of their occupation.

news of the target, the tension of waiting, even the final "good luck" could be said, and the operation scrubbed. Everyone would he ready, physically and emotionally and the bubble was pricked. Rarely would such a cancellation release any jubilation; most of us went about our duties with no mention of fears or anxieties, just tried to make as many trips as possible, learning to build a shell against emotion. But inwardly we were bound to think.

Long before you reached the target area you would see ahead of you a confusing maze of searchlights quartering the sky, some in small groups, others stacked in cones of twenty or more. These often had a victim transfixed, as if pinned to the sky, their apex filled with red bursts of heavy flak. The ground would soon be lit with lines of reconnaissance flares like suspended street lights, here and there illuminating water, perhaps a section of river, that you would frantically try to identify. As the raid developed, sticks of incendiaries crisscrossed the ground sparkling incandescent white, until a red glow would show the start of a fire.

The Germans liberally sprayed the ground with dummy incendiaries and imitation fire blocks in the neighbourhood of important targets, hoping to attract a share of the bombs. Gun flashes, photoflashes, bomb-bursts, streams of tracer of all colours, and everywhere searchlights – it was all very confusing, especially when the air gunners were directing the pilot to avoid flak and searchlights in all directions at the same time.

Pilot Officer Jerrold Morris, 419 Sqadron, RCAF,

The fuselage behind me was burning

Flight Lieutenant S.B. Brackenbury, pilot of a Hampden bomber of 408 Squadron, was caught by radar-directed searchlights on the last raid of 1942. He survived the crash and spent three years in a prisoner of war camp.

The moon was nearly full, and vis[ibility] was very good. About 30 minutes away from the target, Huls, we could see a large fire directly on track, we identified canal that led up to target, and proceeded to glide in from 14,000 feet. The flak was right over target, and we did a steady glide at 180 miles an hour. The Nav. released his bombs at 9,000 feet and I started to climb. There was a great fire burning. Having climbed to 14,000 feet again we were over searchlight belt. Stray searchlights picked us up but on turning into them, [I] put them off. Then a bluish searchlight picked us up and I couldn't shake it off. I climbed, dived, and did 90 degree turns, but to no avail. Then more and more searchlights coned me and it was impossible to look out as it was momentarily blinding. There was no flak [but] I warned the crew to look out for fighters. I flew a straight course to get out of the cone. The Wireless/Operator reported an a/c on the starboard. quarter high. We were still in the searchlights when the fighter attacked ... I heard the guns at the back give a burst and just then a white tracer went by. I turned sharply into the attack and then straightened up. I called up the crew but there was no answer, the intercom was OK. The next attack was made shortly [after] and it was in the same quarter high. As soon as I saw the tracer I again turned into it. I could hear the cannon fire hitting the a/c and then saw port engine burst into flames. I pressed the [extinguishing] button, but nothing happened. I called on the i/c but it was unserviceable. The fuselage behind me was burning, and I think the fire was caused by the flares, which had not been released, having been hit by the cannon fire. The third attack was from the same place. I had no crew to tell me when to take evasive action, so I turned into the attack when I saw tracer. The fourth attack was from the stern. The tracer was going over and by each side, the fuselage was burning, and the engine. I decided to try a crash-landing, but at 5,000 feet I decided I couldn't make it. In case any other crew was alive I pushed the call light button then bailed out. I saw the trail of flame hit the ground and little red balls rolling on the ground. I lit safely in a pine tree.

S.B. Brackenbury, pilot of a twin-engined
Hampden, December 28/29, 1941

Take up ditching positions...

Then-Flight Lieutenant John Fauquier of 405 Squadron bombed Berlin on the night of November 7, 1941. He returned safely but strong headwinds forced him to land at a non-operational airfield, where the Home Guard surrounded the plane, suspecting they were spies.

Finally, we reached the point where we thought, and hoped, Berlin lay ... dropped our bombs and turned for home. It wasn't long before I realized we were in trouble

because the winds had increased greatly in strength and were almost dead ahead. Eventually, I lost height down to a few hundred feet – to avoid icing conditions and to save fuel since the head wind would be less strong.

Wing Commander John Fauquier at the controls of a bomber.

I have seen the North Sea in many moods but never more ferocious than that night. Huge waves of solid green water were lifted from the surface and carried hundreds of feet by the wind. After what seemed like hours in these appalling conditions I realised we were unlikely to make base. I had little or no fuel left and told the crew to take up ditching positions.... It was then I saw briefly one of those wonderful homing lights and made a bee-line straight for it.

John Fauquier, November 7, 1941

The Singleton Report, May 20, 1942

Mr. Justice Singleton was asked to offer independent advice to the British war cabinet on the prospects of the bombing offensive.

I do not think it [the bombing offensive] ought to be regarded as *of itself* sufficient to win the war or to produce decisive results; the area is too vast for the effort we can put forth: on the other hand, if Germany does not achieve great success on land before the winter it may well turn out to have a decisive effect, and in the meantime, if carried out on the lines suggested, it must impede Germany and help Russia. If Germany succeeds in her attack on Russia there will be little apparent gain from our bombing policy in six months' time, but the drain on Germany will be present all the time: and if Russia stands it will remain a powerful weapon on our hands. It is impossible to say what its effect will be in twelve or eighteen months without considering the position of Russia. If Russia can hold Germany on land I doubt whether Germany will stand twelve or eighteen months' continuous, intensified and increased bombing, affecting, as it must, her war production, her power of resistance, her industries and her will to resist (by which I mean morale).

lingtons and then the "unsatisfactory Halifax," giving rise to complaints that Harris favoured the RAF. However, as the Canadian official history notes, seniority, not nationality, was the guiding principle in allocating the newer Lancaster bombers.

RCAF squadrons suffered the same steady drain of casualties as other elements of Bomber Command. Out of every 100 aircrew, 51 were killed in operations, 9 were killed in training, 12 became prisoners of war, 3 were wounded, and just 25 made it through their tour safely. Twenty per cent of those who served in Bomber Command were Canadians.

THE HOME FRONT

Public affairs in Canada were marred by disputes about the Hong Kong expedition and bitter recriminations over the issue of conscription, but for most Canadians political quarrels were less important than the impact of the war on daily life. The government introduced a National Selective Service program in March 1942, which enforced regulations designed to channel men and women into essential occupations. Able-bodied men of military age were prohibited from working in fifty "restricted occupations" and no man or woman was allowed to change jobs without a permit. The Women's Division of the NSS organized a compulsory registration of twenty- to twenty-four-year-old women. Almost a quarter of a million women registered and fifty thousand subsequently volunteered for jobs in war industry.

The introduction of National Selective Service was paralleled by major changes in the regulations for home defence conscription. Until March 1942 only single men ages twenty-one to twenty-four had been called up; now the age limits were expanded to include nineteen- to thirty-year-olds. Fewer than 32,000 men had been drafted in 1941, but 70,504 conscripts were enrolled in 1942.

Conscientious objection to military service was possible if you fell into either of two basic categories. One was for Mennonites and Doukhobors, who had historic rights to exemption. The other category defined a conscientious objector as one who had a personal belief against

bearing arms and belonged to a religious denomination whose articles of faith prohibited combat service. This second condition made it difficult for anyone except Quakers to qualify. Those who were exempted performed alternate service in reforestation and other public projects.

With virtually everyone in the country at work or in the armed forces, the government had two major economic concerns: preventing the new purchasing power from causing inflation and the growth of a black market, and financing the enormous cost of the war effort. The main methods of diverting income from immediate spending were the Victory Loan campaigns and major changes to the Income Tax Act.

NATIONAL ARCHIVES OF CANADA/C29451

BOTH: WESTERN CANADA PICTORIAL INDEX

Movie stars helped to publicize Victory Bond drives. Shirley Temple is seen with Mackenzie King as she kicks off a Victory loan campaign on Parliament Hill. In Winnipeg, "If Day" actors dressed as Nazi soldiers raise the swastika over Lower Fort Garry and arrest Premier John Bracken and other provincial cabinet ministers. Whether the latter action stirred the desired emotions in the public is unknown.

EVERY CANADIAN
MUST FIGHT

NATIONAL ARCHIVES OF CANADA

Posters urged Canadians to fight not only overseas but on the home front.

BACK THEM UP!

CANAV COL.

Almost four million Canadians bought Victory Bonds in 1942, providing the government with $700 million. Corporations, including banks, purchased another $1.8 billion in bonds, meeting most of Ottawa's borrowing needs. Victory Bonds, War Savings Certificates and War Saving Stamps helped to meet short-term financial needs and limit consumers' purchasing power, but the loans would have to be repaid after the war. Canada had to pay for most of its expenditures out of tax revenue or the national debt would get out of hand.

In 1939 a married man with a wife and two children paid no income tax unless he was in the top income brackets. At earnings of $3,000 – double the average income – the tax was just $10. By 1943 the levy at $3,000 was $334 plus an equal amount in compulsory savings. An unskilled worker who made $1,500 paid $48, half of it refundable after the war. A man earning $10,000 – there were very few of these – paid $3,346 and a further $1,200 was taken as compulsory savings. This sharply progressive income tax and excess profits tax helped convince Canadians that everyone was contributing to the war effort.

Rules, regulations, rationing, taxes, long hours of work – it all sounded a bit grim, but the war years were anything but that. Wartime Canada was full of energy and excitement. People travelled to take up new jobs; the trains were crowded with soldiers, sailors and airmen on leave or off to a new posting. Rationing did not seriously affect the supply of beer, liquor or tobacco. Tea and sugar were rationed, but coffee sales soared; so did milk consumption. In fact, people ate more and better food than had been available in the 1930s, and the overall health of the population improved dramatically.

Relations between the sexes were freer and more open than they had ever been. Women were finally granted the vote in Quebec, and there were signs they might find greater equality in the workplace. Unions insisted that when women performed "men's work" they had to be paid at men's rates. Of course, most female workers still worked in traditional low-wage jobs, but a new principle with far-reaching implications had been established.

Canadian soldiers meet the local
girls in rural England.

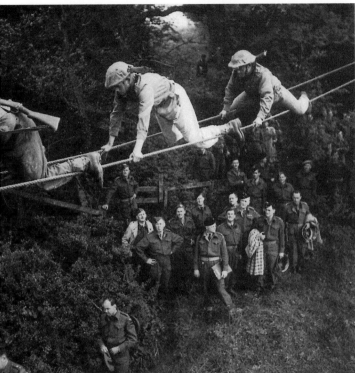

Training in England.
(Above) Training exer-
cises at Barnard Castle
and at the Canadian
Assault School at
Bordon, Hampshire.
(Right) The Black
Watch carry out a
landing exercise.
Among the key as-
pects of a suitable
landing beach are a
satisfactory surface
and adequate exits to
enable the invaders to
get off the beach and
inland as soon as
possible.

THE DIEPPE RAID – PLANNING

On the morning of August 19, 1942, a naval task force composed of 237 ships and landing craft, assisted by 16 minesweepers, reached the coast of France at Dieppe. More than 6,000 soldiers – 4,963 Canadian, 1,075 British, 50 American and 15 French nationals – prepared to launch a raid against Nazi-occupied France.

The origins of the raid are well understood. In October 1941, Lord Louis Mountbatten had been made Advisor on Combined Operations with a mandate "to evolve the technique, policy and equipment for the employment of the three services in combined operations to effect a landing against opposition." Staff officers at COHQ had been at work on these problems previously, but Mountbatten's appointment signalled Prime Minister Winston Churchill's desire to give a higher priority to commando raids against "Fortress Europe."

During the first four months of 1942, British and American planners were trying to develop a program for implementing the "Europe First" strategy agreed upon before Pearl Harbor. The American view was presented by General George C. Marshall, the U.S. Chief of Staff, and Dwight D. Eisenhower, then Chief of the Operations Division. It called for the invasion of Europe, Operation "Roundup," to take place in 1943. A limited diversionary operation, "Sledgehammer," was also to be readied for September 1942, but was only to be implemented if a Russian collapse appeared likely, or if the German position in Western Europe became "critically weakened." Marshall also called for "repeated Commando-type raids – to harass the enemy and give experience to Allied troops."

The British Chiefs of Staff endorsed "Roundup" and "raids – on the largest scale that the available

Admiral Lord Louis Mountbatten, Chief of Combined Operations from March 1942, originally proposed a raid on Dieppe as a training operation to practise air, land and naval forces in a rehearsal for the invasion of Europe.

CANAPRESS

equipment will permit," but they were firmly opposed to "Sledgehammer," even as a contingency plan. If resources were allocated to "Sledgehammer," they would not be available to pursue new initiatives in the Mediterranean. Churchill was committed to action in this theatre and persuaded Roosevelt that "Torch," the invasion of French North Africa, was the ideal joint operation for 1942.

Churchill was willing to gamble that the Soviet armies could withstand a renewed Nazi offensive. He insisted that no real purpose would be served by launching a premature "Second Front" in France. Hitler would be defeated by a strategy of wearing down Germany through blockade, bombing, losses on the eastern front and defeat in the Mediterranean. Raids on the coast of France, preferably large-scale, might help in the wearing-down process by luring the German air force into a major air battle. If Fighter Command could inflict serious losses on the Luftwaffe, aircraft would have to be diverted from the eastern front.

All of these factors combined to make the British chiefs of staff receptive to Mountbatten's proposal of May 13, 1942, to conduct a raid on Dieppe. The town was an important port within the effective range of RAF Spitfires and Hurricanes. The Luftwaffe would surely respond to such an attack and much could be learned about an amphibious assault against the kind of port everyone believed would be a necessary objective when the real invasion came.

General Bernard Montgomery was asked to select a division from his South-Eastern Command to undertake the raid. Despite pressure to employ a composite British-Canadian force, he selected 2nd Canadian Division as the troops best suited to carry out the raid. Senior Canadian officers were enthusiastic. They had long been anxious to gain experience for themselves and their men. The outline plan was eagerly embraced and detailed preparation began immediately. The corps commander, Lieutenant-General Harry Crerar, and Major-General Ham Roberts, the divisional commander, were satisfied with "Rutter," as the original version of the Dieppe raid was called. The plan also won Montgomery's approval. "I am satisfied," he wrote, "that the operation as planned is a possible one and has good prospects of success given: a) Favourable weather; b) Average luck; c) That the Navy put us ashore roughly in the right places and at the right times.... The Canadians are 1st class chaps; if anyone can pull it off they can."

The Canadians and the commandos underwent extensive training on the Isle of Wight for the operation, and on July 2 they boarded their infantry landing ships. After several postponements the raid was cancelled, and the men returned to their bases. The weather had prevented what surely would have been a military catastrophe from taking place. "Rutter" called for a frontal assault on Dieppe, Puys and Pourville, with tanks limited to the main beach. The flanks at Varengeville and Berneval were to be attacked by airborne troops who lacked experience in such a complex night operation. The assault on Dieppe was to be carried out by infantry battalions imbued with the offensive spirit after two months of intensive training. Commando-like skills, high morale and surprise were to overcome an entrenched enemy. No supporting artillery was available and the Royal Canadian Artillery personnel who em-

NATIONAL ARCHIVES OF CANADA/PA153193

Lieutenant-General B.L.M. Montgomery and Lieutenant-General H.D.G. Crerar. Both men were First World War veterans who became their nation's leading soldier. Crerar had the difficult task of representing the Canadian government as well as commanding troops, and he frequently clashed with Montgomery. In 1942 both men endorsed the original plan for the Dieppe raid.

barked were trained to use captured German weapons. The air battle, which was one of the main objectives of the raid, was to be conducted as a separate operation with no provision for communication between the men on the beaches and the air force. The navy's support was limited to six small destroyers.

A great deal of careful preparation had gone into the Dieppe raid. An elaborate "Confidential Book" with topographical detail, beach and tide reports and information on defences was constantly updated through photo-reconnaissance. The guns in the cliffs of the eastern headland were identified, as were the roadblocks on the Boulevard Verdun which prevented tanks from entering the town and shielded anti-tank guns. No definite information on guns in cavelike positions on the western cliffs was available but their presence must have seemed probable. Before "Rutter" was to be launched the decision to limit the operation to one tide, that is, to eight hours ashore, was made, as was the very sensible decision to cancel the bombing raid, the purpose of which was never clear.

How could professional soldiers have allowed such a flawed scheme to go forward? The simple truth is that in the summer of 1942 neither the British nor the Canadian

Montgomery described Major-General J.H. "Ham" Roberts as "the best divisional commander" in the Canadian army and reported that his chief staff officer, Lieutenant-Colonel Church Mann was "first class." These judgements meant 2nd Division was selected for Dieppe. Roberts continued in command after the raid but was replaced in 1943 after criticism of his performance in Exercise "Spartan," a large-scale rehearsal for Normandy.

army, not to mention the Americans, had a realistic idea of the kind of fire support that was required in offensive operations against prepared positions. As C.P. Stacey, the official historian of the Canadian armed forces, has pointed out, all plans for large- and small-scale raids, including the "emergency" invasion of the Cherbourg Peninsula, Operation "Sledgehammer," were based on surprise, speed and the promise of air cover. The artillery-based battle doctrine that emerged in North Africa and which came to dominate Allied military planning for the rest of the war was quite foreign to Allied generals in 1942. Senior British officers, including Montgomery, were still planning exercises in which armoured and infantry brigades, without continuous artillery support, advanced over great distances, rehearsing the "encounter" battle. Montgomery, who left for North Africa before the Dieppe raid, adapted quickly once he examined the lessons learned by the Eighth Army, but no one with any current experience was available to examine the Dieppe plan with a clear eye.

The revival of the raid, as Operation "Jubilee," was strongly influenced by the need to offer the Soviets some evidence of our commitment to sharing the burden as German armies were once again on the march in Russia. But pressure to remount the operation also came from Combined Operations and from senior officers of the Canadian army. Combined Operations needed a major test of the enemy's coast defences to fulfil its mandate, and the Canadian generals desperately wanted battle experience. The RAF was also anxious to revive the raid, hoping to justify their policy of bringing the Luftwaffe to battle in France.

The decision to go ahead with the Dieppe raid has been criticized by participants and historians since 1942. Both groups should remember that on the morning of August 19 everyone believed that the raid had a good chance of success. Mountbatten, Montgomery, Crerar and the divisional commander, Roberts, may properly be accused of inexperience and wishful thinking, but everyone was attempting to further the cause of the liberation of Europe and no one foresaw a tragedy of the kind that occurred that day.

The South Saskatchewan Regiment leaves Weyburn on its way to England, May 1940. The "South Sasks," with the Queen's Own Cameron Highlanders of Canada from Winnipeg and the Fusiliers Mont-Royal, were assigned to 6th Brigade as part of 2nd Division.

DIEPPE – THE BATTLE

The plan called for five assaults on a front of ten miles. No. 4 Commando landed at "Orange Beach" west of Varengeville. Their task was to destroy a coastal battery with one company engaging the position frontally while a second, under the command of Lord Lovat, attacked from the rear. This operation was completely successful.

At Berneval on the left flank, the Commandos ran into a German coastal convoy and were badly scattered. Just seven of the twenty-three craft landed. At Petit Berneval the enemy overwhelmed the attackers, taking eighty-two prisoners. A second landing, a mile to the west, was made by one landing craft. Major Peter Young, with a force totalling twenty men, advanced on the Berneval battery and neutralized it for two hours by sniping at all movement from a distance of 200 yards.

The planners who had designed the assault at Puys, "Blue Beach," must have read too many adventure stories. The beach had only one exit and that was known to be blocked. Not to have fortified the east cliff, which

commanded the beach, would have been foolish and the German army was not given to foolishness. The delays that made the first wave thirty-five minutes late and later landings as much as an hour behind schedule destroyed any chance of surprise – "the effect of darkness and smoke screen was entirely lost." The defenders at Puys were fully alert and opened fire as the landing craft touched down. "In five minutes' time the Royal Regiment was changed from an assaulting battalion on the offensive to something less than two companies on the defensive being hammered by fire we could not locate."

Lieutenant-Colonel Catto, commander of the Royal Regiment of Canada, led a party of men up the cliff at the western end of the sea wall, clearing two houses at the top. The purpose of the Puys landing was to destroy the gun battery on the eastern headland of Dieppe, and Catto's group started west to carry out their task, but they encountered German reinforcements directed at Puys and were unable to proceed. On the beach casualties mounted, and at 0830 hours the

The invasion fleet departs for Dieppe. The flotilla carrying No. 3 Commando collided with a German coastal convoy, alerting the defenders at "Blue" beach.

GREEN BEACH
South
Saskatchewan
Regiment

Queen's Own
Cameron
Highlanders

Pourville

Dieppe

Dieppe

BLUE BEACH
Royal
Regiment
of Canada

Puys

N

N

The Dieppe landing places.

Royals surrendered. Out of 554 men embarked, 67 returned to England. A total of 199 were killed and the balance taken prisoner.

The landing on the western flank at Pourville was initially successful. The South Saskatchewan Regiment began to land at "Green Beach" at 0452 hours, almost exactly on time. The enemy was taken by surprise and no fire was encountered in the approach or as the men hit the beaches. Unfortunately, the landing craft that were supposed to bring two companies to the east side of the

River Scie arrived at the western beach, creating confusion and delaying the companies which were to seize the radar station east of Pourville and the high ground. By the time "A" and "D" companies reached the bridge the enemy was fully alert and machine-gun fire stopped the advance. Lieutenant-Colonel Cec Merritt, commander of the South Sasks, came forward and led his men across the bridge, winning a Victoria Cross for his heroism. Unfortunately, it proved impossible to reach objectives on the high ground, as enemy mortar and machine-gun fire

WHITE
BEACH

Dieppe

Ruins of
the Casino

WHITE
BEACH

Royal Hamilton Light Infantry

Essex Scottish

Fusiliers Mont-Royal

14th Canadian Army Tank
Regiment (Calgary Regiment)

Royal Marine "A" Commando

N→

AERIAL PHOTOS: LCMSDS/WILFRID LAURIER UNIVERSITY

of supporting tanks from the Dieppe beaches, so Law ordered a withdrawal. His judgement was quickly confirmed when a brigade order to withdraw was issued. The two battalions disengaged and withdrew to the beaches but they suffered heavy losses as German mortar and artillery fire from the high ground hampered their evacuation. Of the 1,026 men that landed at Green Beach, 154 were killed in action or died of wounds, 269 were wounded, 256 were taken prisoner and 601 (including wounded) were successfully evacuated. Without support from tanks, the prospects of success at Green Beach were slim. The heroism of individuals could only accomplish minor miracles and more was required.

The frontal assault on Dieppe had always been scheduled for H+30, half an hour after the flank attacks were to begin. The four-inch guns of the destroyers, assisted by RAF

could not be countered by troops who lacked armour or artillery.

The Cameron Highlanders of Canada landed late at 0530 hours and were quickly caught up in the fire-fight around the bridge. The South Sasks had successfully overcome the enemy in Pourville village and Major A.T. Law led the Camerons south towards their objective. The battalion reached the bridge at Bas d'Hautot but German artillery was covering the crossing. The Camerons had no firepower beyond personal weapons, and there was no sign

Hurricanes, were supposed to suppress enemy fire during the run-in, and tanks were to land simultaneously with the infantry to provide direct support. On August 19 the infantry were put ashore at the right place at the right time and both the naval fire plan and the air attack were properly executed. The tanks were fifteen minutes late, which certainly didn't help, but more importantly the scale of supporting fire available was completely inadequate for the task. The Royal Hamilton Light Infantry fought their way into the casino and two small groups

Bodies of Canadian soldiers lie among damaged landing craft and Churchill tanks of the Calgary Regiment on the beach at Dieppe, August 19, 1942.

penetrated into the town, but nothing significant could be accomplished against the well-entrenched enemy. The Essex Scottish, landing on the open eastern flank, were pinned to the sea wall, though one small group got across the Boulevard Verdun and cleared several houses.

The Calgary Tank Regiment approached the beach in two waves. Twenty-nine Churchill tanks left the landing craft, two sank in deep water and twelve were unable to advance beyond the beach. The fifteen tanks that crossed the sea wall (a higher percentage than at several of the D-Day beaches) provided effective support to the infantry with their machine guns. However, the Churchill's main gun could only fire solid armour-piercing shot, of little use in supporting infantry against mortars and machine guns. The tank crews fought with great valour even after their vehicles were immobilized. Enemy 37-mm anti-tank guns couldn't penetrate the tanks' armour, so there were few fatal casualties among tank crews. They stayed to the

last assisting the withdrawal, and many were taken prisoner.

The battle for a foothold in Dieppe had been raging for a full hour when Major-General Roberts decided to land his "Floating Reserve" – Les Fusiliers Mont-Royal. A radio report received at 0610 hours that the Essex Scottish were across the beach and into the houses may have led Roberts to believe progress was being made, but he was also influenced by a message he interpreted as meaning that the Royal Regiment had not landed and was still available as a further reinforcement for the main beach. In other words, the fog of war was total and Roberts chose to act on the fragments of unconfirmed information available to him. The FMRs landed shortly after 0700 hours, scattered along the beach front. The majority were set down at the far western end under the cliffs and were immediately pinned down. Other small groups entered the town via the Rue de Sygogne, and one party moved

Canadian prisoners of war are marched through the streets of Dieppe by their captors. 1,874 Canadians became prisoners of war, including 568 who were wounded. Seventy-two men died while in captivity.

east to the port area. General Roberts, still quite unaware of what was taking place, sent his last reserves, a Royal Marines Commando, to join the battle on the main beach. Fortunately, most of their landing craft were turned back at the last moment.

The Canadians suffered 3,367 casualties at Dieppe, including 901 fatal casualties and 1,946 prisoners of war. British casualties were just less than 300, while there were 550 casualties to naval personnel. The great Dieppe air battle was initially thought to be a triumph for the RAF, based on pilot claims of German planes destroyed. In fact, August 19 brought the RAF its heaviest losses in a single day of the whole war, 106 aircraft. The Luftwaffe was, however, brought to battle, and its actual losses of 48 aircraft destroyed and 24 damaged were substantial.

The last word may be given to a report from the Headquarters of German Fifteenth Army:

> The enemy, almost entirely Canadian soldiers, fought – so far as he was able to fight at all – well and bravely. The chief reasons for the large number of prisoners and casualties are probably:
>
> 1. Lack of artillery support,
> 2. Underestimation of the strength of the defences,
> 3. The effect of our own defensive weapons,
> 4. The craft provided for re-embarkation were almost all hit and sank.

An explosion of joy and enthusiasm

The men welcomed the announcement that the target was Dieppe with loud cheers. An explosion of joy and enthusiasm like I've never seen before in my life and probably will never see again. Mass and communion. Seventy-five went to communion. I was two hours hearing confessions of almost all, even the tough guys.

There was never a Mass for me like this Mass, on the bow of the ship on the eve of battle. The Consecration struck me with terrific solemnity. I had told them to say the words of Consecration with me: "This is My Body, this is My Blood. Take our bodies and souls, oh Lord, that being united with Yours on the altar of sacrifice we may merit victory and salvation for our souls."

When I returned to my ship I replenished supplies of Victory Crosses and Sacred Heart badges, recalling great victories in history won in the shadow of the Cross.

Padre Armand Sabourin, Les Fusiliers Mont-Royal

Something was terribly wrong

In 1942, Denis Whitaker, a captain in the Royal Hamilton Light Infantry, fought his way off the beach through the Casino and into Dieppe. He returned to England. Wounded in Normandy,

he rejoined the "Rileys" as commanding officer in September 1944 and led the regiment for the rest of the war, winning a bar to the DSO awarded for bravery at Dieppe. He retired from the army as a brigadier.

As our LCA moved toward shore, the sun was just rising and I could see the dim outline of the buildings along the Dieppe front. We cruised on; the shore came into focus.

We looked at one another. Something was terribly wrong. Everything was intact! We expected a town shattered by the RAF's saturation bombing the previous night....

Half-standing in the centre of the bow of the boat, I was able to peer over the top of the ramp. Smoke had been laid down to mask our approaches. Now, through wisps of smoke, I could see the rocky beach backed by the sea wall, the buildings and hotels on the far side of the green esplanade, and the casino immediately ahead on the right. That was White Beach, my battalion's objective....

On the right, the west headland loomed darkly. An awesome-looking castle crowned its heights. The west cliffs were dotted with caves. They would make ideal locations for defensive weapons.... What frightened me most was the way the headlands on both sides were wrapped around the beach. Enfilade fire from both flanks could make it a terrible killing ground....

Major Bud Matchett, who commanded C Company, had to clear the casino, climb the hill through the town, and then knock out or capture all the enemy positions, including a hotel, a post office, and Gestapo Headquarters. Bud Bowery's D Company was to climb the cliff and take the castle, afterwards hooking to the west headland to destroy the anti-aircraft and artillery batteries before they began firing on the troops landing on the main beach. Then he had to make contact with the South Saskatchewans.

Some objective for two small companies, each with only one hundred men! The other units had similarly unrealistic assignments....

Enemy machine gun bullets smashed against the sides of the LCA or cracked just overhead. The smoke screen laid down on the headlands by the Bostons and Blenheims had quickly dissipated. The Hurricane attack – a single swipe – had only a momentary effect, now lost, of subduing the German fire....

The ramp dropped. I led the thirty-odd men of my platoon in a charge about twenty-five yards up the stony beach. We fanned out and flopped down just short of a huge wire obstacle. Bullets flew everywhere. Enemy mortar bombs started to crash down. Around me, men were being hit and bodies were piling up, one on top of the other. It was terrifying.

Captain W. Denis Whitaker,
Royal Hamilton Light Infantry,
later to become Brigadier-General,
DSO and Bar, CM, ED, CD

Teach any man what fear is

The smoke from our shells mixed with the artificial smoke so that soon the whole valley of Dieppe lay under a white carpet out of which the houses appeared like shadows. Enemy aircraft had damaged our whole communications network....

I looked on the beach; the artificial fog [was] growing thinner. The picture which presented itself could teach any man what fear is. The beach was strewn with infantry equipment: machine guns, packs, grenade throwers, munitions.... Two whole regiments were clinging tightly against the concrete wall, seeking protection from our artillery fire and from the machine gun fire of the beach company, and tank upon tank stood at the water's edge. Everywhere along the whole strand our shells were exploding, their effect multiplied ten times by the exploding stone splinters.

On the green grass between the concrete wall and the edge of town, where the beach company had dug out their trenches, tanks were twisting and turning ... trying to get through into the town. Well, they could try forever! The commander of our division had closed all the streets leading from the beach to the town with a tank-proof concrete wall.

Captain H.H. Ditz, Battery Commander,
302nd German Infantry Division

Like a razor cut to the face

Lieutenant-Colonel Dollard Ménard commanded a battalion of 600 men, the Fusiliers Mont-Royal. Because of garbled communications, they were sent ashore to reinforce the Essex Scottish in the mistaken belief that the Essex Scottish had made a breakthrough. In fact, that regiment was pinned down on the beach and the FMR landed into a hail of fire.

The last fifty yards were the worst. Our landing ships were already within each of the Nazi canons. I could feel my throat tighten. I wanted to do something, to fight, but I was trapped in this damned barge. As soon as the barge landed I leapt out and took with me a group of sappers to cut the barbed wire. My first objective was to clear a parapet some hundred yards along the beach.

I think that I must have made no more than three steps before I was hit by a bullet for the first time. We always say "hit by a bullet" – that's false. A bullet is like a razor cut to the face. At first you don't feel the pain. I was hit in the right shoulder and knocked to the ground. One of my men came to my aid, but I told him, "Go ahead. I'm unharmed." I don't know why I said that. I groped for

MEN of VALOR
They fight for you

LT.-COL. DOLLARD MÉNARD, D.S.O.,
O.C. LES FUSILIERS DU MONT-ROYAL AT DIEPPE.

Wounded five times by intensive enemy fire, he maintained his attack throughout. During withdrawal, exhausted by loss of blood, he still insisted on organizing defences against enemy aircraft and looking after his men.

KEN BELL/DND/NATIONAL ARCHIVES OF CANADA/PA131232

Private E.W. Pritchard examines a German pillbox at Dieppe after Canadians had re-entered the town in 1944.

my first aid kit with my left hand and wondered, "How in the devil am I going to be able to make a bandage." All this while I was on the beach fully exposed to enemy fire. That's when I was hit a second time. It seemed to explode all around me, and I was no longer sure I was still in one piece. The bullet had hit me in the cheek and tore my face pretty badly. I managed to get up and get as far as the parapet, when I was hit for the third time, this time in my right wrist. But I was able to continue with the advance. I was leaving the beach when I was hit in the right leg just below the knee, but I continued on trying to reach the shelter of the town. The last bullet hit me below the right ankle and nailed me to the ground for good. I began to pray.

Later, some of my men collected me and carried me to a barge returning to England. But once on board, a couple of bombers tried to blast us out of the water. I noticed that I was stretched out on some crates of munitions. But all I could say was "To the devil with them, they have not got me yet and they never will."

Lieutenant-Colonel Dollard Ménard
Les Fusiliers Mont-Royal

Our first casualty...

The Cameron Highlanders were piped ashore by piper Corporal Alec Graham.

Our first casualty was C Company's sergeant major. He got hit right in the head and was killed instantly. It was through him that Colonel Gostling was killed. He looked over and saw that the CSM was hit but he didn't know he was dead. He stood up and yelled, "Stretcher-bearer, stretcher-bearer!" Just then he was shot.

Private
Herbert Webber,
Queen's Own
Cameron Highlanders
of Canada

Chances of leaving were minimal...

We received a call for tanks to return to the beach, to be prepared to lay down a smoke screen to cover the landing of evacuation boats. Because my three tanks were to be part of the rearguard that day, I think my crews knew that their chances of leaving the beach were minimal. As the boats appeared they came under very intense fire. There was a rush of men for the boats. Some were swamped by too many men, sunk by gunfire or forced to turn back with partial loads. Casualties on the beach and in the water were unbelievable.

Lieutenant Jack Dunlap
Calgary Tank Regiment

A question of need

Padre John Foote of the Royal Hamilton Light Infantry tended the wounded and dying throughout the battle and refused all offers to be evacuated.

It seemed to me the men ashore would need me more than those going home.

Padre John Foote, RHLI

F.L. DUBERVILLE/DND/NATIONAL ARCHIVES OF CANADA/PA136022

A view of the beach taken in 1944, showing the ruins of the Casino in the foreground.

THE FIGHTER WAR

Fighter Command, which became the Commonwealth's most celebrated military force after its victory in the Battle of Britain, could not play a significant role defending Britain during the Blitz. Hurricanes and Spitfires were short-range, daylight fighters unsuited for operations against night bombers; they were now needed largely as insurance against a revival of German plans to invade England. This role, which involved much patience and little action, was not easy to accept and Fighter Command quickly developed plans for offensive action.

The idea was to combine the necessary training of fighter pilots with attacks on Luftwaffe squadrons in France. "Rhubarbs," in which two or three pilots sought action, "Rodeos," which involved larger fighter sweeps, and "Circuses," which added twin-engined bombers as bait to bring the Luftwaffe into the air, did provide combat training but the cost was high. The German air force now had the same advantages of radar and proximity to home base that Fighter Command had enjoyed in the Battle of Britain.

After June 1941 Fighter Command was called upon to do whatever it could to take pressure off the Soviets. A policy of stepped-up raids might force the Luftwaffe to direct fighters from the eastern front. This was what Fighter Command had in mind when Air Marshal Sholto Douglas argued in favour of remounting the raid on Dieppe. He knew the Luftwaffe would have to intervene and was confident that Fighter Command, equipped with the new Spitfire IX, could win a major victory. He was right about the German response, but the RAF/RCAF lost ninety-nine aircraft to a German total of forty-eight. Eight RCAF squadrons were involved in the battle, including two Army Co-operation units (Nos. 400 and 414) flying Mustangs.

Day-fighter squadrons were active in all theatres of war and RCAF pilots were involved in every one. The most famous individual pilot was "Buzz" Beurling, who became Canada's top-scoring fighter-pilot while flying his Spitfire in defence of the besieged island of Malta. He was credited with shooting down twenty-nine German aircraft.

One of the most dramatic stories of the air war occurred in the cockpit of a Catalina flying boat of No. 413 squadron, which was based in Ceylon. Flight-Lieutenant Len Birchall was flying a routine patrol south of the island on April 4, 1942, when he encountered the Japanese fleet headed for Colombo. Japanese "Zeroes" quickly caught up with the slow patrol plane and shot it down, but his wireless message got through and the British fleet dispersed, avoiding another Pearl Harbor. Birchall was taken prisoner and ended the war as senior Allied officer in a prisoner of war camp in Japan.

Canadians were also involved in night-fighter and intruder operations as pilots in RAF squadrons or in one of the three RCAF units, 406, 409 and 410. Flying Officer Robert Fumerton and his radar observer, Sergeant Pat Bing, were the leading night-fighter aces, destroying fourteen aircraft while flying Beaufighters against German night bombers.

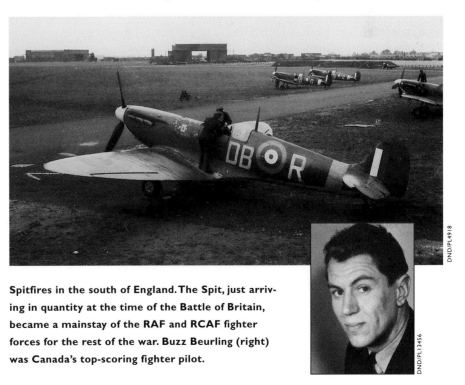

Spitfires in the south of England. The Spit, just arriving in quantity at the time of the Battle of Britain, became a mainstay of the RAF and RCAF fighter forces for the rest of the war. Buzz Beurling (right) was Canada's top-scoring fighter pilot.

DND/PL13456

DND/PL4918

THE BATTLE OF THE ATLANTIC

British success in cracking late U-boat Enigma codes provided the Royal Navy with breathing space in 1941, but the declaration of war against the United States offered Admiral Dönitz an opportunity to abandon the North Atlantic and sever the Allied lifeline in American waters. The United States Navy was ill-equipped for anti-submarine warfare and its attention was focused on the Pacific. Months passed before convoys were organized or air cover provided. The coastal cities failed to implement a blackout and U-boats preyed on vessels silhouetted against the bright lights of American cities.

The U-boat captains called this phase of the war "the American turkey shoot" and Allied shipping losses quickly rose to frightening levels. The U-boats also tried their luck in Canadian waters. On the night of May 11, 1942, two merchant ships were sunk in the Gulf of St. Lawrence. By the end of the year fourteen more had been torpedoed, as had two corvettes. Despite the organization of a St. Lawrence Escort Force, based at the port of Gaspé, the shallow waters of the Gulf proved ideal for U-boat operations. The Ger-

mans abandoned their campaign only after merchant ships were kept out of the river and the pickings became too slim. The last, and worst, incident of the year came in October when a U-boat sank the passenger ferry *Caribou* travelling between Sydney, Nova Scotia, and Port-aux-Basques, Newfoundland. Among the 137 passengers who died were many women and children.

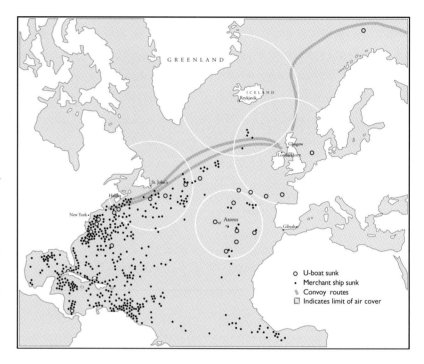

The Battle of the Atlantic, 1942. Germany's declaration of war against the United States led to a highly successful U-boat campaign off the east coast of North America. U-boats also operated in the St. Lawrence River, sinking merchant ships without the loss of or damage to a single U-boat.

This view of HMCS *Gaspé* with some of the crew on the foredeck gives a good idea of just how small the corvettes were that escorted convoys across the North Atlantic.

With convoys organized and escort groups improvised in the coastal regions, the U-boats moved back into the Atlantic to operate in the "black hole" south of Greenland where there was no Allied air cover. Admiral Dönitz now had the three hundred U-boats he had declared sufficient to close the Atlantic, and for a time it looked as if he might succeed. The German navy had added a "wheel" to their Enigma machines in February, creating an Ultra blackout for the rest of 1942. So convoys could not be easily routed away from wolf-packs.

The Royal Canadian Navy had begun convoy escort operations in 1941 with inadequate ships, untrained crews and poor equipment. This was evident to all by September 1941 when convoy SC42, escorted by just four RCN corvettes and one destroyer, lost sixteen merchant ships. The RCN agreed to increase its escort groups to a minimum of six ships including two destroyers, but this meant there was less time for training, rest or refits. As soon as a corvette had undergone a shakedown and some initial training it was sent to sea, ready or not.

The "American turkey shoot" took the pressure off the Mid-Ocean Escort Force and the RCN was able to begin some anti-submarine warfare training in the spring of 1942, including practice against a British submarine. Unfortunately, the emphasis was on hunting U-boats

HMCS *Assiniboine*, part of convoy Escort Group C1, rammed and sank U-210 on August 6, 1942, after a wild running fight through thick fog. No fewer than eighteen U-boats attacked convoy SC194, sinking eleven of thirty-six ships.

rather than on simply protecting a convoy, and the Canadians acquired a reputation for being too ready to take offensive action.

Problems with inadequate radar and sonar continued to plague the RCN, but as historian Marc Milner puts it, "The great need for 1942 was for escorts of any descrip-

Crew watch a movie on the mess deck of a Royal Canadian Navy ship. During the war most naval volunteers were enlisted in the RCNVR, the Royal Canadian Naval Volunteer Reserve, known as the "Wavy Navy" after the distinguishing stripes on their officers' jacket cuffs. The RCN, Royal Canadian Navy, was the permanent force, while RCNR was used to designate officers and men who had served in the Merchant Navy before joining up. The vast majority of naval personnel were RCNVR and their song "Roll Along Wavy Navy" was the unofficial anthem of the men who fought the Battle of the Atlantic.

tion." Attempts to check the growth of the navy to allow time to improve performance were "overwhelmed by the operational emergency," and in the last six months of 1942 the Canadians "bore the brunt of the German assault." Through sheer bad luck Canadian-escorted convoys were intercepted twice as often as British ones. Sixteen convoys lost ships in the air gap during the last half of 1942 and eleven of these were escorted by Canadian groups.

There were important victories – in August alone three U-boats were sunk by RCN ships – but by the end of 1942 it was evident that the time had come to withdraw the Canadians from the mid-Atlantic for re-equipment and training. Winston Churchill conveyed this message to Mackenzie King on December 17, 1942.

"I appreciate the grand contribution of the Royal Canadian Navy," Churchill wrote, "but the expansion of the RCN has created a training problem which must take some time to solve." What Churchill and the Royal Navy proposed made very good sense, but there was naturally some resentment in Ottawa. No one, British or Canadian, knew that the climax of the Battle of the Atlantic would occur when the RCN was away from the centre of action.

"THE UNKNOWN NAVY"

It is with good reason that a recent book on the Canadian Merchant Navy, written by Robert G. Halford, has been titled *The Unknown Navy.* One of the keys to the survival of Britain during the Second World War was the transport of food, goods and weapons from North America. The struggle to accomplish this, known as the Battle of the Atlantic, has been told many times. Accounts of the chess match between the Allied escorts and the German U-boats as they fought their desperate struggle over the merchant ships has portrayed the merchantmen as mere pawns in a greater struggle. These pawns, however, have a story of their own to tell. The Canadian Merchant Navy, and the industry behind it, played a major role in the Allied war effort.

Early in the war, as the full implications of the U-boat threat began to materialize, the British began to look for options. One of the earliest expedients was the transfer of twenty-five shallow-draft Great Lakes boats in the spring of 1940 to England to replace British coastal ships lost to the Germans. Six of these ships were immediately put to good use in evacuating the remnants of the British Expeditionary Force from Dunkirk. Later that year, a mission was sent to North America to seek out shipbuilding yards to replace the steadily increasing losses. Though the Canadian industry had declined from its heyday in the 1920s, the war had stimulated tremendous growth. The British mission placed an order for twenty 10,000-ton dry cargo vessels, followed shortly by a Canadian order

NATIONAL ARCHIVES OF CANADA/PA116455

Survivors of a vessel torpedoed in the North Atlantic, photographed at St. John's, September 15, 1942.

for an additional eighty-eight vessels. By the time the last wartime ship was launched, 354 10,000-ton and 43 4,700-ton vessels would be produced. This was in addition to the construction of nearly 500 destroyers, frigates, corvettes and minesweepers for the navy. In 1944, merchant ships were being launched at a rate of almost two per week. To put this in perspective, the 10,000 ton Park/Fort class of merchant ship produced in Canadian yards, which was nearly identical to its more famous American cousin, the Liberty ship, was being produced at a faster rate based on population and at a lower per unit cost. Nearly half of the ocean-going vessels of the Commonwealth, including those of Great Britain, were built in Canada. Canadian government expenditures and the workforce devoted to the creation of the merchant fleet were larger than those of the aircraft industry. What an amazing accomplishment for a country considered an economic lightweight prior to the start of the war.

The Canadian Merchant Navy evolved into the world's fourth largest wartime fleet with a force of over 12,000 men. The majority of the ships in the fleet were Canadian-built. Over the course of the war, sixty-seven Canadian-flagged vessels were sunk by enemy action. The toll of merchant seamen lost was 1,578, a rate much higher than experienced by the navy. In addition, there were losses not related to enemy action.

The contributions of this fleet are immeasurable. After the war the British government had nothing but praise for the accomplishments of the Canadian Merchant Navy. Rear Admiral Leornard W. Murray, Commander-in-Chief of the Canadian Northwest Atlantic, stated that the Battle of the Atlantic was won by "the courage, fortitude and determination of the British and Allied Merchant Navy." Well deserved praise for the pawns of the "Unknown Navy."

In spite of my brave words...

Admiral Leonard Murray was Flag Officer, Newfoundland, until September 1942, when he was appointed Commanding Officer, Atlantic Coast, with headquarters in Halifax.

In order to encourage the captains of the merchant ships of all countries which carry the lifeblood of the U.K., I made it a point to attend the briefing conference of all captains and chief engineers before their departure. During the winter of '42–'43, when sinkings were at their worst, I could see when I told them of the measures by escort and air cover that were being taken for their protection and safety; I could see that they knew very well, and that they knew I knew in spite of my brave words, that anything up to 25 per cent of them would probably not arrive in the U.K. in their own ships, and that probably half of that number would not arrive in the U.K. at all. But there was never a waver in their resolve.

That such bravery should be found in what many look upon as an undisciplined service fills me with the greatest admiration. During that period, the casualties in convoy was in the nature of 25 per cent in ships and 12 ½ per cent in personnel. Think that over, and remember that the much-flaunted Luftwaffe cracked and had to call off the Battle of Britain when the rate was only 7 per cent.

Admiral Leonard Murray, Royal Canadian Navy

To scare away scurvy

Conditions were terrible that winter. Groups were worked on a thirty-five-day cycle, which entailed twenty-nine days away from St. John's, twenty-seven days away from fresh bread, twenty-five days away from fresh meat, added to which, at the northern end of their beat, there was no sunlight to speak of in the winter. We had to revert to the old rations of Nelson's time, barrelled salt beef and lime juice or tomato juice to scare away scurvy.

Admiral Leonard Murray, RCN

The most revolting scene I've ever witnessed

Chief Petty Officer Jim Liddy of Saint John kept a daily diary which he later transcribed into a book for his children and grandchildren. At the outbreak of war he applied to join the navy.

I received word that my application for a commission in the Canadian Navy had been turned down due to the number of people applying. They suggested application should be made in six months to a year's time. It was quite a disappointment....

An urgent call came over the airwaves. The Navy needed anyone who had knowledge of Morse code, semaphore and the International Code of Signals, and this was right in my line....

Having made all arrangements with Lil, my wife of a little more than two years, I joined the Saint John Division of the RCNVR on October 7, 1939, with the rating of Ordinary Signalman....

After attending Signal School at HMCS Stadacona *in Halifax, Liddy embarked on his first convoy.*

Our movements were clouded in secrecy. We were not told what ship we would be sailing on until the harbour craft brought us alongside, and after that we were not allowed to communicate with the shore. This was as it should be, no doubt, but it caused a source of worry to Lil back home, who imagined the worst every time a British ship was reported sunk. The ship we now boarded was the SS *Comedian*....

At first light on Wednesday, October 25 (eighteen days after joining up), I looked out over Bedford Basin ... crowded with merchant ships of all shapes and sizes, and realized that this was no great adventure, but a deadly serious business of moving all the valuable cargoes these ships contained across the Atlantic to England, where they were badly needed....

For the first several days at sea, at nighttime all ships would be on their proper stations. At first light the next morning a great many of them were scattered, like a bunch of sheep, all over the visible ocean. This happened until a lot of the captains got used to sailing so close to other ships in the dark.

Liddy's first convoy reached Liverpool without mishap. On a later convoy he was not so fortunate.

We ran into some exceptionally heavy weather, which got worse as the day progressed, until by nightfall the winds had increased to hurricane force, driving snow mixed with ice pellets, bringing visibility to zero. At around 0230 on Monday, we were jolted awake by a terrific crash and rending noise, after which the ship took a heavy list to starboard. I do not remember ever having moved faster in my life. In a few seconds I was out on deck just in time to see the outline of another ship drifting off astern. I knew then what had happened; we had been rammed.

Going back to the room, I quickly jumped into my heavy duffel coat (we slept almost fully dressed), put on a lifejacket, grabbed the small leather case and headed for my station along the boat deck.... A huge gaping hole yawned in the ship's side to well below the waterline. Peering down the engine-room skylight, I saw that the water was rising to a level with the top of the engines, and steam was escaping from the stokehold where the fires were being doused by the steadily rising water.

No. 2 port lifeboat was the first to be lowered with two men in it at the "falls." When it was let go, one of them jammed at the David-block, causing the boat to hang vertically down the ship's side. One of the men in her was catapulted out but managed to grab the rope ladder and climb back on board. Meanwhile the falls had been cleared and the boat lowered, only to find that someone had let the "painter" (mooring rope) go, and she drifted astern with her lone occupant. He however had the presence of mind to grab the log-line trailing from the stern and hung on till a heavier rope was thrown to him and the boat hauled around to the starboard side.

This one was soon filled and, in charge of Commodore MacKinnon, started away for the ship that had rammed us, lying some distance off, showing brilliant cargo clusters.

The next boat to be lowered was No. 1 Port, into which I had thrown my small case and also one that belonged to Commodore MacKinnon that he had entrusted to me. I clambered in after them along with the majority of the navy signal ratings, three or four officers and quite a few Lascar firemen.

When we pushed away from the ship's side, I took the starboard bow oar and along with all the others realized we would never make it to the other ship trying to row at an angle to the 50- to 60-foot-high waves which every minute threatened to swamp us. We became content to just try to keep her head-on to the waves and wait till daylight.

I will never forget the experience we had in that small boat as those huge combers rolled at us, cresting at the top so high above us, then up, up and over, sliding down into the trough below. The blowing sleet in the screeching wind tore at our clothes and faces. We were continually drenched with ice-cold water. A lot of the men were desperately sick, and the sound of vomiting on empty stomachs added to the discomfort of the subzero temperature....

As dawn broke, the other ship spotted us and steamed slowly to where we were, providing a lee from the still howling wind. She had one rope ladder over the side and was in the process of putting another over when we came alongside. As we did so, one of the Lascars jumped out and grabbed the bottom of the ladder, just as our boat dropped off about 40 feet in the trough of a wave. He was so numb with the cold he couldn't hang on till the boat came up on the next wave, and down he came between the boat and the ship, to be crushed between the two.

This was a hard lesson for all the rest of us – to grab the ladder on the highest point of the wave, so that we could get our feet onto it too, and only one man at a time.

By then, they had the second ladder lowered, and members of the crew climbed down it and helped us up the other one. In our cramped and half frozen condition we really needed the assistance to climb over on the deck of the RMS *Oropesa*, the ship that had rammed us and picked us up. A hot drink of rum and coffee sent the blood tingling all through it and revived me somewhat.

Commodore MacKinnon's boat was the first to be picked up, half an hour before us.... The third one had met the fate that we were so afraid of; it had capsized. Most of the people in it managed to climb on to the upturned boat and hang on for dear life. There were nine that didn't make it. Among these were the chief engineer and one of the young apprentices who I'd exchanged books with the day before. We saw their bodies floating around, their lifejackets keeping them on the surface, and the scavengers of the sea, the seagulls, making a meal out of that part of them that was above water – their faces. This was the most revolting scene I've ever witnessed and I hope I'll never see it again.

Chief Petty Officer Jim Liddy, RCNVR

Marvellous feats of acrobatics

Harry Ferns to William "Pat" Patterson, February 1, 1942
Dear Pat,
The plebiscite has the Tories howling mad largely because it has confused them badly. Mr. King made a very long and tiresome speech on Monday last. He and Hanson [Conservative House Leader] put 23,000 words on the record in the course of the afternoon and evening. Nonetheless, the PM's performance was one of his best from an intellectual point of view, and he very fairly brought together all the relevant points for the purpose of putting the conscriptionist arguments in their proper proportion. He studiously avoided saying whether a vote to free the government from its pledge meant a vote for conscription. In the province of Quebec the Liberal party is absolutely neutral. The candidate in Montreal–St. Mary's is running on an anti-conscription ticket. Godbout made a speech which on the basis of excerpts might be described as anti-conscriptionist, but when read in its entirety was really strong advocacy of the policy of supporting King against the threat of Meighen. All the boys are performing marvellous feats of acrobatics.

I understand that the Cabinet is completely unanimous, and the bulk of the party more or less so.... Coldwell [CCF] declared himself ready to support the plebiscite, urged the government to tell the people how to vote, and moved an amendment about the conscription of wealth....

Turnbull and Pickersgill have become great manufacturers of propaganda. Because they are fighting "Big Business" they are busy digging up such items as Drew's criticism of the Red Army in 1937, Hepburn's record of hatred for the working class, etc. I get the impression I am working in the Agitprop section of the Comintern....

I don't think that the hold of the Liberals on power is being very seriously shaken. The opposition can't overcome the basic fact that Canada is making a very considerable effort in this war, that the need for men in the army is not a major need either for Canada or for the Allies with their superabundance of men and their paucity of equipment and brains everywhere except in the U.S.S.R. And, more important, Canada is still remote from the theatres of real war; the Canadian people are not genuinely frightened yet....

Harry Ferns

I am now a bit fed up...

By the summer of 1942, some elements of the Canadian Army had been stationed in England for two and a half years, and had seen no action.

April 26, 1940
The military life continues to fascinate me – continually I learn things about people of which I remained in complete ignorance as long as I was merely reading books. There are certain complicated artillery schemes which it is easy to learn while reading in the manuals of instruction, but very hard to perform while out in the countryside doing practical exercises. And so it is simple to evolve political theories when one is studying philosophy at the university, but they must be greatly revised when one has had experience of real flesh-and-blood humanity....

October 13, 1941
For two whole years now, I have lived in army camps and worn a khaki uniform and suffered army discipline, and I am now a bit fed up, and I would like to go home, please....

Let me make use of my irritation for a moment or two to ask one question. Why not conscription in Canada, or at least in Canada save Quebec? Why should the better part of the younger generation put up with these discomforts, and the larger more selfish part stay comfortably at home making themselves secure in all the good jobs?

G. Hamilton Southam

PART IV

FIRST STRIKE – 1943

Troops of the Princess Patricia's Canadian Light Infantry in action near Valguarnera, Italy, July 20, 1943.

If, in Churchill's phrase, 1942 was "the end of the beginning," 1943 was the year in which the Allies struck the blows that marked the beginning of the end for Nazi Germany. The most important events occurred on the eastern front, starting with the surrender of Sixth Army at Stalingrad in February 1943. The loss of a quarter of a million men and the forced retreat of the other German armies to the startline of the 1942 offensive did not mean that Germany had lost the war, but it did suggest that a compromise peace was Hitler's best hope in the east.

Hitler agreed to consider this compromise but only after the German army had regained the initiative in an operation which would prove that while winter belonged to the Russians, Germany could still win victories in the summer months. Operation "Citadel," which began in July, involved converging attacks by two powerful armies equipped with the new Panther and Tiger tanks, but Soviet resistance could not be overcome, and after two weeks of costly fighting "Citadel" was called off. This was bad enough for the Germans, but when the Red Army launched massive counterattacks, the Germans were pushed back an average of 150 miles along the entire front. From now on a separate peace with Stalin would mean the removal of Hitler and junior-partner status for Germany in a Soviet-dominated Europe. The Nazis much preferred the total defeat of Germany to such a compromise, and after the fall of 1943 Hitler argued that if the German people failed him they did not deserve to survive.

British Commonwealth and U.S. forces also won important victories in 1943. General Bernard Montgomery's Eighth Army, with its Australian, British, Indian, New Zealand and South African divisions, overwhelmed Rommel's Afrika Corps at El Alamein, then advanced west to join up with British and American troops landing in North Africa. Hitler transformed this minor setback into a military disaster by reinforcing Tunisia, sacrificing a large German army and further weakening the Luftwaffe when every aircraft was needed on the eastern front. Some 275,000 German and Italian soldiers held out until May, but less than a thousand managed to escape. This was a surrender on the same scale as Stalingrad, and Hitler's only comfort was his belief that he had tied down the Allies for the first half of 1943.

The reality was that the British and Americans had not been able to agree on plans to confront the German army in 1943. When Churchill persuaded Roosevelt to support Operation "Torch," the invasion of North Africa, General Marshall had stated the obvious, "If Torch, No Roundup," meaning that a commitment of the best troops, with extensive naval and air resources, to the Mediterranean would make the promised invasion of France, code-named "Roundup," impossible in 1943. Without "Roundup" there was no agreed strategy for employing the Commonwealth and American armies.

Churchill and Roosevelt met at Casablanca in January 1943 to try to develop new plans for the defeat of Germany. The war situation gave them little choice. The U-boat offensive was jeopardizing the supply of food, fuel and munitions to England and threatening to cut off the buildup of American troops in the U.K. The Battle of the Atlantic simply had to have priority, so the U.S. Navy agreed to divert escort-carriers and destroyers to the anti-U-boat war, and Very Long Range "VLR" Liberator bombers were to be transferred to the RAF and RCAF so that the Greenland air gap could be closed.

With this issue settled, the question of what to do

Churchill, visiting Canadian troops in England in May 1944, inspects the soup.

with their armies had to be confronted. Churchill argued for the invasion of Sicily as the logical next step. It would open the Mediterranean, making it possible to use the Suez Canal instead of the Cape of Good Hope route to India and Australia. This British strategic objective was of little interest to the United States but there was no real alternative. The American military accepted Operation "Husky" but refused to support an invasion of the Italian mainland, and insisted on British agreement that the invasion of northwest Europe would take place in 1944.

If the Commonwealth and the United States were to have any real impact on the German military machine in 1943, it was clearly up to Bomber Command and the United States Eighth Air Force to establish a "second front" in the skies over Germany. The invasion of Sicily would absorb all of two German divisions; the bomber offensive could tie down much of the Luftwaffe and a large part of the German war effort.

For Canadians, 1943 was the year in which their armed forces began to play a more visible and vital role in the war. The 1st Canadian Division entered combat in Sicily, Admiral Leonard Murray and the RCN took control of their own theatre of war, the northwest Atlantic, and Canadian bomber squadrons, supplied with graduates of the British Commonwealth Air Training Plan, formed No. 6 Group, Royal Canadian Air Force. Canadians were set to join in the first great offensive strikes against Hitler's Reich.

STRATEGIC BOMBING

After 1942, the bombing offensive was a joint campaign conducted by the RAF/RCAF and the United States Army Air Force. Both air forces were committed to variants of a strategic bombing doctrine as the path to victory. The Air Officer Commanding (AOC) Bomber Command, Air Marshal Sir Arthur Harris, was the foremost champion of the night bomber and the area bombing offensive. According to Harris a "speedy and complete victory" could be won if Bomber Command was given unconditional priority in the production and allocation of aircraft.

Harris desperately wanted the Americans to join the night offensive but U.S. bomber doctrine called for "precision" daylight raids, and General "Hap" Arnold was a firm believer in the American policy. Churchill urged the two "bomber barons" to develop a

"**The bomber will always get through.**" Air Marshal Sir Arthur Trenchard (left), seen here with Montgomery, was a strong proponent of mass bombing, believing it had revolutionized the nature of war.

co-ordinated offensive so that a night raid by a thousand bombers could be followed by a daylight raid on the same target. Even those who doubted that bombing could destroy German industry or break civilian morale believed that around-the-clock bombing would devastate the German air force, as the Luftwaffe was bound to respond with an all-out defensive effort.

The sceptics had other reasons for supporting a powerful air offensive. General Alan Brooke, the professional head of the British army, opposed all claims to priority for the RAF, but he noted that the bomber would "bring the horrors of war home to the German people" and make them realize that "aggression did not pay." This in itself was, he thought, a worthwhile aim.

The decision to mount a combined bomber offensive was announced at the Casablanca Conference and given the code name "Pointblank." The primary objective was the reduction of German fighter strength to obtain command of the air for an invasion and to allow for more precise bombing of specific targets. This goal was to be accomplished by attacks on German aircraft factories as well as the attrition of combat.

Air Marshal Harris was unhappy with the list of specific objectives for "Pointblank" and interpreted the directive in his own way, attacking any important German city within reach of his bombers. Bomber Command continued to improve its navigation and target-marking

The Mosquito, one of the most potent and versatile aircraft of the war, first entered operations in 1941. More than 1,100 of these moulded-plywood fighter-bombers were produced at de Havilland in Toronto. Shown here are the third and fourth to reach Britain, in 1943.

with the introduction of Pathfinder squadrons and the development of new navigation devices. Harris genuinely believed that Germany could not survive the crescendo of bombing that would strike her cities and he was quite sincere when he claimed that air power could end the war in 1943. Those who portray Harris as a heartless "butcher" of civilians and aircrew should at least take note of the fact that Harris was trying to end the war quickly, avoiding the much heavier casualties involved in invading Europe.

Harris was sincere but mistaken: he failed to consider the German response to heavy assaults on their cities. The battle of the Ruhr, March to July 1943, consisted of forty-three major attacks led by Pathfinder Mosquitoes which marked targets using Oboe, a blind bombing device or H2S, airborne radar. The Germans reacted by dispersing industry, organizing new civil defence measures and improving their defences. Flak towers for the vaunted 88-mm anti-aircraft gun were built and the radar-controlled night-fighter defences improved.

Bomber Command losses throughout the period averaged 4.7 per cent, meaning that 872 bombers failed to return in just over 18,000 sorties. This loss rate could not be allowed to continue so permission was granted to make use of "Window," strips of aluminum foil which were known to confuse radar. The use of "window" had been forbidden out of fear that the enemy would employ

it against England or in the Allied invasion of Sicily. Now it was decided to use it in a series of raids that would begin as soon as the Sicilian landings were complete.

Hamburg, the large north German port which provided a clear radar "signature," was selected as the principal objective. Window proved effective in the first attack but little damage was done and daylight raids by the U.S. Eighth Air Force were even less accurate. On the night of July 27 a combination of freakish weather conditions and concentrated bombing in the city centre produced a fire storm of unprecedented fury. More than 40,000 were killed and the core of the city was destroyed.

Nazi Germany had suffered a major catastrophe. Albert Speer, Hitler's armaments chief, told his Führer that raids of similar intensity on six more cities "would bring Germany's armaments production to a total halt." Major resources were now diverted to civil defence, anti-aircraft guns, new radar networks and night-fighters. Bomber Command had opened a second front in the skies over Germany.

By the end of 1943 the U.S. Eighth Air Force, which had discovered that it could not conduct daylight bombing without suffering unacceptable loses, was using long-range fighter-interceptors to accompany its deep raids. The famous P-51 Mustang, an aircraft with the range of a bomber and the performance of the best fighters, struck the final blows against the Luftwaffe, establishing abso-

Speech by Field-Marshal Milch at a Conference on the Problems of Aircraft Production, August 25, 1943

I will take this opportunity to explain the basis of our policy. We are firmly convinced that our only chance of maintaining Germany's arms industry and labour lies in our hitting back at the enemy both by day and by night harder than before and above all harder than until a week ago. If we fail and the percentage of enemy aircraft shot down remains at the same level as up to the first half of July, we shall be crushed. I think it is idle to make long-term plans for U-boats, tanks, aircraft and so on. Programmes of this nature can never be fulfilled; Germany would be brought to her knees.

There is only one remedy. That is for our fighters to hit the enemy so hard day and night that he is forced to abandon the policy of destroying our arms production.

Enemy bomber losses in May and June amounted to about 4.4% of the total raiding force. In July there was a slight increase, the figure being 6.4%. It is clear that these losses are not enough to deter an enemy as resolute as ours. You know that the defence of our country is now in the forefront of our strategy. A large number of S/E and T/E fighter Gruppen has been brought back to Germany. In my opinion this is absurdly late in the day, but at last it has been done. Field-Marshal Göring, too, is now bringing pressure to bear in this matter.

My own attitude is this: I would tell the front that Germany itself is the real front line, and that the mass of fighters must go for home defence.

Albert Speer to Martin Bormann on the reconstruction of oil plants, September 16, 1944:

We must not allow ourselves to give up hope that we must eventually be successful in gaining mastery over the enemy air forces over Reich territory, and developments during the last few days have shown that a large number of bombers can be destroyed by the use of a comparatively small number of fighters. A few weeks quiet in the air will show a considerable increase in our fighter strength.

Interrogation of Reichsminister Albert Speer:

Q. At what stage of the war did strategic bombing begin to cause the German High Command and Government real concern, and why?
A. The first heavy attack on Hamburg in August 1943 made an extraordinary impression. We were of the opinion that a raid repetition of this type of attack upon another six German towns would inevitably cripple the will to sustain armaments manufacture and war production. It was I who first verbally reported to the Führer at that time that a continuation of these attacks might bring about a rapid end to the war. At first, however, the raids were not repeated with the same weight and in the meantime it became possible for the civilians to adapt themselves to these air attacks both from the point of view of morale and the experience gained, whilst at the same time the armaments industry was able to gather useful experience.

This enlarged section of an air photo taken August 12, 1943, shows the extent of damage to the central area of Hamburg. The burnt-out shells of roofless houses can be readily identified.

Ready to go. The cavernous bomb bay of a Lancaster.

Ground crews... a hell of a life

Many of the ground trades really worked hard and had a hell of a life on a bomber station. The fitters and riggers repaired aircraft and engines night and day in all kinds of weather. They worked out in the open or under a bit of canvas shelter. The armourers hauled and loaded bombs, changed bomb loads, fused and defused bombs, rain or shine, at all hours of the day ... [When a raid was laid on the] armourers would manhandle the [bomb] trolleys under the plane and raise the bombs into the bomb bay. They had a hydraulic-powered winch most of the time but on occasion it was powered by hand. The fuel trucks ... loaded the specified amount of fuel to get the plane to the target and back. There was never very much to spare.... Another truck would deliver the type and amount of Window.... While all this was going on members of the ground crew who looked after an aircraft had to check it thoroughly. Engines would be run up and tested; radio men, radar men and instrument men would call at each aircraft and check the various pieces of equipment and instruments. The camera would be checked and loaded with film. Ammunition would be put in the turrets. The many thousands of rounds for the tail turret were carried in canisters near the bomb bay, and ammo tracks ... ran along the fuselage to the tail turret.

Stoking up at the NAAFI mobile canteen.

More work for the repair crews. The pilot managed to bring in this Mosquito with most of its rudder surface burned away.

lute air superiority in daylight over the skies of western Europe.

The combined bomber offensive had not been able to force a German surrender or prevent German war production from increasing, but it had forced Hitler to divert crucial resources away from the eastern front. It also fulfilled the Casablanca directive by eliminating the German air force and making the invasion of Europe possible.

NO. 6 GROUP RCAF

Throughout the Second World War, the Canadian government tried to maintain a separate Canadian military identity while offering full cooperation to British and American senior commanders. A nation of eleven million could not expect to play a role in the determination of grand strategy, but wherever and whenever possible Canadian forces were to be commanded and controlled by Canadians. General Andrew McNaughton had forced the British army to recognize his status as the senior officer of a Canadian contingent and his nationalism was one of the reasons behind his dismissal in 1943. The RCN, which might have benefitted from closer integration with the Royal Navy, was even more committed to operational autonomy. The RCAF was, however, deeply divided on the issue of Canadianization, since most vet-

erans preferred to stick with their British and Commonwealth squadrons. But the rapid expansion of the RAF was only possible because of the British Commonwealth Air Training Plan, and by the end of 1942, 37 per cent of the pilots in Bomber Command were Canadians, Australians or New Zealanders. About 60 per cent of these were Canadian. By January 1945, 46 per cent wore Commonwealth shoulder flashes and 55 per cent of these were

The stately homes of England were pressed into war service. Allerton Hall was headquarters for No. 6 Bomber Group.

members of the RCAF. Pressure to create a separate RCAF bomber group, commanded by a Canadian air marshal, was inevitable, and when Sir Arthur Harris offered his support, matters moved quickly. The new group became operational January 1943, flying from seven bases in Yorkshire: Croft, Dalton, Dishforth, East Moor, Leeming, Middleton St. George and Topcliffe. The Air Officer Commanding, Air Vice Marshal G.E. Brookes, had served in the Royal Flying Corps in the First World War and joined the RCAF in 1924 when it was first established.

No. 6 Group grew to include fifteen squadrons flying from eleven bases. Throughout 1943 and on to the very last operations over Germany in April 1945, the group played a major role in the defeat of Germany. The

A senior-level briefing at Canadian Bomber Group headquarters: Air Vice Marshal G.E. Brookes, Air Officer Commanding, and Group Captain C.R. Slemon, senior Air Staff officer, explain tactics to group and staff officers.

From an airman's album – Flight Lieutenant John R. Harding

(Below) The crew of W-Willie, March 1943. From left: F/Sgt Les Brady, RCAF, mid-upper gunner, Sgt Spence Cartwright, RAF, bombardier, Sgt Bob McCrae, RAF, rear gunner, Sgt Pat Baird, RAF, wireless operator, Sgt Sid Burton, RAF, pilot, Sgt Ron Squire, RAF, flight engineer, and me, F/Sgt John Harding, RCAF, navigator.

As a sergeant navigator-observer (brevet is an O with a single wing), August 1942. We have recently arrived in Lossiemouth, Scotland, for further crew training. Of my class of 27 Canadians, 17 will be killed in action within a year flying with Bomber Command.

December 1942, I am on squadron (103, RAF, Elsham Wolds, Lincs.). My field service cap is folded and tucked in my left epaulet. This blue battle dress is our normal working garb and is what we wear on sorties (or "missions," as the Americans call bombing trips). On this photo sent to my mother in Windsor, the censor erased the squadron Ident letters (PM-W) on the Lanc for security reasons.

September 20, 1944. After 50 bombing sorties (two tours) and with a DFC, I am back in Canada, based at Rockcliffe, Ottawa. Here I'm navigator in a B-17 Flying Fortress with 168 Heavy Transport Squadron. Our main duty is to run military mail across to London (Biggin Hill), then up to the front lines in Europe.

(Left) March 30, 1944, on my second tour. I'm with 550 Squadron, RAF, North Killingholme, Yorks. This photo was taken just before the ill-fated Nuremberg raid, wherein the RAF lost some 93 aircraft (including 14 lost by Canadians). I carry aboard my helmet and oxygen mask on my left shoulder, a metal case containing sextant and a large satchel of maps, charts and plotting instruments in my right hand, and my parachute harness, with chest-pack fitting, in my left hand.

(Below) In October 1944, I am posted to Biggin Hill in Britain to help run mail consignments in Dakotas (DC-3s) up to the lines. Near the end of our tour of duty, our crew volunteers to check out a new crew. Here took place the crash that landed me in Dr. Tilley's burns unit at East Grinstead.

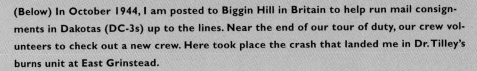

The first Canadian-built Lancaster bomber prepares to leave Victory Aircraft in Toronto on its trip to England. The Lanc was the most effective heavy bomber for most of the war, flying thousands of sorties over Germany. It was the aircraft flown by the Dam Busters, who breeched the dams in the Ruhr Valley.

initial teething problems of a new group were overcome, and as new Lancasters from Victory Aircraft in Toronto arrived in 1944, RCAF squadrons were among the best in Bomber Command.

VICTORY IN THE ATLANTIC

The worst period of the Battle of the Atlantic was the dark winter months of 1942–43. An Ultra blackout was an important factor in the growing success of the U-boats, and the diversion of ships, especially escort-carriers, to support Operation "Torch" was also significant. However, the primary cause was the increase in the number of operational submarines, as became clear after Ultra intelligence was again available, for it was no longer possible to reroute every convoy away from the numerous wolf-packs.

To counter this threat Churchill established a high-profile Anti-U-boat Committee under his own chairmanship and appointed an aggressive new commander, Admiral Max Horton, to oversee the battle. Horton was able to build upon the work of the Admiralty's operational research scientists under the physicist P.M.S. Blackett. Blackett's scientists had determined that nine escorts were more effective at protecting sixty ships than six were in guarding thirty. Doubling the size of convoys released escorts to form hunter-killer groups which could be sent to the aid of convoys when they were under attack. Blackett was also instrumental in convincing the navy that air cover reduced losses by 65 per cent, reinforcing demands for very-long-range aircraft to close the air gap.

The crisis of the battle began before these and other measures were fully implemented. Merchant ship losses, ninety-five in the first twenty days of March 1943, were so heavy that the possibility of a lengthy halt to convoy sailings had to be considered. Instead the tide of battle

The B-24 Liberator, equipped with airborne radar and the Leigh Light for illuminating surfaced U-boats, was a formidable weapon against enemy submarines. The VLR Liberator permanently closed the gap in the air cover south of Greenland.

A U-boat under attack with depth charges.

quickly turned and within two months the U-boats suffered a total defeat.

The first sign of possible victory came in early April when a USN escort group with the carrier *Bogue* provided effective cover in the Greenland air gap. Five new Royal Navy support groups, including one with the carrier HMS *Biter*, joined the battle, as did new land-based aircraft. The Royal Canadian Air Force was scheduled to receive twenty new Liberators but it was an old, slow, RCAF Catalina that began the attack on wolf-pack "Fink" in early May, sinking U-630 at its station in front of a storm-battered convoy. In the next few days, six more submarines were sunk by escorts and two were lost colliding with each other. The next convoy had even better cover and the full attention of a support group as well as its own escort. Five U-boats were sunk and not a single merchantman was lost. By the end of May the Germans had lost forty-three U-boats, more than twice the number lost in any previous month of the war. On May 24 Admiral Dönitz ordered his U-boats to abandon the offensive. In his memoirs he wrote, "We had lost the Battle of the Atlantic."

THE CANADIANS IN BRITAIN

During the Second World War close to half a million Canadians were stationed in the United Kingdom, some of them for most of the war. By 1943, the army had sent all five of its divisions plus two armoured brigades, a total of 240,000 men to Britain, while the overseas strength of the RCAF had risen to 42,000 ground and air crew.

Everyone who tries to describe the relationship between the Canadians and their British hosts quickly discovers that there are almost half a million different stories to tell. When 1st Division was quartered at Aldershot in the winter of 1939–40, many of the men found the local population as cold and unwelcoming as their unheated barracks, while others quickly made friends. The winter was exceptionally cold and the ordinary miseries of army existence were complicated by the blackout and what Canadians saw as a shortage of food that they didn't much like anyway.

Battle of the Atlantic, 1943–45. The defeat of the U-boat is graphically illustrated by this map. Compare it with the map on page 104.

For the Canadian soldiers passing the years in Britain, life was a constant round of drill, inspections and training, with time off to discover the delights of English pubs and to fraternise with the locals. But an army can only train for so long. In the photo at top, the King and Queen inspect the 3rd Canadian Division at Aldershot, 1941.

121

They did like the beer and the English pubs that sold it. Coming from a country that made the public consumption of alcoholic beverages as uncomfortable as possible, young Canadians quickly adapted to the relaxed atmosphere of pub life. Many would say they adapted too well, for there were frequent complaints of drunkenness from local authorities. Canadians were better paid than their British counterparts, and this discrepancy was said to be one of the reasons for the occasional dust-up with British "Tommies."

Given the age distribution of the army population, the record suggests that over the five years the Canadians were in England, relations were remarkably good and crime rates incredibly low. Tens of thousands of young men away from their homes and families in a strange country were bound to drink and fight and go absent without leave. By 1944, very few soldiers had unblemished records, but the "crimes" noted on their personnel records were largely minor offences against military regulations, incidents that would have been considered normal in civilian life.

The army did its best to keep the men busy and much energy was devoted to concerts, Saturday night dances and a host of other activities designed to boost morale. Organized sports were the most important form of officially sanctioned recreation and unit war diaries are full of reports on hockey and football games. The most famous football game of the war years was played in 1944 when 30,000 people gathered to watch the "Tea Bowl," a contest between the Canadian Army "Mustangs" and the U.S. Army "Pirates." The Canadians, captained by former Hamilton Tiger Cat quarterback Major Denis Whitaker, included Captain George Hees of the Toronto

Group Captain Ross Tilley (left) with British plastic surgery pioneer Sir Archibald McIndoe.

No one stares in East Grinstead

With the escalation of the air war over Germany in 1943, casualties in Bomber Command climbed. A quarter of all Canadians killed in the war would be bomber crew. The air war also brought a painful and psychologically devastating injury, "airmen's burn," a flash burn caused by intense dry heat from burning fuel. At the Queen Victoria Hospital in East Grinstead, Sussex, Group Captain Ross Tilley, a Canadian plastic surgeon in charge of the fifty-bed RCAF Canadian wing of the hospital, performed hundreds of operations to restore hands, feet and, especially, the faces of burn victims.

With our heads swathed in surgical dressings and bandages, leaving only two eyelets and a small hole to eat and drink through, we must have presented a strange sight. All the hair on my head had been completely burned away. I had no eyebrows or lashes. My ears were like two potato chips. I had no distinct lip line. I must admit that the pain was such that during the earlier days in hospital, my will to live was very low.

Flight Lieutenant John R. Harding, RCAF

Allowed to wear their uniforms instead of the standard hospital blues, the airmen at Queen Victoria were encouraged to mingle in the community. Nano Pennefather visited the hospital.

Sunday we went out to one of the plastic surgery hospitals at East Grinstead. Some of us go out each weekend. The boys appreciate it, I think, and it does us a lot of good. They are really wonderful. Their spirit is marvellous. Some of them have been there for a couple of years, but they have complete confidence in their doctor – a Canadian – and know he'll fix them up. I made up my mind not to complain any more after seeing those kids.

Nano Pennefather, Women's Division, RCAF

Eighty per cent of the burned airmen treated by Dr. Tilley and his staff returned to flying duty, and sixteen of these would be killed in action.

Patient with Pedicle, charcoal drawing by Charles Goldhamer. Rebuilding a badly burned nose might require a temporary bridge of tissue between chest and nose to encourage growth of skin and blood vessels.

NATIONAL ARCHIVES OF CANADA/PA137316

Wayne and Shuster – rare is the photo in which this inventive pair are *not* mugging for the camera.

Argonauts and other professional players from Winnipeg and Ottawa. The Canadians won 16-6 in a much-talked-about triumph.

A lot of effort went into organizing entertainment with Canadian content. The British "Ensa" shows with their vulgar and, to Canadians, unfunny humour were widely disliked and all three Canadian services sponsored their own touring shows. "The Tin Hats," "The Kit Bags," "The Blackouts," "The Air Screw" – the list goes on. After 1943, the Army Show, with Sergeants John Wayne and Frank Shuster, was much in demand. In 1945, the RCN sent its "Meet the Navy" show to the London Hippodrome. It starred the dancers Alan and Blanche Lund and a young singer named John Pratt who brought sold-out crowds to their feet with his song "You'll Get Used to It," which grabbed everyone in a war-weary nation:

You'll get used to it, you'll get used to it
The first year is the worst year.
Then you'll get used to it.

The most important unofficially sanctioned activity was meeting and often marrying British women. Despite the military's attempts to limit such marriages, more than 40,000 wives and 20,000 children sailed to Canada at war's end, the vast majority from Britain.

Canadian women also served in the United Kingdom – almost 2,000 CWACs, 1,300 members of the RCAF Women's Division and 503 Canadian Wrens. The army nursing service helped to staff the ten Royal Canadian Army Medical Corps hospitals in Britain and served in all twelve of the units established behind the armies on the continent. Canadian women were also active in the Red Cross and other volunteer organizations.

SICILY

The plans for the invasion of Sicily were strongly influenced by the experience of the Dieppe raid and the surprising confusion of the landings in North Africa. General Dwight D. Eisenhower, the Commander-in-Chief, and his deputy, General Harold Alexander, were determined to take the time to rehearse the assault troops and ensure that overwhelming naval and air support were available. General Bernard Montgomery, now famous as the victor of El Alamein, insisted that he needed "the entire Eighth Army" because "we must plan the operation on the assumption that resistance will be fierce and a prolonged dog-fight will follow the initial assault." General George Patton, commanding U.S. Seventh Army, could hardly settle for less.

With an attack on this scale, two of the seven assault divisions had to be brought directly from Britain and the United States as the port facilities in North Africa were not large enough. The Canadian government, sensitive to criticism in the press that Canadian troops were still inactive in England in the fourth year of the war, persuaded Churchill to substitute 1st Canadian for 3rd British Division as the unit to sail from England.

General McNaughton, who would have preferred to keep First Canadian Army together for the invasion of northwest Europe, supported the policy for purely military reasons. He hoped that 1st Division would gain valuable experience that would benefit the entire army when it returned to take part in the cross-Channel invasion. McNaughton's concern with obtaining combat experience, especially for officers and NCOs, had led him to send 348 Canadians to serve with First British Army in Tunisia. Valuable as such experience was, it was no substitute for the lessons to be learned employing a division with all its supporting troops in large-scale operations.

Sicily was defended by Italian Sixth Army with more than 200,000 men, supported by two German divisions, but the invasion achieved operational surprise and a beachhead was quickly secured. Some Italian units fought with determination, but most of Mussolini's conscript army was quite ready to surrender at the earliest opportunity. The Germans, reinforced by a Panzer grenadier division and two paratroop regiments, fought a skilful delaying action before retreating to the mainland.

The campaign, which began on July 10 and ended on August 17, has been judged harshly by historians because the Germans were able to withdraw their forces to fight another day. But if the purposes of "Husky" were to capture Sicily and knock Italy out of the war, then it was highly successful. Mussolini was ousted from power a week after the landings and the new Italian government began secret negotiations to sign a surrender. The invasion of Sicily also contributed to Hitler's decision to end all offensive operations in Russia and diverted resources away from the eastern front. Germany had suffered a major military and political defeat.

The Canadians in Sicily lived up to their First World War reputation, fighting with skill and determination. The worst setback occurred before the landings when two ships carrying divisional signals equipment and artil-

lery were sunk by U-boats. Fifty-eight Canadian soldiers were among the missing. The landings on "Sugar" and "Roger" beaches south of Pachino were virtually unopposed. Major-General Guy Simonds, commanding 1st Division, was able to report that all objectives had been captured by nightfall. "Morale high and troops very confident of themselves," he signalled. "Success mainly due to excellent co-operation Royal Navy and RAF."

The invasion was big news throughout the world but official announcements failed to mention the Canadian role. Mackenzie King blamed the British government for this oversight but the decision to use the terms "Allied" or "Anglo-American" forces had been made by General Eisenhower, who thought specific mention of the Canadians would break security. This omission was quite unacceptable in Ottawa and King made a radio broadcast announcing the invasion. "All Canada," he told his listeners, "will be justifiably proud to know units of the Canadian Army are a part of the Allied force...."

The first encounter with the Germans came at

Canadian troops and equipment come ashore in Sicily as barrage balloons float overhead.

DND

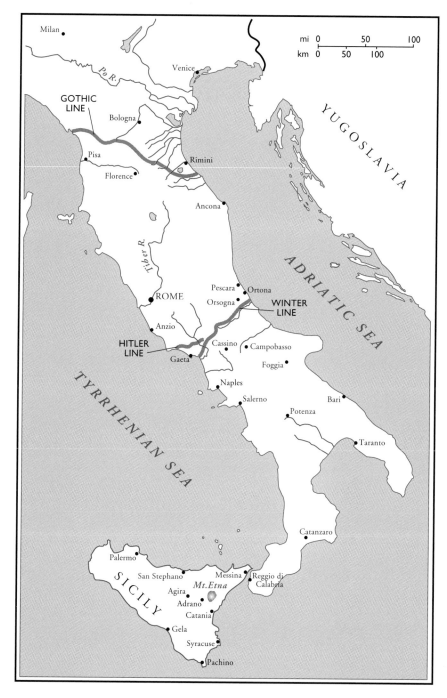

Sicily and the Italian peninsula. The 1st Canadian Division landed near Pachino in Sicily in July 1943. Joined by 5th Canadian Armoured Division, they reached Rimini in December 1944 before rejoining First Canadian Army in Holland in March 1945.

to flee. The Germans now withdrew to defensive positions based on Mount Etna, while Montgomery's Eighth Army worked its way forward cautiously. The Canadians, on the left flank, encountered heavy opposition in difficult mountain terrain. The battles for Assoro, Leonforte, Agira and Regalbuto involved seventeen days of hard fighting.

The "Hasty Pees" pulled off one of the most extraordinary exploits of the campaign at Assoro. Carrying little except rifles and Bren guns, they scaled the mountain terraces single file in partial moonlight. After a forty-minute climb on goat tracks they dug in on the edge of town, inflicting heavy casualties on the enemy when counterattacks were mounted.

Leonforte fell to the 2nd Brigade after a night of hard house-to-house fighting. Agira was an even tougher problem and could not be captured until the Loyal Edmonton Regiment and the Seaforth Highlanders scaled peaks overlooking the town. Agira cost the Canadians 438 casualties, their heaviest losses of the Sicilian campaign. The Canadians were in action until August 6, the day the Germans decided to evacuate the island. General Patton's advance along the north coast was threatening the escape route at Messina and the Germans had no choice but to withdraw.

Grammichele, a seventeenth-century planned city built as a hexagon and perched on a long ridge. The crack of 88-mm guns greeted the Three Rivers Tank Regiment and a fierce battle erupted. The Hastings and Prince Edward Regiment, the "Hasty Pees," converged on the town with tank and artillery support, forcing the enemy

General Simonds and his men had won the admiration of the veteran Eighth Army. Lieutenant-General Oliver Leese, the Corps Commander, was lavish in his praise of the division's battle training, artillery and engineer support, and staff work. The "Red Patch" Division had won its spurs.

(Facing page) Tanks of a Canadian armoured unit rumble through the streets of Regalbuto, Sicily.

Princess Patricia's Canadian Light Infantry (above) march through the streets of Valguarnera, Sicily, July 19, 1943. Once the front line has moved through, civil authority has to be organized. In the second photo the chief of police of Valguarnera reads a proclamation to the people of the town. With him are Captain George Hart, ex-Metropolitan Police inspector of London, England, now civil authority officer, and Captain W. Cooper of Toronto, Field Security Officer.

Too big to talk about...

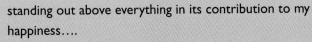

Lieutenant Frank Hall wrote to his wife while he was en route to Sicily, July 3, 1943.

Darling:

If my handwriting in this letter is worse than usual, it is because of the throbbing of the ship's engines and not my nerves....The reason why I am on board a ship will be old news by the time you get this letter, so I need not (even if I could) tell you anything about it....

Occasionally one feels fear, as a sort of painful hurt in the stomach. It is a definite *physical* feeling, and a damned unpleasant one, but there is a cure for it. The cure is just to do something to occupy your mind. Anyway, fear is not a very frequent visitor. I suppose it will be, later on....

The big things are, at this moment, too big to talk about. If I say I love you, I am just saying what I have said a hundred times before and the word has no connection with what I feel now. It is hopelessly insufficient, no matter how it is dressed up.

I remember all our life together, not as a series of incidents, but as a sort of single, all-encompassing event standing out above everything in its contribution to my happiness....

Just to say "I love you" sounds flaccid – almost a cliché.

Please don't wear the widow's weeds too long, if I go West.... Death doesn't mean a thing beyond getting rid of the encumbering fogs and fumes of the body....I do believe in the indestructibility of the human spirit....Nothing is ever *destroyed* in the Universe: it simply changes form – and why should life be an exception to this rule?...

Finally (and then I will drop the subject) we all have to die sometime and

> How can man die better
> Than by facing fearful odds
> For the ashes of his fathers
> And the temples of his Gods?

Macaulay has an ancestor of our enemies say this, so we can hardly dare have a lesser sentiment!

If this turns out to be a post-mortem letter, don't let it get you down, and if it doesn't, by the time you get it I will be an "old soldier." Old soldiers, you know, never die....

All my love, darling, for always and always,

Frank

Lieutenant F.C. Hall, Seaforth Highlanders of Canada, was killed August 5, 1943.

THE INVASION OF ITALY

The decision to invade the mainland of Italy was made at the "Trident" conference of May 1943. Churchill had again travelled to Washington to persuade Roosevelt that further operations in the Mediterranean would not jeopardize the invasion of France in 1944. Agreement was reached "to mount such operations as are best calculated to eliminate Italy from the war and to contain the maximum number of German divisions," but such activity was not to interfere with the buildup for an assault on western Europe which was now set for May 1944 and given the code-name "Overlord."

This was a reasonable compromise between British ambition and American suspicion. Marshall and Eisenhower made it clear that there would be no "all-out campaign" in Italy but they accepted the idea of invading southern Italy to secure the port of Naples and the Foggia airfields. Churchill, determined to have the last word, suggested that the capture of Rome was the real objective.

Before the invasion could be mounted, Churchill, Roosevelt and their military advisors met in Canada at the First Quebec Conference, August 1943. Churchill suggested that the Canadians attend the plenary sessions but Roosevelt argued that all the smaller Allied nations would claim the same right. Mackenzie King, who had no wish to be involved in debates over grand strategy, readily agreed to host the meetings and be available for photo opportunities. The debate on European strategy at Quebec revealed the deep mistrust that had developed between the British and Americans over strategic issues, but in the end the commitment to "Overlord" and limited operations in Italy was reaffirmed.

The plan for the invasion of Italy called for Eighth Army to attack the heel and toe of the peninsula six days before U.S. Fifth Army, with one American and one British corps, landed at Salerno, south of Naples. This operation, code-named "Avalanche," ran into serious difficulties as the Germans mounted large-scale counterattacks. Montgomery's forces met little resistance, but the desperate situation at Salerno forced Eighth Army to change direction and come to the aid of Fifth Army. The Canadians were ordered to seize Potenza, a town to the east of Salerno, as part of the rescue attempt. Simonds decided to form a battalion battle group to lead this advance, and "Boforce," named after Lieutenant-Colonel Bogert, Commanding Officer of the West Nova Scotia Regiment, started north on September 17. Potenza was captured on September 20 in an impressive feat of arms, but by then the situation in the bridgehead had been brought under control with the help of naval guns and the 82nd Airborne Division.

Roosevelt, King and Churchill at the Quebec Conference. Behind them, at the left, British Foreign Secretary Anthony Eden gazes across the river.

October was a month of short, sharp encounters with an enemy that was withdrawing in good order. Third Brigade remained in action throughout November, but the rest of the division was out of the line enjoying the delights of "Maple Leaf City," a recreation centre established in the town of Campobasso.

As the Allies advanced beyond Naples, Hitler changed his mind about the campaign in Italy. Rommel, his favourite general, had advised withdrawing the German armies north of Rome, but Hitler, ever reluctant to give up ground, approved General Albert Kesselring's proposals to halt the Allied advance south of the city on a series of lines that encompassed Monte Cassino and a small Adriatic port called Ortona.

THE ROAD TO ORTONA

The struggle for Ortona is one of the best known battles fought by Canadians in the Second World War. Matthew Halton, the CBC's chief radio correspondent in Italy, made "Moro River" and "Ortona" household words in 1943, and since then veterans as well as war correspondents and historians have offered numerous accounts of

The bullet meant for me

My batman, Private Harry Armitage, got a sniper's bullet in the throat as the two of us peered through some kind of hedge as I pointed out the spot I would be making for. I am sure the bullet was meant for me, as my cap badge made a gleaming aiming mark. Armitage, who was more or less cheek-by-jowl with me looking through the gap in the hedge, was the victim of my folly. Of course, it was he who had the night before polished my cap badge. But it was I who wore it and furnished the target.

Major Strome Galloway,
Royal Canadian Regiment

that December in Abruzzi.

The Allies had invaded the Italian mainland to force Italy out of the war, to establish air bases for the strategic bombers, and to draw off the maximum number of German troops. Hitler's decision to stand south of Rome was all that sensible Allied planners could have hoped for. The Foggia plains were suitable for air bases and the Germans poured resources into Italy to meet the Allied advance and into the Balkans to replace the Italian army.

Hitler gave Kesselring specific orders to fight a "delaying action only as far as the line Gaeta–Ortona. This line will be held," the Führer insisted. Eisenhower, though still in command of overall Allied operations in Italy, saw the theatre increasingly in terms of its significance for Operation "Overlord." On October 25 he informed Winston Churchill that:

Lieutenant-General Harold Alexander, known to all as "Alex," commanded the Allied armies in Sicily and Italy. As Field-Marshal Viscount Alexander of Tunis he served as the last British-born Governor General of Canada.

General Harold Alexander was left with the task of devising a plan that would meet Eisenhower's objectives even if it failed to fully realize Churchill's dreams. He developed a three-phased scheme which required Lieutenant-General Bernard Montgomery's Eighth Army to advance north across the Sangro River to capture Pescara and gain control of the important Rome–Pescara highway. Eighth Army was then to turn west, attacking Rome from the flank while Lieutenant-General Mark Clark's Fifth Army attacked towards Rome through the Liri Valley. Finally, a seaborne landing at Anzio, south of Rome, would secure the Alban Hills, outflanking the Germans from the west. If all went well the Allies would be in Rome for Christmas or early January, but even if the terrain, the weather and the enemy

> My principal commanders and I are in complete agreement that it is essential for us to retain the initiative until the time approaches for mounting Overlord, otherwise the enemy will himself seize the initiative and may force us on the defensive prematurely thus enabling him to withdraw divisions from our front in time to oppose Overlord. If we can keep him on his heels until early spring, then the more divisions he uses in a counter-offensive against us the better it will be for Overlord and it then makes little difference what happens to us if Overlord is a success.

This clear and realistic appraisal of the purposes of the Italian campaign did not appeal to Churchill. The Prime Minister was still fearful of Overlord and anxious for a major victory in Italy, which would allow him to argue against the withdrawal of troops and landing craft for the projected invasion of the south of France.

Position warfare

Our battlefield changed drastically after the end of October 1943. We no longer fought in sun-drenched hill country, advancing through orchards of ripe fruit or vineyards heavy with grapes, or along dried-up river beds, or rutted roads inches deep in white dust, or climbing mountains in crisp autumn air. Our battleground was now the low-lying, muddy no-man's land separating our barbed-wire-encircled strong-points, our scattering of waterlogged slit trenches, and our sandbagged ruined peasant cottages, from enemy positions probably much the same as ours. It was "position warfare."

Major Strome Galloway,
Royal Canadian Regiment

Mud became a major obstacle as the winter rains came down. Here Sergeant-Major Jimmy Walker gets a push from Bombardier W. J. Black, San Pietro, November 26, 1943.

a series of sharp counterattacks, but San Leonardo was finally taken by a battle group from the Calgary Tanks and Seaforth Highlanders.

The German defence of the Moro had to this point been a skilled and successful delaying operation. But the enemy now decided to wipe out the Canadian bridgehead, which controlled the coastal highway. The attack by the 90th Panzer Grenadiers' reserve battalions demonstrated the difficulties faced by the attacking force in Italy. The Hastings and Prince Edward Regiment were "behind well-prepared defence zones which had been carefully registered for artillery and mortar fire and covered by machine-guns set up to fire on fixed lines." The German attack was cut to pieces by mortars and disciplined small-arms and machine-gun fire. The loss of close to two hundred men forced the German corps commander to order a withdrawal to the edge of Ortona behind a deep ravine the Canadians would call the "Gully." The Canadians spent eight days forcing this position, at the cost of 1,000 casualties.

denied capture of the Italian capital, the continuing purpose of the campaign would still be fulfilled.

Eighth Army began its attack on November 28 and in less than two days British, Indian and New Zealand troops had cracked through the Bernhardt Line, shattering the 76th Panzer Corps and forcing Kesselring to send reinforcements to re-establish the Adriatic front north of the Moro River. Montgomery concluded that a further push to Pescara was impossible without a pause to build up supplies and work on the bridges across the Sangro, which was threatened by heavy rains.

The New Zealand Division led off the renewed offensive, but its objective, Orsogna, could not be captured easily. The Canadians were ordered into action early to relieve some of the pressure on the New Zealanders and on the night of December 5/6, 1st and 2nd brigades attacked across the Moro. The initial battles for Villa Rozatti (the Princess Patricia's Canadian Light Infantry – PPCLI) and San Leonardo (Seaforth Highlanders) led the enemy to commit a panzer grenadier regiment to

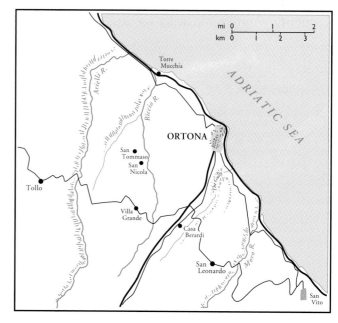

The Moro River, the "Gully" and Ortona – the famous Canadian battlefields of 1943.

A group of officers of the Royal 22nd Regiment. Captain Paul Triquet (standing second from left) won the Victoria Cross serving with this regiment, the "Van Doos." Triquet led his company, about fifty men, supported by six tanks of the Ontario Regiment, in an attack on Casa Berardi, a fortified hamlet overlooking the road to Ortona. Triquet displayed extraordinary bravery in leading the attack and then deployed his remaining men to defend the Casa against counterattacks. He told his men, "Ils ne passeront pas" (They shall not pass), and inspired them to hold on until reinforcements arrived.

The collapse of the German position at the Gully ought to have led to a general withdrawal to a ridge line north of the Tesoro and Arielli rivers. This is certainly what Montgomery anticipated but for reasons that remain unclear, General Herr, commanding 76 Panzer Corps, decided to defend Ortona with two parachute battalions. It has been suggested that the Canadians should have simply bypassed Ortona, but in fact no such choice existed. Ortona and the coastal highway were essential objectives if the advance north was to be continued and sustained logistically.

ORTONA – THE BATTLE

Ortona is an ancient city said to have been founded by the Trojans after the fall of Troy. The northern part, called the Old Town, consists of extremely narrow streets with most buildings connected by common walls. The town is dominated by two massive towers, a fifteenth-century fortress perched on the promontory above the harbour, and the cathedral of St. Thomas about 200 metres inland. In 1943 the coastal highway entered the built-up area about 800 metres from the centre of the city.

The first day's fighting had brought the Edmontons and "C" squadron of the Three Rivers Regiment to the Piazza Vittoria at the southern edge of the Old Town. Here they discovered that the German engineers had blocked the side streets with rubble from demolished houses. The "paras" hoped to entice the Canadians to advance down the Corso Vittorio Emanuele to the Piazza Municipale, which would become a killing ground. Lieutenant-Colonel J.C. Jefferson had other ideas. He insisted that the companies take their time planning platoon-size operations against one or two houses. Where possible, a tank would be used to blast down walls at short range. More often, the Edmonton's six-pounder anti-tank guns were brought into play. A platoon commander explains their role:

We used the anti-tanks in a unique way. The shells could not penetrate the granite walls, sometimes four feet thick. So we just put them through the windows and they bounced around inside much like they would in an enemy tank, doing horrible damage.

It was a battle of great innovation and adaptation. All the hardware of the infantryman was brought to bear against his entrenched foe.

We preferred to clear houses from the upstairs down. If we couldn't get through the windows, we "mouse-holed." The "Beehive" charges we used would kill any Germans in the adjacent rooms and we followed right through immediately. The "36" grenades could be dropped downstairs before we carried on to clear the lower rooms. This was a basic difference between our approach and the Jerry tactics. When they came into a house it was on the ground floor. Trying to return the favour of our grenades was disastrous for them. Their old "potato mashers" would rattle back down the stairs to explode at their feet.

On December 24, resistance stiffened. Major-General Vokes asked General Hoffmeister if further operations should be cancelled or delayed, but Hoffmeister was con-fident. The German paratroopers, he told Vokes, were taking a dreadful beating and brigade morale would suffer if they were not allowed to finish the job.

The "job" ended on December 28 when patrols reported the town "clear of the Hun." Ortona cost the Loyal Edmonton Regiment 172 casualties, of which 63 were fatal. The Seaforth Highlanders lost 41 killed and 62 wounded. The German parachute troops, who were in their own eyes the elite of the German army, had made the defence of Ortono a point of honour. They now withdrew with heavy and irreplaceable losses from a battle they could not win against troops who would not quit. War, after all, is not about capturing territory; it is about imposing your will on the enemy. After December 1943, the 1st Parachute Division and the rest of the German army were forced to recognize that the Allies might be delayed but they could not be defeated.

Men of the 48th Highlanders in the Ortona sector, December 1943.

I regret to inform you...

Alton Kjosness was a private with the Saskatchewan Light Infantry.

Dear Mother,
I suppose you know by now that I am in Italy, and that I was all through the Sicily campaign. I've seen some interesting sights and also have been in some pretty tough scrapes, but I'm still in one piece and all okay, so I guess I'll last as long as the next man....

The weather is pretty cold and rainy now, so it's battle dress and greatcoats and canvas tents. Yesterday, it took us all afternoon to battle through a three-mile detour because Jerry had blown so many bridges.

Alton

Dear Mrs. Kjosness,
I deeply regret to inform you that your son, M45520 Private Alton Kjosness, gave his life in the Service of his Country in the Mediterranean Theatre of War on the 15th Day of December, 1943.

From official information we have received, your son died as the result of wounds received in action against the enemy.

Captain S.C. Smith, Saskatchewan Light Infantry

Dear Captain Smith,
If you have time, please write to me and tell me all you can about how Alton got hurt, and his last words, if any. Was his face hurt, or his hands?

My name is Mary. When Alton died, I saw him in my dreams — he was standing in the entry with a smile on his face, and I said to him, "Are you home on furlough?" and he answered, "No, I'm home to stay." But we did not know he was dead until the telegram came. His sister Hope okays the telegrams, so imagine how she felt sending her mother and father that news. Alton went to Heaven to spend Christmas, which is far better.

Mary Kjosness

Chaplain Major Roy C.H. Durnford conducts a burial service at San Leonardo di Ortona, December 10, 1943. Men wear helmets because of heavy shelling; they had been told to run for cover if danger was imminent.

Alton Kjosness was in a tank on the road to Ortona when it struck a land mine. His mother wrote to her mother and her sister in Vancouver:

We received a nice letter from the chaplain that buried Alton. He says, "Alton could not survive the shock. He was buried on the 16th, the day after he was wounded, in a little British cemetery at a place called Fossacesia, a quiet place in an olive orchard overlooking the sea. There are about fifty Canadian lads buried there. No one ever dies in vain, least of all a soldier of Canada...."

Mary Kjosness

Alton Kjosness's remains were later exhumed and reburied at the Moro River Canadian War Cemetery at Ortona. Mary Kjosness would choose this inscription for her son's memorial: "Alton was a poet."

(Below) Personnel of the Edmonton Regiment during street fighting in San Leonardo di Ortona, December 10, 1943.

DND

DND

A tank of the Three Rivers Regiment
rumbles into the main square of
Ortona, December 22, 1943.
(Left) Twenty men of the Loyal Eddies
were buried when a two-storey buiilding
blew up. Lance Corporal Roy Boyd is
rescued after three days under the
wreckage, conscious but unable to move
even his hands.

135

In the facing picture by Lieutenant Terry Rowe, photographer with the Canadian Film and Photo Unit, refugees pick their way through the rubble of the town, December 30, 1943. On a hillside near Ortona (right), regimental padre Major E. J. Bailey conducted a memorial service for the officers and men of the Loyal Edmonton Regiment who fell in one of the fiercest battles of the Italian campaign. Tribute was also paid to Lieutenant Rowe, who was with the Edmontons at Ortona and later met his death at Anzio.

DND

Lili Marlene

One of the nightly events at Campobasso which has fascinated us all is the languorous sexy singing of "Lili Marlene" preceding the German news in English from Radio Belgrade. It is a must for everyone who can get near the Signals truck or a radio.

Our German interrogators sing it in German... most of us have one or another of the many English translations, some with the beauty of poetry, others perversely obscene, all finding consolation in an extraordinary enemy love song which has become the favourite of two opposing armies.

Ortona... a ghostly vapour

From the intervening vineyards rose a ghostly vapour, like a shroud winding itself about the town. The most boisterous and profane among us became silent in the face of what we witnessed. The morbid fascination of destruction held us in its grip as life and its monuments dissolved before our eyes.

Major Charles F. Comfort, war artist, journal

NATIONAL ARCHIVES OF CANADA/PA128286

ROME

As the Canadians fought their way into Ortona, the Allies finalized their plans for 1944. At the Teheran Conference, the first meeting between Churchill, Roosevelt and Stalin, an agreement was made to give priority to "Overlord" and to "Anvil," a landing in the south of France. Italy was a poor third in Allied plans and Alexander's armies were to shrink as divisions were drawn away for the invasion of France. The departure of Eisenhower and Montgomery to command "Overlord" was a further indication that Italy was now a secondary theatre.

Churchill, who was unhappy with these decisions, did win support for one last attempt to capture Rome. An offensive in the Liri Valley was to draw German reserves away from the city before an amphibious assault hit the beaches at Anzio outflanking the German defences. The landings, on January 22, 1944, were initially successful, but strong German reinforcements soon sealed off the beachhead.

Personnel of the Seaforth Highlanders of Canada burying the crew of a knocked-out German tank near Pontecorvo, May 19, 1944.

Hitler understood Allied intentions, which he described in a letter to General Kesselring after the landings:

In a few days from now the Battle for Rome will start: this will decide the fate of central Italy…. But it has even greater significance, for the Anzio landing is the first step in the invasion of Europe planned for 1944.

The enemy's aim is to pin down and to wear out major German forces as far as possible away from the English base in which the main body of the invasion force is being held….

Fortunately Hitler drew the wrong conclusion from his analysis, and instead of conserving troops for the main invasion he urged Kesselring to use all available resources "until the last enemy soldier has been exterminated or driven back into the sea." The battle for Rome became one of the most ferocious battles of the war and one of the most important. German divisions that would have endangered the landings in Normandy were pinned down and worn out far from the decisive battlefield in France.

The Canadians were drawn into the battle after the capture of Monte Cassino. The 5th Canadian Armoured Division, commanded by Major-General Bert Hoffmeister, had joined 1st Division to form I Canadian Corps, and both divisions were committed to action. First Division succeeded in breaking through the Hitler Line defences and 5th Armoured was able to advance through the gap they created, crossing the Melfa

and Liri rivers before being drawn into reserve.

I Canadian Corps did not join in the capture of Rome but Canadian troops of the 1st Special Service Force, a joint U.S.-Canadian unit nicknamed the "Devil's Brigade," were among the first Allied troops to enter the city on June 5, 1944. The Canadian component, originally 2nd Parachute Battalion, fought as 1st Canadian Special Service Battalion in the mountains and the Anzio bridgehead before the advance on Rome. In August, the battalion took part in the "Champagne Campaign" landing on the Riviera near Cannes as advance troops in the invasion of southern France.

Major General Chris Vokes talks to men of the Hastings and Prince Edward Regiment at the Italian front "in the Hyde Park manner on a soapbox. I want you to get to know my face, so that in coming battles you will know me when I visit your unit," he told them.

Major-General B.M. "Bert" Hoffmeister, a militia officer, fought in Sicily as the commanding officer of the Seaforth Highladers. Promoted to brigadier to command 2nd Canadian Infantry Brigade, he won the admiration of all who knew him. Hoffmeister's brigade captured Ortona in December 1943 and he was promoted to major-general in command of 5th Canadian Armoured Division in early 1944. The division, known as "Hoffy's Mighty Maroon Machine," was involved in the battles for Rome and the Gothic Line, ending the war in Holland with the battle for Delfzijl.

General H.D.G. "Harry" Crerar, a regular artillery officer who served with the Canadian Corps in the First World War, was the natural successor to "Andy" McNaughton as commander of First Canadian Army. He served briefly in Italy in command of I Canadian Corps but returned to Britain before the corps went into action. Crerar's lack of experience in command of a brigade, division or corps was a serious handicap, but the government rightly insisted that Canadians must command Canadian troops and Crerar was the best available choice for senior officer.

Lieutenant-General E.L.M. Burns was an intellectual with considerable analytical abilities. He wrote both popular and professional articles and books, including a postwar study of Canada's military manpower problems. Burns was a competent commander but he lacked the ability to inspire or motivate men and was replaced as corps commander in 1944 after he lost the confidence of both British and Canadian senior officers. He went on to a distinguished postwar career as a peacekeeper.

THE GOTHIC LINE

I Canadian Corps had done well in its first operation, but the overall failure to prevent some elements of the German army from escaping led to endless recriminations. General Mark Clark was accused of ignoring orders to cut off the enemy because he wanted American troops to capture "the great prize" – Rome. Oliver Leese, Montgomery's successor at Eighth Army, was criticized for his management of the Liri Valley battle, while he in turn wanted to sack Lieutenant-General E.L.M. Burns, the Canadian corps commander, for failing to exercise better traffic control.

The bickering drew attention away from the real significance of the battle for Rome. Twenty-three German divisions had been held in Italy while the Allies built a firm bridgehead in Normandy. Kesselring's army had suffered such heavy casualties that fewer than ten divisions were left to man a new defensive position in the Apennines known as the Gothic Line. Hitler, who should have devoted every available unit to Normandy, sent seven additional divisions to Kesselring and reinforcements to rebuild the others to their original strength. The Gothic Line would be strongly defended.

At the sharp end, war is a series of isolated moments in which a handful of men draw upon their reserves of courage to overcome the terrain,

Mortars of I Canadian Corps firing at night, April 6, 1944.

the enemy and their own fear. On September 1, 1944, 11 Platoon of the Princess Patricia's Canadian Light Infantry was one of the many small units at the tip of the spear. They were part of Operation "Olive," Eighth Army's attack on the Gothic Line. Tens of thousands of men were involved but 11 Platoon was very much on its own.

The battalion had crossed the River Foglia without meeting any opposition, but between the banks of the river and the Pesaro road the enemy had constructed a barrier of wire obstacles and mines. The West Nova Scotia Regiment had already come to grief on this minefield and 1st Division's advance was in danger of stalling.

Lieutenant Egan Chambers, the platoon commander, went forward on his hands and knees exploring a path that bypassed the obstacles. The trail was sown with Schumines, shoebox-sized boxes with just enough explosive to blow off a man's foot. The Germans had developed these difficult-to-detect mines to maim rather than kill. A wounded soldier had to be helped to safety, taking extra men away from combat.

Chambers organized his platoon in single file, telling each man to follow exactly in his footsteps. The strange procession began to move as the first faint rays of light broke through the darkness. The platoon, and behind them the rest of B Company, advanced step by very careful step. They were almost across the field when mortar and spandau fire began. The last yards were taken at a quick pace and three men were hurt by Schumines. Chambers was knocked down and wounded by one explosion, but he was able to form up the platoon and lead it on a quick attack across an anti-tank ditch and into the village. The buildings were in rubble, providing cover against German artillery. The inevitable counterattack was beaten off with the aid of 5th Division tanks.

Chambers was awarded an immediate Military Cross for his "coolness in action" and "bold and skilful handling" of the platoon.

The PPCLI were not the only Canadian battalion assaulting the Gothic Line, and B Company was not alone in penetrating the outer defences. The Perths took Pt III with a bayonet charge. Other regiments of Bert Hoffmeister's "Mighty Maroon Machine," 5th Canadian Armoured Division, were equally successful. The 8th New Brunswick Hussars and the Cape Breton Regiment cracked one of the key German positions at Monte Marone, where concrete-emplaced anti-tank guns in steel tank turrets covered the approaches. By the afternoon of September 1 the Canadians had broken through the Gothic Line on a mile-wide front. The coastal plain, south of Rimini, was within reach.

Enemy reserves in the form of 26 Panzer Division arrived to try to reclaim Pt 204 but the Perths and Strathconas held off all counterattacks. The next day the "Red Patch" Division was on the move. The Royal 22nd Regiment secured Pt 131 while the Seaforths, working with British tanks, circled north beyond the Gothic Line defences. The Loyal Eddies took the next bound, racing to Monte Luro, which fell as the Irish Regiment entered Tomba Di Pesaro. The chase continued the next morning.

The enemy had been taken by surprise throughout Eighth Army's sector. Kesselring, the German commander-in-chief, was convinced that the Allies were planning another amphibious assault and he had been slow to react. He was persuaded that the coastal advance was the real thing only after learning that both Canadian divisions were involved. Kesselring and his subordinates believed that the Allies would rely on the Canadians to lead any major offensive. As soon as he was certain they were in action, reinforcements were rushed to the Adriatic sector and new defensive lines established.

The first days of September were proud moments for I Canadian Corps. Men shrugged off fatigue, ignored the heat and endured the white dust which lay "like powdered snow" three to four inches deep. It was impossible to see moving tanks, as they were enveloped in turbulent clouds of chalk. So were the men; but despite the choking dust, thirst and danger, "the same old time-worn humour and perpetual good nature" persisted.

Before the battle, Corps Commander Lieutenant-General E.L.M. Burns had urged "everyone ... to press forward until the enemy is destroyed; to strike and pursue until he can fight no longer. Then and only then shall we have won what we, as Canadians, have been fighting for – security, peace and honour for our country." Front-line soldiers are rarely impressed with messages from senior officers but Burns understood the mood of confident expectation within the Canadian Corps. This was to be the battle that ended the Italian campaign.

The hope of a breakthrough soon faded. The assault on the Gothic Line, which began with such promise, bogged down as enemy reinforcements arrived to man new de-

Spitfires of 417 Squadron in Italy, April 1944. Ground crew had to do most of their service work in the open air.

fensive lines. Historian Bill Mc-
Andrew notes that the autumn
rains intervened to immobilize
tanks and limit air support, but he
also insists that the overall plan was
flawed. The Canadians were assigned to the best sector for a break-
out but were denied the necessary
troops. British V Corps had plenty
of resources but its advance was
soon stalled in the mountains.
When the Eighth Army's commander, Oliver Leese, recognized
his error and transferred additional
forces to I Canadian Corps, it was
too late. Allied casualties were
mounting and new German infantry divisions had arrived.

The battlefield was controlled
by artillery and mortars and both sides had enough fire
power to exact a high price for each yard gained, each village won or lost. On September 17 General Harold Alexander, the Allied commander, reported that "the enemy
continues to put in reinforcements … he intends to fight
it out where he stands." There would be another winter
of misery for soldier and civilian alike.

The German forces in Italy, like their counterparts in

Major-General B.H Hoffmeister in his command tank "Vancouver." Fifth Canadian
Armoured Division, known as the "Mighty
Maroon Machine" after the colour of the divisional shoulder patch, owed much of its high
morale to Hoffmeister's leadership.

northwest Europe, had again avoided
final defeat on the battlefield – but to
what purpose? The Nazi regime had
been preserved for another year so
that millions more could die on the
battlefields, in the death camps and in
the cities of Hitler's Reich. As long as
the German armed forces, and indeed
the German people, were willing to
support Hitler's bloody tyranny, the
Allies had no choice except to persist.
If German armies were not attacked
and Germany not bombed, the Reich
might recover and return to the offensive. Their secret weapons – the V2,
the jet aircraft and the schnorkel U-
boat – would help to restore confidence to Germany and the war would
continue to rage.

We need to remind ourselves of this reality whenever
we analyse the last years of the war, and especially when
we think about the Italian campaign. There has always
been debate and bitter controversy over the purpose of
operations in the Mediterranean. American military
leaders were especially suspicious of British motives in
Italy. Was Churchill waging a military campaign coordinated with other attacks on the Third Reich, or was it all
part of a larger strategy to restore British power in the
Mediterranean? It was, of course, both, but its essential
feature was always to contribute to the defeat of Germany.

The soldiers in Italy called themselves the D-Day
Dodgers because so little attention was paid to their efforts after June 6. The campaign in Normandy and
northwest Europe has continued to overshadow their
achievement. There were no great celebrations to mark the
fiftieth anniversary of the liberation of Rome or the battle
for the Gothic Line. The men and women who served in
Italy deserve better from us. They made a vital contribution to the defeat of Hitler's Reich and they helped to
bring us "security, peace and honour for our country."

The Po Swamp

As you can see, Jerry had every conceivable advantage. Dug-in machine guns, observation of the whole
river from the fields behind; he had the whole thing
taped with artillery. The bridge was blown up, it was
seventy feet from one bank to the other, and so
on…. From where I am now, just on the other side
of the former enemy bank, and looking north to
where he is now, in the five miles from us to them,
there are four canals and one river. Lovely, eh? This is
the Po Valley, sometimes called the Po Swamp.

Lieutenant Reg Roy, Cape Breton Highlanders

The D-Day Dodgers

All veterans of the Italian campaign recall the haunting lyrics of the "D-Day Dodgers," sung to the tune of "Lili Marlene." The lyrics were written by a young poet, Hamish Henderson, serving with 51st Highland Division after hearing that Lady Nancy Astor had described the army in Italy as "D-Day Dodgers".

We are the D-Day Dodgers, out in Italy,
Always on the vino, always on the spree.
Eighth Army skivers and their tanks,
We go to war, in ties and slacks,
We are the D-Day Dodgers, in sunny Italy.

We fought in Agira, a holiday with pay;
Jerry brought his bands out to cheer us on our way,
Showed us the sights and gave us tea,
We all sang songs, the beer was free,
We are the D-Day Dodgers, in sunny Italy.

The Moro and Ortona were taken in our stride,
We didn't really fight there, we went there for the ride.
Sleeping 'til noon and playing games,
We live in Rome with lots of dames.
We are the D-Day Dodgers, in sunny Italy.

On our way to Florence, we had a lovely time,
We drove a bus from Rimini, right through the Gothic Line.
Then to Bologna we did go,
We all went swimming in the Po,
We are the D-Day Dodgers, in sunny Italy.

We hear the boys in France are going home on leave
After six months' service, such a shame they're not relieved.
We were told to carry on a few more years,
Because our wives don't shed no tears,
We are the D-Day Dodgers, in sunny Italy.

We are the D-Day Dodgers, way out in Italy.
We're always tight, we cannot fight.
What bloody use are we?

Troopers G.W. Richardson, E. Duncan and S. Montgomery of the Governor General's Horse Guards display new haircuts, Liri Valley, May 26, 1944.

Privates J.W.G. Groves and R. Chisholm enjoy magazines from home, Ortona, April 15, 1944.

At the entrance to a little graveyard in Italy, men of the Seaforth Highlanders of Canada scan the lists of their battalion's casualties since the landing in Sicily.

Some imagined landscape of the moon

The war artist Charles Comfort describes the Monte Cassino sector.

Optimism was running high at Headquarters. The 5th Canadian Armoured Regt. was approaching the Melfa River, seven miles beyond Pontecorvo. In the morning they were across the river and closing in on the town of Ceprano.

This whole area [Cassino-Pignataro lateral] had received the direct impact of our attack ten days ago and was a scene of destruction equal only in my experience to the Berardi sector on the Adriatic, with one striking difference, that the Berardi shelling took place in December and this had happened in May. The destruction of trees in full foliage creates a far more sinister impression of devastation than those destroyed in winter, seeming to evoke responses similar to those when a promising young life is suddenly and unexpectedly ended, symbolizing, in a sense, the disaster of human sacrifice which was taking place in this valley of shadow....

The Benedictine monastery, topping its high hill, still dominated the valley impressively. As we approached more closely, the wasted desolation of its proud ruin became more apparent and one found it difficult to understand why so great a monument should have been destroyed by our own generation.... The parts of the abbey destroyed three months before included rich accretions of the art of the sixteenth, seventeenth and eighteenth centuries.... One trembled to think of the appalling loss because it was obviously all gone....

Rounding the monastery hill, Cassino itself came into view. For sheer horror and utter devastation, I had not set eyes on its equal. The terraced structure of the streets might be discerned, if one searched for structure in that formless heap of calcined stone, but it resembled rather some imagined landscape of the moon....

The town itself was completely silent. Swallows darted aimlessly about, their plaintive shriek the only sound other than the roll of gunfire and the clatter of armour. Unburied dead, protruding from rubble or huddled grotesquely in cellars, still made a grisly spectacle.... In the flats, near the Rapido River, the lands flooded by the enemy bristled with shattered tree stumps, the stagnant surface dull with a heavy brownish algae.... The Pinnacle, a cone-shaped feature topped by mediaevel ruin of Rocca Ianula, where the New Zealanders had paid so dearly, overlooked desolation on all sides. The Roman amphitheatre, the Cappella del Crocifisso, the luxurious Continental, the Baron's Palace, all were reduced to a common denominator.... The ground everywhere was strewn with shell fragments, spent casings, and a litter of German equipment. In a most depressed state of mind, I set up my equipment to one side of Route 6 and sketched what was left of the town.

Major Charles F. Comfort, War Artist

An Italian officer salutes me...

September 3, 1943
An Italian officer ... salutes me and offers his hand. I shake it.... He gives the order to his men to [drop their weapons], pulls out a piece of paper which, half in Italian, half in French, explains that Marshal Badoglio has signed the Armistice.... He lifts his canteen and takes a drink and offers it to me. It's red wine.

October 6, 1943
My journal ... is kept hidden in the bottom of my pack since regulations forbid journals. It's a faithful friend always at my side. Together we take time to recapitulate and consider what is happening in this corner of Italy.

For several days now the enemy has changed tactics; he is moving more slowly, holding his positions and stopping the relatively easy push we have enjoyed since embarking at Reggio di Calabria....

Bodies floating on the water, others lying on their graves. A large man stretched out on the beach seemed unhurt.... I opened his shirt. The bullet went through his heart ... his name ... MacPhearson. Yesterday in Canada, an "anglais"; today, a comrade at my feet.

Lieutenant Claude Châtillon,
Royal 22nd Regiment

I used to think I was in a smalltime job...

September 30, 1942

Dear Folks,

The navy sort of infused a new philosophy of life into me. If ever I hear
anybody talking of a lack of thrills or
adventure in their own or anybody
else's life or job, you'll see a smile begin. I used to think I was in a
smalltime job at CIL, always thinking
of change....To have it again would be
Seventh Heaven. Any place where you
work 9–5, even lots of overtime, but
can go home to relax, talk to ...
friends, go to shows or dances and
have real fun (there's a difference),
have a day and a half off to dig the garden, wash the car,
go to Church, read or sleep – boy, it's going to be appreciated when I get back.... If it doesn't do anything else, this
life will have done that....You don't know how tired you
can get of seeing the same faces day in and day out.

　　　　Sub-Lieutenant Wilfred Bark, RCN, HMCS *Weyburn*

In March 1943, HMCS Weyburn *was heading for England
after six weeks of fighting in the Mediterranean when it was
sunk. The following report was carried in the* Ottawa Citizen:

... Two sub-lieutenants, Wilfred Bark, a Royal Canadian
Naval Volunteer Reserve officer, and J.R.W. Lydekker of
the Royal Naval Reserve, trav-
elling as a passenger, and
Stoker Sidney Day of the res-
cuing destroyer were those
lost in the attempt to rescue
the captain, Lt.-Cmdr. Thomas
Wake Golby, RCNV, of Victoria, B.C., who was knocked unconscious by the blast which
fatally wounded the ship....

Had Bark not delayed aban-
doning ship because he wanted
to help his captain as he had
helped a score of crew members, he might still be alive.
When he finally left the *Weyburn*, his chance of life had
passed and he was last seen clinging to a line from the res-

cue destroyer for a few seconds before an underwater
explosion, which signalled the end of his corvette, took
his life.

　　The majority of the crew was between decks
when the vessel was hit and the lights were ex-
tinguished and the steam pipes burst. Many were
injured in the mess decks but all managed to escape.

　　Two officers off watch below, Lieut. Pat
Milsom, RCNVR, of Toronto, and Sub-Lieut.
Bark, were asleep in their bunks but managed to
make their way up the riven and twisted companionway.

　　Reporting to the bridge, Bark and Milsom
helped revive the unconscious captain....

　　"When I came back," Milsom said, "I found
many of the men already had given their own lifebelts to
supplement those of others who were injured or were
not strong swimmers. That was just like our men, thinking
of the other fellow first."

　　A British destroyer meanwhile had drawn close to the
stricken corvette....

The float crews gradually assembled at their stations.
Some were injured....Twelve men and the dog crowded
into the float.

Slowly the distance between the float and the corvette
widened. The men could see the British destroyer tie up
to the corvette's side. The rescue work was swift but before it could be completed the *Weyburn* was listing consid-
erably. Then she re-
sumed an even keel.

　　"And then," said
one survivor, "we
saw her bow going
up. The captain was
on the bridge and
we could see him
hanging onto the
rail. The bow went
higher and our ship
started to sink by the
stern. It was quick,
damn quick. The captain raised one arm and waved
at us. I guess he was waving good-bye. And then he
and the ship were gone."...

Ottawa Evening Citizen, March 15, 1943

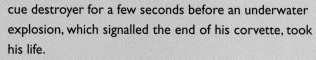

**Three of Weyburn Crew
Died in Rescue Effort**

GIBRALTAR, March 15—(C.P.
Cable)—Survivors of the Canadian corvette Weyburn, torpedoed
or mined in the Mediterranean, today told of the vessel's last minutes and the heroism of three men
who made a vain attempt to rescue the captain as he went down
waving farewell.

The Weyburn's loss was announced March 8 in Ottawa by
Navy Minister Macdonald who

were asleep in their bunks but
managed to make their way up the
riven and twisted companionway.
On deck the officers and crew were
just as cool as they were shortly
before when they were in action
against enemy aircraft, two of
which the Weyburn downed.

Reporting to the bridge, Bark
and Milsom helped revive the unconscious captain. First Lieut.
W. A. B. Garrard, R.C.N.V.R., of
Victoria, ordered Leading Signalman Leonard W. Murphy of Toronto to destroy confidential books
and Coder T. Hind.

Like an amputation of the heart...

On October 27, 1943, G. Hamilton Southam left for the Mediterranean. In a letter home he described his parting from his wife, Jacqueline, and baby son, Peter:

It was like an amputation of the heart.... Jacqueline and I arranged, before we parted, to think of each other particularly between 9:55 and 10 p.m.... each day, and I would like to suggest that you calculate what time that is in Canada, and then join us in thought and prayer....

He writes home about the controversy over sending the "zombies" into action.

February 11, 1944
For us over here, the political frenzy at home has something unreal about it. I am afraid that is because we have

spent so long killing people we disagree with, the spectacle of people merely shouting insults at other people seems childish. It's a mood very dangerous to democracy, the mood of soldiers....

Southam was appointed Intelligence Officer at HQRCA.

October 27, 1944
The three moments of the day when I get a sensation of pleasure are: when my batman brings me a cup of tea in the middle of the morning, when my batman brings me a cup of tea in the middle of the afternoon, and when I crawl into my sleeping bag at night.

Lieutenant Hamilton Southam,
11th Canadian Army Field Regiment, RCA

On cool reflection...

November 20, 1941
Dear Jean,
On cool reflection I have decided that it is now time for me to go on active service and cease being a civilian. Consequently, I am going to follow the matter up at once and see what terms I can reach with the armed forces of Canada....

I have not the faintest idea what lies ahead.... Of one thing we must not lose sight. We have no right and no reason to expect or to ask any more security or privilege of the future than anyone else of our generation. And our generation, my love, is throwing its collective self into the pot....

Please don't think me a damned fool. In some respects, undoubtedly, but in this, I think not. Forgive me if I've caused an upset in your mental plans.... *On verra*, from now on must be our motto.

I'm most pleased what you say about the ring. That ring from now on is the focal centre of my existence, so I hope you will keep it with you always.

Pat Patterson

Dear Pat,
Do as you think best. As for me, I don't know....

The other girls when their lads left consigned them mentally to the care of some good God. I wish I could do

the same for you – unfortunately I can't – you will have to be consigned to luck – who I feel is not the best of guardians.

Jean

William "Pat" Patterson and Jean Partridge were married early in 1942, and Pat was accepted into the RCAF.

Dear Jean,
We were glad to hear Pat got in as a Navigator, since that's what he wants and I'm sure he'll like it. Yes, I'll take care of Pat's clothes. I'll put the trunk upstairs with Harry's....

Love, Mum.

Dear Jean and Pat,
I suppose by now you have received the news of Harry being shot down. Seems no matter how well prepared we think we are, it's still hard to take. It has been hard on Dad, as he had to keep on working. I just couldn't do anything today, but I can't quit and think keeping busy will help a lot. We also got a cable from Harry this morning saying he was well, but that was sent before he was shot down and killed.

Mother

(Overleaf) Coastal Command aircraft patrolled the waters off France throughout 1944, sinking a number of U-boats, destroyers and supply vessels. Bristol Beaufighters equipped with 3-inch rockets carrying a 25-pound armour-piercing warhead were especially effective against surface ships.

U.S. AIR FORCE PHOTO

Escape story

On May 12, 1943, No. 6 Group was ordered to bomb Duisburg. Eight aircraft were lost, including two Wellingtons of No. 426 Squadron. Flight Sergeant O.W. Forland was one of six crew members who bailed out near the Belgian coast – five were captured.

In my haste ... I dropped and lost my second compass. That night I slept in the woods. Next morning, 14 May, I crossed the Spa-Stavelot railway line near Hochai. There I saw a working man. I can speak no language but English, but I showed him my [RAF] badges and he managed to confirm my opinion as to the points of the compass. A little later I came to signposts marked Malmedy and Liège. I followed the post marked Liège.

I now cut off the uppers of my flying boots, and bound the rubber soles to my walking shoes with strips torn from my [escape] purse. Though I realized the risk I ran, I decided to walk along the road even though [it was] in broad daylight.

About 1630 hrs I met a man pushing a bicycle. I showed him my map, and said inquiringly "Liège?" He took me a little off the road, and indicated to me that I was twenty kilometres from Liège. He also was obviously warning me to avoid Spa, as it was full of German troops. He offered me one hundred Belgian francs, and eventually himself took me to an isolated farm nearby. Here I showed the farmer my identity discs, and was given food and made welcome. Next morning, 15 May, a woman came to see me. She spoke to me in German and then in English, took away my identity discs, and asked me a number of questions about the aircraft, and the names of the other members of my crew. She seemed very doubtful of my identity. Finally I showed her some Canadian cigarettes, which appeared to convince her. Later she told me that had I been a German masquerading as a Canadian, I would not have resisted the temptation to smoke these myself.

She then removed my RAF uniform, and the farmer gave me civilian clothes. I retained my Oxford walking shoes [which were worn under the Canadian pattern flying boots]. I remained here till 1 June 1943. During this time I was photographed by the woman, who visited me several times. She told me that one member of my crew had been captured by a German forest guard immediately after landing, and had unfortunately told his captor that the crew comprised six persons instead of the normal complement of five. Since the Germans found one dead body in the aircraft, and later captured three other members of the crew, they continued to conduct a local search for the sixth man, who was myself. For this reason I had to spend a good deal of my time sleeping in the woods rather than in the farmhouse. The farmer told me that German m[otor]c[ycle] police with binoculars constantly patrolled the district during daylight.

On 1 June 1943 my subsequent journey from here was arranged for me.

Flight Sergeant O.W. Forland, RCAF

Stared at... pointed at... the prisoner of war

Carlton Younger describes his feelings of relief at reaching a prisoner of war camp.

Having been stared at, pointed at, segregated from those around him by special guards, perhaps interrogated for long hours, he was among his own people. The sound of his own language raised his spirit and he could laugh once more without a guilty feeling that he was fraternising with the enemy; within the limits of the camp he could move how and where he pleased.

When these first sensations had worn off, others took their place. The mere fact of being a prisoner offered endless possibilities. A man might dream of reading Shakespeare, of learning languages, of playing the piano, of doing some of the things he had often longed to do but for which he had never found time.

There were men for whom the barbed wire was a symbol of security. As a prisoner of war, they reasoned, there were no responsibilities. You neither looked for your food nor paid for it. You could read, paint, act, or play the trombone, sleep for long hours and eat when you felt like it. You did not have to go anywhere or get dressed for Sunday. You were never alone.... Laws and regulations were not multifarious and complex, but rigid and easy to understand.

Carlton Younger, RAF,
No Flight from the Cage

"One of the nicest boys I'd met..."

The letters of Sergeant Nano Pennefather of Montreal, who was serving in London with the RCAF Women's Service, recorded the social scene in the capital as thousands of young people far from home sought company and entertainment in their off-duty hours. All too often friendships were short and poignant.

Dear Mom,
Well, another Christmas season has come and gone....

Saturday we went to a tea dance at the Royal Empire Club Society.... There Clare and I met Michael Patterson of Victoria and Warren Freeland of Peace River. In the

evening we all went to another dance at the Overseas League.... [the next] Saturday we met Warren and Mike at the Royal Empire Society for another tea dance....

Monday, Warren and I ... went to see a Noël Coward play, *Blithe Spirit*, a bit risqué but very funny. Tuesday evening was the Head-

quarters dance. I had a whale of a time. The RCAF Band which used to play at the Red Triangle Club in Ottawa is over here now. I was on the dance committee....

New Year's afternoon we went out to have tea with Dr. and Mrs. McGregor, Gene and John, a simply sweet couple. Warren and his brothers and Wilf spend all their leaves there. We had a delicious tea and I just hated to have to go, but I had promised to meet some friends for dinner.

Warren walked with me to the Tube station. It was quite a stormy night. His leave was up, so I said goodbye to him with mixed feelings. He was one of the nicest boys I'd met over here and we had some awfully good times....

Your loving daughter

January 4, 1943
My Dear Penny,
Just a note to let you now that I have arrived back in camp....

I wished you could have stayed with us on New Year's day, but a date is a date and must be kept. I would have liked to have kissed you goodbye, but you have done something to me and I was not sure of my grounds for the first time in my life. I don't like this feeling and am annoyed with myself – so there.

I have been down to the village pub to try and drown my sorrows, but it doesn't help any....

The Stirling is a huge aircraft and we have lots to learn about it. So we sit in the classroom all day, which will last for a week.

Yours with lots of love and maybe a little kiss.

Warren

January 8, 1943
Dear Warren,
I think that was the best way to say goodbye, just like that – as though we were going to see each other the next day. Because you know you told me you didn't want to fall for anyone again (especially a gal who is as fickle as the wind, she really is, you know).

We certainly had an awful lot of fun, Warren, while you were in town. I didn't have time to miss being home for Christmas, as I thought I might....

Penny

January 19, 1943
Dear Penny,
I just got back from a week's course at an operational station, where I have been doing fighter affiliation with a Spitfire and a camera gun. I liked it real well – it gives me lots of confidence that I can shoot okay....

I received a letter from Gene. She told me that she had phoned you. I am glad, it will make a swell place for you to go. One does miss the home life doesn't one....

Warren is on the right.

You're not fickle, Penny, you just haven't really fallen in love with anyone yet. I'll envy that lucky person. But we won't talk about that when we get together. We'll just have a lot of fun and go places together....

We had a Stirling prang (crash) and go up in flames. Everyone managed to get out. I can't see how they made it as the kite (aircraft) is an awful mess....

Warren

Waterbeach, Cambs, January 29, 1943
Dear Penny,
This is just going to be a start at writing as I have to go flying at 11 and it's 10:30 now. It's a great day so I think I will enjoy it. We have been doing a lot of flying lately. My

skipper is a great pilot so we will be through here soon. Yesterday we got tired of doing circuits and bumps so decided to do a little low flying. It's lots of fun to fly right down on the deck, weaving in and out amongst the trees. It's kind of dangerous though as someone might report us and then we'd be grounded and have a strip torn off. Well, my dear, I will have to close till later. Duty calls....

... I am back from flying. We were practising some more circuits and bumps. Gee, it's a dull life. We got tired so decided to go out and shoot the countryside up and give some farmers a scare. We had a great time. Once we flew up a river and scared a flock of ducks up. One flew into the wing and got killed, which was kind of tough luck.

CANAV COLLECTION

The air force gathers for a pint.

Another got caught in the slipstream and made a crash landing in the water. I yelled, "Dinghy, dinghy." We circled around to see if it was hurt, but I guess that duck didn't practise his drill because we never saw it again. I have to fly tonight. If we get lots of hours in, we will soon be through here....

Warren

February 10, 1943
Dear Warren,
Hi chum, about time I answered your last letter. It came just as I was going on leave.

Peter and I went to Somerset and had a wonderful time, eating and sleeping and going for walks. Eggs for breakfast and chicken – but I better stop or I'll be making you jealous....

Penny

Oakington, near Cambridge, February 21, 1943
Dear Penny,
I bet you had a nice leave with your brother. I am glad you had a good rest as I am coming to London and hope to see quite a bit of you....

Gee it's 24.15 hours and time I went to bed. I was kind of waiting for my skipper to come in. He is on ops tonight as 2nd pilot. I hope he is okay.

Warren

RCAF Overseas Headquarters, April 4, 1943
Dear Mom and all the kids,
A year ago today I arrived in Toronto to begin life in the Air Force. It's been a wonderful year. I've done and seen so many things I'd never even dreamt of. I wonder where I'll be in another year – home again I hope....

The other day going up the escalator in Waterloo Station there were two Canadian naval officers and an English WAAF. I could hear them saying, "Yes, she is," "No, she isn't." I turned around and said, "Yes, she is ... a Canadian" and in two minutes we discovered that one of the boys was practically a relation. He is a nephew of Aunt Kit who married Uncle Archie MacDonell. His English friend asked, "Are all Canadians related?"...

One of the boys I met at Christmas and went out with a lot, Warren, was reported missing. However, we are quite hopeful that he may be reported prisoner of war. The last time he was in London we went over to Gene and John McGregor's for dinner and there was an air raid so we put on our tin helmets and went out to see it. He hadn't been on ops yet and wanted to see if he'd be afraid. I don't think he was.

He was the most thoughtful boy I've ever known....

Penny

Warren Freeland's letter of February 21 was never sent. It was found in his kit on the station by his brother Carl after Sergeant Warren Freeland, Gunner, Bomber Command, RAF, was killed in action.

PART V

LIBERATION

The view from one of the invasion craft at dawn on D-Day, June 6, 1944.

WHEN FRANKLIN ROOSEVELT AND Winston Churchill left the Quebec Conference in August 1943, the long and frequently bitter debate over the timing of a "Second Front" in northwest Europe was finally over. Since the spring of 1942 the two allies had been at odds over the most fundamental questions of grand strategy. Churchill and the British chiefs of staff, fearing casualties similar to those experienced in the First World War, sought ways of weakening Germany before the major offensive was launched. They wanted to disperse German military power by attacking in the Mediterranean while their heavy bombers reduced German production and morale. With luck they might even avoid the need for an invasion of France.

U.S. military leaders, on the other hand, were reluctant to wait and suspicious of what they saw as Britain's imperial interest in the Mediterranean. General Marshall, in particular, was convinced that the only sound strategy was a direct attack on Germany by the shortest possible route. The debate was played out against the background of events in Russia. The British feared a repetition of the Russian collapse of 1917 and the prospect of the entire weight of the German army being directed against the Allied forces. The Americans replied that an early invasion of Europe was the best way to prevent a Russian defeat.

The plan for the invasion was drawn up by a staff working under the direction of Britain's Lieutenant-General Frederick Morgan. He had been appointed Chief of Staff to the Supreme Allied Commander (COSSAC) in May 1943 but there was no agreement on who that Supreme Commander should be. The planners confronted a very difficult

General Dwight D. Eisenhower, here visiting the Polish Armoured Division, successfully led the Anglo-American forces in both the Mediterranean and northwest Europe. Eisenhower integrated British and American officers, insisting that they work toward common goals despite strategic differences.

B.J. GLOSTER/DND/NATIONAL ARCHIVES OF CANADA/PA115879

task. Though they had gained experience in assault landings at Dieppe, North Africa and Sicily, "Neptune," the assault phase of "Overlord," presented some special problems. Morgan was forced to work within guidelines that allowed for a three-division (plus airborne) initial attack. The key to success was, therefore, rapid landings of additional troops and supplies on the captured beachhead.

The Calvados coast of Normandy contained only minor ports, so the planners had worked out an extraordinary scheme of creating two manmade harbours – "Mulberries" – and a number of artificial breakwaters called "Gooseberries." Everyone agreed that the early capture of Cherbourg was vital to success and it was hoped that the prefabricated harbours would allow for continuous unloading of supplies into the beachhead while Cherbourg was liberated and its port repaired.

Apart from the problem of supply, COSSAC had established four criteria which had to be met if the landings were to be successful: (1) The enemy must remain ignorant of the proposed landing site; (2) he must be prevented from bringing up reinforcements quickly once the Allies had landed; (3) there must be complete Allied air and naval superiority in the English Channel; and (4) the local defences must be largely destroyed by air and sea bombardment.

A series of deception plans was used to draw enemy attention to a variety of possible landing sites and eventually to persuade them that the main landings would take place in the Pas de Calais.

By January 1944, Supreme Commander General Dwight D. Eisenhower and his own Chief of Staff, Walter Bedell Smith, had taken over the direction of planning "Overlord" with General Morgan acting as

Smith's deputy. Eisenhower had brought Air Chief Marshal Arthur Tedder with him from the Mediterranean as his deputy commander and co-ordinator of the Allied air effort. Admiral Bertram Ramsay of the Royal Navy controlled the naval forces. For ground commander, Eisenhower had asked for General Harold Alexander, another member of his successful team in the Mediterranean. Instead he got Bernard L. Montgomery, the victor of El Alamein and the most famous British general of the war.

Supreme Headquarters Allied Expeditionary Force (SHAEF) quickly got down to work on the details of the plan. A five-division front was authorized and the methods of preventing the Germans from reinforcing the front line were worked out with the various air force commanders. The air plan called for the disruption of the French railway network and the destruction of rail and road bridges across the rivers Seine and Loire. The railway marshalling yards and bridges were struck with considerable precision, wreaking havoc with the French transportation system, but no pattern to the raids could be determined by the Germans, and they read the destruction of the Seine bridges as designed to prevent their troops in Normandy from moving north to the Pas de Calais.

A fictitious American army group, with a busy radio network and General Patton in command, was set up in eastern England. The countryside was dotted with unoccupied tent encampments, dummy tanks, transports and glider aircraft, and preparations for embarking non-existent troops continued through June and July 1944. A landing in the Pas de Calais area fitted into the German General Staff's appreciation that this area offered the Allies the shortest way across the Channel and the best route into Germany; it also flattered Hitler into believing that the Allies considered his "V" weapons to be so important that they would plan their landings with a view to destroying their launching sites, in the Pas de Calais area, as quickly as possible. So thoroughly convinced was the German High Command that it continued to believe in June and part of July that the Normandy landing was a diversionary attack, and it therefore refused to weaken the defences in the Pas de Calais area until it was too late

to affect the outcome of the battle for Normandy. The Allied planners were confident that their deception schemes were confusing the enemy. Ultra kept the Allies informed of broad enemy strategy and provided detailed information on the location of all the main Panzer formations in the west.

The establishment of absolute air and naval superiority in the Channel was a requirement because the size and numbers of the convoys involved in the landing operation would make them very vulnerable targets. The amount of shipping required for the assault and supply was enormous – 4,126 landing ships and craft, 864 merchant ships and 736 ancillary ships – a large portion of which sailed virtually simultaneously through well-defined channels which had to be cleared of mines. Any attacker, whether U-boat, surface vessel or aircraft, which managed to penetrate the escorts would be almost assured of a victim. The extent of the casualties which could be inflicted had been well-illustrated when E-boats had penetrated an escort screen during an American landing exercise at Slapton Sands in the spring of 1944. They had sunk just two ships, but had killed over 700 troops and sailors.

The danger was real and SHAEF demanded and got the largest modern fleet ever assembled, 1,213 Allied warships, including the bombarding squadrons, which doubled as escorts, but excluding the distant cover of the Home Fleet, which watched for the possible intervention of the larger surface units of the German fleet. The greatest danger remained the German mines, particularly the new pressure mines which were difficult to sweep and for which no proper countermeasures were developed until after a mine had been captured intact on June 9. Given the size of the target presented, the losses sustained by the huge convoys at the hands of German naval forces were remarkably small.

The Luftwaffe retained, in 1944, a more fearsome reputation than the German navy had ever had. Consequently, control of the airspace over the convoys and the beaches was regarded as essential. To achieve control the Allied Command gathered together an air umbrella of

Detailed information on the Normandy beach defences was obtained from shots like this, taken from a U.S. P-38. Defences included timber ramps with mines or saw-toothed blades to tear the bottoms out of landing craft. Pump and hose for blasting holes can be seen, as can soldiers fleeing from the buzzing aircraft.

truly gigantic proportions. On D-Day and throughout the "Neptune" assault phase, SHAEF could employ some 11,590 aircraft (excluding 3,500 gliders) out of the roughly 13,000 operational aircraft stationed in England. An elaborate plan for D-Day was developed which established long-range fighter patrols over areas of France as far east as Calais and as far south as Le Mans – then another continuous screen around the Normandy Peninsula, and finally a low and high altitude cover over the beaches and far back to the assembly areas of the convoys off the Isle of Wight; all told, 3,700 fighters were committed. There were fighter bombers, rocket-firing Typhoons, twin-engined Mosquitoes and B-25s available for close support, as well as 3,500 heavies of Bomber Command and the 8th U.S. Air Force ready to lay down bomb carpets to overwhelm the defences. The 3rd German Air Force stationed in France had scarcely 200 operational fighters and few bombers; although it flew a few sorties during the first few days of the invasion, their effect was minimal. In the air, as on the sea, Allied superiority was simply not challengeable.

The Canadians were to play a significant role in "Overlord" and the campaign in northwest Europe. No. 6 (RCAF) Bomber Group was first into action, sharing the responsibility for isolating the battlefield. Sixteen RCAF

fighter squadrons of 2nd Tactical Air Force were united in No. 83 Group, which was to support Second British Army from Normandy to Germany. The Royal Canadian Navy was strongly represented in the "Neptune" plan. RCN destroyers, frigates and corvettes were heavily committed, and five RCN landing craft flotillas brought Canadian and British soldiers to the beachhead.

The buildup of the Canadian army overseas was complete by the spring of 1943. The size of the Canadian contingent had led to the establishment of First Canadian Army, composed of two corps containing five divisions, two independent tank brigades and the scores of support units required to make up the largest type of military formation in the Allied armies. First Canadian Army was the creation of General Andrew McNaughton, who was the closest thing to a national hero this country was to have during the war.

McNaughton's successor, Lieutenant-General H.D.G. "Harry" Crerar, possessed none of the charismatic qualities that had made "Andy" a popular figure. Crerar was intelligent, hard-working and well-trained, but he was a shy, private individual and was quite incapable of playing the role of inspirational leader. Lieutenant-General Guy Simonds, who had led the 1st Division in Sicily and returned to England to assume command of II Canadian

Corps, was quite a different type. Simonds was a protégé of Montgomery's, who later described him as "the best general the Allies produced during the war." Tall, lean and humourless, Simonds was a forceful and creative soldier with a personality "as cold as ice." Everyone respected Simonds but he inspired little affection.

The 3rd Canadian Division had been selected for the Normandy invasion in the summer of 1943. It would form part of Lieutenant-General J.T. Crocker's I British Corps until II Canadian Corps was landed in France. The division was commanded by R.F.L. "Rod" Keller, an energetic regular army officer who had risen from major to major-general since the outbreak of war. At forty-two, Keller was too young to have seen action in the First World War and he had not taken part in the campaign in Italy. The decision to leave him in command instead of replacing him with a Mediterranean veteran was a tribute to the standard of training and high morale of the entire division.

During the first months of 1944, the Canadians, like the other assault units, found themselves caught up in a training programme which became more and more detailed. The plans for "Overlord" filled volumes of paper, all stamped "Bigot," the special, super-top-secret code for the invasion. Apart from the exercises, it was a staff officer's war. No detail was too small. Decisions were made about how much rum (whiskey for officers and NCOs) should be carried and where. The battle gear of the individual soldier was weighed, assessed, reduced, weighed again. Gas respirators were discarded by some brigades, carried by others. Would one or two 24-hour ration packs be necessary? Eye shields were issued for troops who had to ride on tanks. Other equipment, identified in marvellously precise military terminology as "Knives fighting," "Paint phospherence luminous," "Tape tracing" and "Jerkins assault," was indented for.

Experiments on waterproofing vehicles produced good results though it took 246 man-hours to do one ve-

The "Overlord" plan. The Allies believed that the assault landing phase of "Overlord" would be the most difficult part of the battle, but once ashore they found that the struggle had just begun.

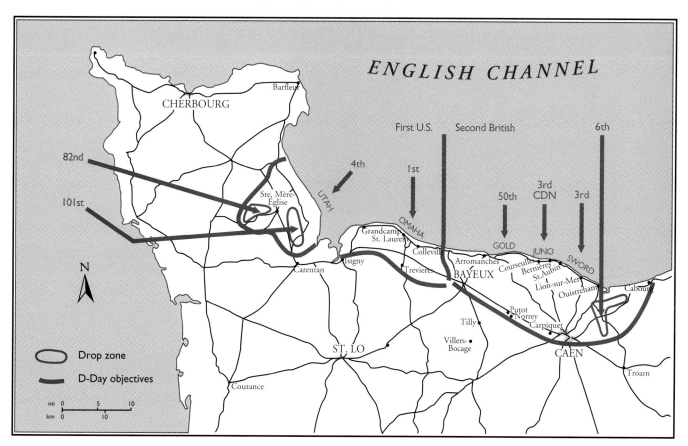

The Allied air forces were given a number of objectives after air superiority was won. A key requirement was interdiction to isolate the Normandy battlefield by wrecking the French rail system and destroying bridges over the rivers Seine and Loire. This railway yard was attacked by heavy bombers.

hicle, and more time and practice de-waterproofing. Folding bicycles were a much-debated item; it was decided that the soldiers of the reserve brigades would carry them. (Most soldiers carried the bikes as far as the beach before dumping them.) The planners planned and the soldiers rehearsed.

How they did rehearse! Squadrons of the 1st Hussars and Fort Garry Horse went off to school to learn to navigate their DD (Duplex Drive) tanks. The division assaulted the long-suffering coastline of the south of England in Exercise "Fabius III," which closely simulated the plan for the first two days of the campaign. As the troops headed for the sealed embarkation area to receive their final briefings, there was a collective sigh of relief that at least the rehearsals were over.

During the night of June 5/6 the enormous weight of Allied sea and air power was brought to bear on the roughly fifty-five miles of coastline that made up the invasion front. Air activity increased all along that front before midnight, and then a few minutes past midnight the airborne troops began their descent on Normandy. Both British and U.S. air-landings ran into the usual problems of planes losing their way and men and equipment becoming separated. In the dark, company and battalion commanders found it difficult to gather their men together and to locate their objectives. Despite this confusion and considerable loss of strength, the main tasks allotted to these divisions were fulfilled. The U.S. divisions established themselves in the area in front of the beach called "Utah," while the British staked a claim on the eastern side of the Orne River which would not have to be given up again. Some of the further objectives were not held but considerable damage was done.

The 1st Canadian Parachute Battalion was part of the British 6th Airborne Division's 3rd Brigade, and "C" company landed in the most easterly drop-zone near Varville, blowing up a bridge across the Divette River, destroying a German strong-point and then moving back about four miles to le Mesnil, a village at an important road junction east of the Orne River. The other companies also completed their tasks before concentrating in the le Mesnil area. The troops landing on "Sword" beach linked up with the airborne units in the area of the Benouville–Ranville bridges in the first hours after the landing. The possession of these bridges and the le Mesnil road junction would force German reinforcements from the east to detour around Caen, which meant considerable delay in reaching the front north of the city.

Four years previously, almost to the day, the small ships of the British fleet had disappeared westwards across the Channel carrying the last soldiers without their equipment from the smoke-choked beaches of Dunkirk; now they loomed out of the morning mists, bringing back to France the most modern mechanized armies the arsenals of democracy could provide.

D-DAY

The German defences on the coast of France have been compared to a length of rope with a series of knots tied along it. The knots were powerful coastal batteries and concrete fortifications, but in between strong-points and "resistance nests" were long stretches where the rope became thin and frayed. The coast of Normandy was one area where the so-called Atlantic Wall was far from complete. General Erwin Rommel had tried to correct the problem in the spring of 1944 by increasing the number of beach obstacles, but if the Allies attacked at low tide they would be of limited value. Of the five Allied landing areas only the beach designated "Omaha" provided natural defences. Here the U.S. 1st and 29th divisions would have to climb high cliffs that the Germans could easily defend. Elsewhere, at "Utah," "Gold," "Sword" and the Canadian beach "Juno," the assault troops broke through the Atlantic Wall in the first hour of the landings.

Success did not come from the overwhelming application of brute force as some historians have contended. Bad weather forced the bombers to unload well inland for fear of hitting the landing craft flotillas, and while naval fire helped to demoralize the enemy and keep heads down, it did not destroy a single forward gun position. The artillery field regiments – shooting from the

KEN BELL/DND/NATIONAL ARCHIVES OF CANADA/PA190144

Soldiers eat aboard ship on the way to the D-Day invasion.

A healthy body of fighting men

1st Canadian Parachute Battalion, part of 6th British Airborne Division, was given the vital task of seizing the le Mesnil crossroads to prevent the enemy from using these highways to attack the bridgehead.

By the time this letter reaches you ... the papers should really have splashed the invasion news about, and I can visualize your feelings when you read that an airborne invasion has taken place. We have just been given the liberty of divulging the fact that for the past two weeks we have been in a transit camp, awaiting our plane ride to meet the "Foe."...

Please don't picture me in the vainglorious role of a hero. Many's the time these past few days, fitting 'chutes, priming grenades, cleaning weapons, that I have felt the qualms associated with an invasion.... My mind has been buzzing with all kinds of thoughts since we have first been briefed, telling us what our jobs were, and how much it would affect the course of the beachhead. You can't help but feel these little pangs of pride.... Millions of people know that tomorrow great events will take place, and yet, it is only in our hearts that we know it will happen. This letter is being repeated countless times throughout the entire country; millions of soldiers, no doubt, feel as I do, and are writing as I am....

We all want this war to end – and no one more than the other, and whatever qualms we will naturally feel, will be quite orderly, and to be expected....

All I ask of you is to take this letter as it's being written. I am looking at things level-headedly, and am certain that nothing has been left to chance. We are a healthy body of fighting men, and have no doubts that we will take good care of ourselves.... Your continued, steady writing is all I ask for. It is the best medicine any person craves, especially those with invasion nerves....

So for now, Goodnight, and pardon the indifference, if any, you may have noticed in this letter. I mentioned I didn't feel like waxing sentimental, and I hope you will understand.

All my love, Alec

Lance Corporal Alec Flexer was killed in action June 6, 1944.

Le Régiment de la Chaudière, 8th Brigade's reserve battalion, prepares to go ashore to advance through the Queen's Own Rifles, who have broken through the Atlantic Wall. The "Chauds" advanced inland, capturing Beny-sur-Mer.

D. SULLIVAN/DND/NATIONAL ARCHIVES OF CANADA/PA132790

(Left) Troops head for shore by LCA (Landing Craft, Assault) from HMCS _Prince Henry_.

(Overleaf) Rough weather had delayed the landings and the tide covered many of the mined obstacles. The beach at Bernières-sur-Mer was the only one available when the 9th Brigade, including the North Nova Scotia Highlanders, the Highland Light Infantry, the Stormont, Dundas and Glengarry Highlanders and the Sherbrooke Fusiliers, was ordered to land and start inland to Carpiquet.

G.A. MILNE/DND/NATIONAL ARCHIVES OF CANADA/PA116533

decks of pitching landing craft – were unable to fire accurately. This meant the defences had to be overcome in close combat, with infantry, combat engineers and armour cooperating to capture the fortified positions.

The North Shore (New Brunswick) Regiment landing at St. Aubin-sur-Mer got through the forward defences in a series of "breathless rushes" across the sand. The sea wall prevented the tanks from leaving the beach until "C" Squadron of the Fort Garry Horse forced an exit through a minefield at the cost of three tanks. By 11:00 a.m. things were under control and the Royal Marine Commando assigned to link "Juno" and "Sword" beaches landed. By this time the reserve companies of the North Shores were moving inland.

The Queen's Own Riffles had the roughest experience of all the Canadian battalions. The DD amphibious tanks were late and played no part in overcoming the first line of resistance. "A" Company landed well away from the resistance nest and got off the beach quickly, but "B" Company's landing craft were blown off course by the wind and beached the men directly in front of the machine guns. These soldiers had to draw upon all their reserves of courage to save the situation. Three men, Lieutenant Herbert, Corporal Tessier and Rifleman Chicosky, were awarded medals for their work in destroying the main pillbox. Bernières-sur-Mer was captured after a two-hour battle but German anti-tank guns held up the advance inland, creating an enormous traffic

jam in the streets of the village. The Régiment de la Chaudière, the reserve battalion, and 9th Brigade, the force assigned to reach Carpiquet, were held up for most of the day, and everyone gave thanks for the air force and the achievement of air superiority.

The 7th "Western" Brigade landed on both sides of the River Seulles at Courseulles-sur-Mer. The town encompassed a strong-point, the most heavily fortified portion on "Juno" beach. The Regina Rifle Regiment on the east side and the Royal Winnipeg Rifles to the west achieved miracles in overcoming a series of concrete emplacements that were fiercely defended. The tanks of the 1st Hussars and the reserve battalion, the Canadian Scottish, joined the advance inland by mid-morning. The landings on "Juno" were an extraordinary success, one of the great achievements of the Canadian army, but one that Canadians have been strangely reluctant to recognize.

> ### Thin on the ground
>
> None of us really grasped, at that point, spread across such a large front, just how thin on the ground we all were. Each single one of us, from Elliott Dalton, our Commanding Officer, who was leader of his boat, to the ordinary soldier, was suddenly on the run at top speed. We were all riflemen on the assault.
>
> Company Sergeant-Major Charlie Martin,
> Queen's Own Rifles

Recollections of D-Day

A new position was added to each battle company in the 3rd Canadian Division, an intelligence man. The idea was General Montgomery's as a way to improve the communication of tactical intelligence in the heat of battle. In the Queen's Own Rifles, Rifleman Les Wagar was chosen to fill this role with one of the four companies.

A British or Canadian assault division for the Normandy invasion was an augmented division of over 30,000 troops, especially equipped to overcome fortified beaches, move inland quickly, repel expected armoured counterattacks, and hold a perimeter while major forces built up behind them. An assault company had a complement of about 90 men, rather than the usual 110, in order to fit into three assault landing craft....

June 6, before dawn
The Channel was black and drizzly, rolling in the black swells of yesterday's storm.... But this was no flat-bottomed LCI – this was a real ship, an LSI [Landing Ship, Infantry], equipped to feed, billet and transport an entire beach assault group, ringed with climbing nets and LCAs [Landing Craft, Assault] slung from the davits. We'd been aboard her since the 4th, waiting....

Reveille was early....The LSI was still ploughing ahead into the darkness. I don't remember eating.... I remember lining up for rum ration, but only because someone talked me into it: Since I was so queasy in the stomach, at least I could be a good pal and get an extra shot for a drinkin' man. The drinkin' man was smarter than I was. He poured both mine and his into his canteen, which was already half full – a little something he was saving up for a party when the time was right.

Then official noises began coming over the intercom, people started giving orders, the engines slowed. We got into our gear and lined up on deck beside our designated LCA. The sky was just beginning to lighten as the LCAs were dropped into the swells, and we climbed down the nets to get on board.

At that point I don't remember anyone saying anything. Each man's job had been set and memorized days before....We knew the width of the beach we had to cross, the jackmines we had to avoid, the bunkers, the gun positions, the wall we had to get over or through, the streets and the buildings of the town we had to take, the minefields, the possible enemy strength, the perimeter we had to establish for the next wave to go forward....

June 6, dawn
H-Hour at Bernières was 0730. A and B companies would take the beach and the wall. C and D would land 20 minutes later to take the town. Now we began to pick out the features of Bernières ahead. Support started up. Shells from battleships we couldn't see began hissing high over-

Ships that had taken the invading force over to France brought the wounded back. Here casualties are carried ashore in England, June 8. The Royal Canadian Army Medical Corps was well prepared to deal with casualties. The discovery of penicillin was one factor in lowering the mortality rate but the organization of front-line Field Dressing Stations and rapid evacuation to well equipped hospitals also contributed to saving the lives of more than 90 per cent of the wounded.

DEAN/DND/NATIONAL ARCHIVES OF CANADA/PA131437

head, exploding somewhere inland on targets we couldn't see. A line of four Spitfires swept low along the line of the coast, blazing away at God knows what. To our left, someone pressed the firing button on a long, converted LCT bristling with bank after bank of heavy mortars. We watched nests of mortar shells lobbing up and over and down, and the town blowing up in slow motion. Someone – it had to be the CO, Major Nickson – cursed, "Damn! They're supposed to be hitting the beach." Now the Spitfires were coming back along the coast, higher up, and swinging out over us, heading home. The last one in line was on a collison course with the last nest of mortar shells lobbing up from the LCT. I watched their trajectories closing and wondered if the guy would know what hit him. The plane exploded and fell into the water just off shore. The CO was up, trying to pick things out with his binoculars – I think it was him – and suddenly blurted, "My God! There's a Frenchman in a boat out there, pulling the pilot out of the water." The unreality of things was creeping in. With our heads down as ordered, tucked safely behind the shelter of steel plates, and all Hell breaking loose around us, here was a mere civilian who didn't know he was in a war – just knew that somebody had to get a man out of the water, and he was elected…

… Our tank support had been slowed down by the heavy seas and hadn't arrived yet. Able and Baker had been turned around about a half-hour ago. H-Hour was now tentatively one hour later and someone had forgotten to tell us…. About 1,000 yards offshore we turned again and started doing slow circles, waiting. The odd shell began throwing up waterspouts nearby. Any help the earlier support fire had given us was rapidly disappearing.

Now the order came to go; all the tanks hadn't arrived, but we were going to have to go with what we had. The tide was coming in, and keeping clear of the jackmines was going to become a bigger problem for the assault craft the higher the tide moved up the beach….

The ramp dropped, and we poured off in single file into waves up to our waists, running….

Company HQ set up beside the wall, near a jagged split where one man at a time could climb to the waterfront road. Most of the company were already in the town when some sniper filtered back into the near houses and lined up on the road. A lttle panic in the rear until the sniper was taken out. Wounded were coming back with stories of snipers holding things up in town…. Word passed down that A and B companies had a lot of casualties….

… A few stunned civilians were peering out of doorways as we moved into the cobbled streets. Now the platoon commanders were reporting that they were digging in on their objectives on the perimeter of town….

Rifleman J.L. Wagar, Queen's Own Rifles,
Canadian 3rd Division

(Left) Medical and nursing staff followed soon after the landings. Here Private F. Madore has dressings checked by Sister M.F. Giles, June 16.

(Right) Privates Gaston Daigneault and Robert Bonneau of le Régiment de la Chaudière escort a youthful German prisoner, June 15.

KEN BELL/DND/NATIONAL ARCHIVES OF CANADA/PA 131427

F.L. DUBERVILL/DND/NATIONAL ARCHIVES OF CANADA/PA 114495

CAEN

Beyond the Atlantic Wall, the "Overlord" plan called for an advance inland and the organization of defensive positions capable of withstanding counterattacks by German Panzer divisions. The beachhead had to be deep enough to allow room for the buildup of supplies and the deployment of additional divisions and to provide airfields for the Tactical Air Force. Montgomery hoped to base his defences on Caen and the railway line west to Bayeux; but on D-Day 21st Panzer Division had stopped British 3rd Division in front of the city and the next day 12 SS Panzer Division was able to check the advance of 9th Canadian Brigade before it could reach Carpiquet. The only formations able to carry out Montgomery's directives were the 7th "Western" Canadian Brigade, which seized its objectives along the railway line, and 50th British Division, which liberated Bayeux.

Lieutenant-Colonel F.M. Matheson, D.S.O., Regina Rifle Regiment. Matheson was just one of a number of militia officers who proved to be superb leaders in Normandy. He commanded the Regina Rifles from D-Day to the end of the Battle of the Scheldt.

The Canadian position, which controlled the main Caen–Cherbourg highway as well as the railway line, soon came under attack. The 12th SS "Hitler Youth" Division was confident that it would throw what Kurt "Panzer" Meyer called the "little fish" back into the sea and Meyer helped to lead a series of attacks on the 7th Brigade "fortress." The first attempt came on the night of June 7 with attacks on Putot and Norrey. The Germans committed two battalions at Norrey, but a torrent of small arms and artillery fire forced the Panzer grenadiers to abandon their plan. The Reginas' war diary, underestimating both German intentions and the effectiveness of Canadian artillery fire, dismissed this assault as a minor counterattack. Pressure continued throughout June 8, especially at Putot, where the 12th SS was able to cross the railway and outflank the Royal Winnipeg Rifles. Putot was lost late in the day and then recovered through a carefully orchestrated

The Normandy battlefield. Third Canadian Infantry Division with 2nd Canadian Armoured Brigade landed on D-Day and entered Caen more than a month later on July 9. Second Infantry Division entered the battle south of Caen, assaulting Verrières Ridge on July 19 and 25. At the end of the month 4th Canadian and 1st Polish Armoured divisions joined in the advance to Falaise and the "gap" between Trun and Chambois.

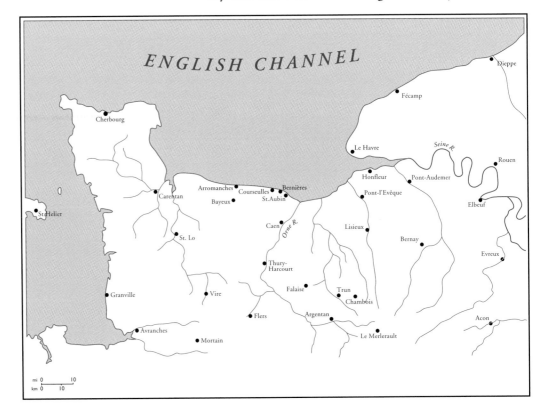

counterattack. The Canscots and 1st Hussars – using an artillery barrage provided by 12th and 13th field regiments – were in Putot before the enemy could recover.

Just as the Canscots were clearing the last holdouts in Putot, Kurt Meyer's regiment launched a new attack on the Regina Rifles. Panther tanks advanced down the highway to the edge of Bretteville before the Canadians opened fire. At dawn on June 9, Meyer withdrew his defeated forces to Rots. He did not, however, give up, deciding to use the one company of Panther tanks that had not been in action to overcome the Reginas' key position in Norrey.

This time the attack was to be in broad daylight, timed for noon when the tactical air forces – still based in England – might be absent. The Germans were relying on speed and left their infantry to follow. Suddenly, one Panther was struck a jolting blow. In the next four minutes, five more Panthers were destroyed by 17-

LCMSDS/WLU

A popular German magazine published photographs of the 12th SS Hitler Youth Division preparing to counter attack the Canadians. The text reads "Invasion! The German Army prepares countermeasures."

pounder Sherman Firefly tanks of the 1st Hussars. The 12th SS had suffered a severe defeat and there was no more talk of throwing "little fish" back into the sea.

The battles fought by 7th Brigade in the first days of the Normandy landings are the stuff of which legends are made. The Canadian victory was of vital importance in securing the Allied bridgehead. Canadian operations, and especially those of the Regina Rifles, demonstrated a level of professionalism that is rarely mentioned in histories of our volunteer army.

If German armour could not overcome Canadian defences, it was unlikely that the thinly armoured and undergunned Shermans of 2nd Canadian Armoured Brigade could succeed against the German armour, but the 1st Hussars and Queen's Own Rifles were told to try. The battle at le Mesnil-Patry, known to veterans as the "Charge of the

A pistol shot to the temple

The Regina Rifles had captured Norrey-en-Bassin and we were to move from there to capture Le Mesnil-Patry seven miles forward. There was an ominous lack of information. Both companies rode tanks forward until suddenly we came under heavy fire from German 88s, and riding the tanks became like riding a wild bull. Whoever nicknamed the Sherman tanks "Ronsons," after the cigarette lighter, had a good reason. The 88 was the most successful gun of the war, efficient against aircraft, tanks or infantry. In fifteen minutes they knocked out nineteen of the Shermans of the 1st Hussars. We were sitting ducks. In all, we lost eighty-seven killed or wounded, and B Squadron of the Hussars, sixty.

The next morning things seemed strangely quiet, so we took a patrol into Le Mesnil-Patry. We discovered enormous dug-in tank positions, cleverly camouflaged. The villagers told us that there had been eighty heavy

tanks and many infantry, and lighter armour – too much for a holding operation. The enemy had been preparing to launch an attack against the beaches.

Was that why our attack had been so badly prepared and so quickly mounted – to forestall theirs? In any case, our action had prompted their withdrawal so that while we lost hundreds, we might have saved thousands. It's always easy to criticize orders when you're the one being shot at. But you don't know what the High Command knows. My view is that somebody had made a very difficult, but necessary, decision.

On moving forward that second day, we came across Tommy McLaughlin and his section. There were six bodies, each with a pistol shot to the temple. The image of our murdered men – wounded and in field dressings, all of them prisoners, their weapons gone – would stay with us.

Company Sergeant-Major Charlie Martin,
Queen's Own Rifles

Anxious to get at the enemy

The Highland Light Infantry of Canada from Waterloo County, Ontario, attacked Buron, one of the fortified villages ringing Caen. The battalion war diary records the battle.

July 7, 1944. Morale 100% as men are anxious to get at the enemy in Buron who have mortared and shelled us for over one month.

July 8, 1944. At 0730 hrs the two assaulting companies crossed the start line and travelled down their axis of advance towards the objective....

The forward edge of the village was strongly held by a ring of defensive positions most of which contained MMGs. These brought down continuous and devastating fire on our troops and it was almost impossible to advance through. Many times our troops were pinned to the ground by it only to get up and go on as soon as it let up. The tanks had to be called forward on several occasions to aid the infantry forward.

"D" Company under Major J.H. Anderson was the first company into the village. The tanks were not able to follow them in as they struck a minefield on the right flank, "D" Company had to smash its way through alone and clean out all the trenches that comprised the defensive system. They suffered heavy casualties doing this and progressed on to the orchard on the right forward side of the village with only half a company.

In the orchard Sgt. Herchenratter organized the remnants of two platoons and led the attack at clearing out the orchard. Cpl. Weitzel, already wounded, here distinguished himself by leading the two men left of his section into an attack on two well sited MG posts. When both of them were hit he continued on and knocked out both posts before he himself was killed.

Meanwhile, "B" Company was encountering heavy opposition on the left flank. They charged again and again but were faced with a strong reinforced company equipped with at least double the usual number of automatic weapons. Tanks were called for but were out of communication. When contact was finally made the tanks feared to move forward because of the minefields. It was sometime before they could be told that the left flank was free.

At 1130 hrs the C.O. was able to get his Company Commands in by means of a runner and learned the state of affairs. "D" Company had only one officer (Major Anderson) and 38 O.Rs; "B" Company had one officer (Mr. Chantler) and about 1/3 strength; "C" Company was about 50% strength and "A" Company about 66% of their strength. All had reached and taken their objective and were consolidating. Mortaring and shelling by the enemy from St. Contest and Bitot on the left flank were exacting a heavy toll by the minute. So continuous and severe was the shelling that even the slit trenches were not safe. The enemy followed his old habits of bringing to bear all the fire he possessed on his own position once it was overrun.

The LOBs (left out of battle) were sent for and the Battalion was reorganized. They dug in completely to hold what they had taken and endeavoured to get the rest of their casualties out.

Night fell on a quiet, smoking village which had witnessed one of the fiercest battles ever fought in the history of war. It was the HLIs first big fight and the 8 July will go down in its memoirs as a day to be remembered. The ranks were sadly depleted and reorganization showed them to be thin on the ground – too thin to stave off a counterattack in the night. Yet they doggedly dug in, determined that their day's work would not be in vain and though dead tired ready to go on to Caen the next day if the opportunity presented itself. One hundred percent stand-to was maintained during the night but the enemy had expended all his energy during the day and with the exception of a few snipers trapped behind the lines all was quiet and the night passed without event.

Light Brigade," should have ended attempts to use Blitzkrieg tactics in 1944, but Montgomery tried a larger attack using 7th Armoured Division. When this thrust was thrown back by a company of Tiger tanks, the struggle in the Caen sector, like the one behind the American beaches, turned into a battle of attrition.

Such a battle was bound to lead to the defeat of the German armies if the Allies could maintain continuous pressure using the full weight of artillery and air power to assist the infantry and tanks. This approach to combat has been widely criticized by historians and military strategists who insist that bolder measures should have

(Facing page) Canadian troops entering Caen, July 10, 1944. Much of the town was destroyed by Allied artillery and especially Allied bombers, which struck the city in preparation for Operation "Charnwood," the attack on Caen on July 8.

I don't know what you say...

I saw him sitting in the lee of a hedge at the side of the road, his jacket draped loosely over his shoulders, the bandaged remainder of a shattered arm wrapped to his chest. He'd been looked after, just waiting for the jeep to come back up for him.

I don't know what you say to a friend with a wound like that – but I said something, and my pain was showing. He said, "Hey, don't be sorry for me. I'm the lucky one. I've got my boatride home. I'm sorry for you guys. You're the ones who hafta stay here."

I said, "Lucky it's your left arm, anyway."

He laughed, "Yeah. There's lots o' things a guy can do with one hand. And no one worries any more. They'll be looking after guys like me back there."

I had to go. "Good luck, anyway. Maybe see you again, sometime, back in Toronto."

"Good luck to you guys. I'll be thinkin' of you over here."

Rifleman J.L. Wagar, Canadian 3rd Division

This man hated me...

What many feared more than death was a lifetime of suffering. John Burwell Hillsman, a surgeon with the No. 8 Field Surgical Unit, wrote of one such wounding.

This man hated me. I kept away from him as much as possible, but his eyes seemed to follow me, brimming with resentment.

Unloading casualties evacuated from France by RAF Dakota aircraft.

NATIONAL ARCHIVES OF CANADA/PA128184

When he came in he didn't want to live. I hoped he would die too. A shell had burst in front of him and blown off his arms just below the shoulders.

Now he was a lump beneath the blanket. No legs, no arms, just a body with a head on one end. That was the trouble, that head – he could think.

But what could I do? I was a surgeon, not an executioner.

Dr. John Burwell Hillsman, 8th Field Surgical Unit

been used. John Ellis, an influential British historian, accuses the Allied commanders of "battering" the Germans to death "with a blunt instrument" and argues that Montgomery's operations were "ponderous and slow." The war was won, he maintains, by overwhelming numerical and material superiority, not by good leadership and military effectiveness.

No Allied soldier who served at the "sharp end" would agree with this view. The simple truth is that numerical and material superiority in the form of powerful air forces and large navies meant little on the battlefield. The Allies were seldom able to concentrate enough troops to obtain the 3:1 or 4:1 force ratio necessary to overcome a well-equipped, well-dug-in enemy, so a temporary stalemate developed. Hitler could not trade space for time in France and Allied advances were invariably met with fierce counterattacks. It was in these clashes that the German armies in Normandy were destroyed.

For the Canadians the three weeks between le Mesnil-Patry and the July 4 attack on Carpiquet airfield were a period of frustration involving long hours under enemy mortar fire, constant night patrols and the first signs of a "battle exhaustion" crisis. Battle exhaustion, the Second World War equivalent of the "shell shock" of the Great War or today's Combat Stress Reaction, had been a major problem for all three Allied armies in Italy, and the medical services were well prepared to deal with it in Normandy. Soldiers who broke under the pressure of battle usually suffered panic states that they could not control. Evacuated to Casualty Clearing Stations set aside for this purpose, the soldier was given twenty-four hours to rest and recuperate. A psychiatrist then tried to determine if he was fit to return to his unit or needed to be posted to a communications job away from combat.

By the middle of July, one in four non-fatal casualties was due to battle exhaustion and some officers questioned the humanitarian approach taken by the medical

Canadian officers watch a Typhoon taking off. This potent rocket-armed aircraft supported the troops on the ground from bases just behind the front lines.

Battle exhaustion

The term "battle exhaustion," which covered a range of emotional and mental states of breakdown, suggested the condition was temporary and could be improved by a brief period of rest and, if necessary, sedation, away from the front at a forward aid station.

Major Burdett McNeel, a medical doctor and psychiatrist, commanded 1st Canadian Exhaustion Unit in Normandy. He made the following entries in the war diary.

13 July 1944: The first twelve patients arrived at 1200 hrs. The majority of these were from the RRC [Royal Regiment of Canada] which had been in action two days…. Histories were taken, each man was given three grains of Sodium Amytal and put to bed.

14 July 1944: Forty-one patients were admitted today. About 15 of these are cases which have been out of the line for about a week … cases seen yesterday and today have shown chiefly anxiety symptoms…. The precipitation factor in most cases is said to be blast – mortar more frequently than shell.

15 July 1944: Twenty-six patients were admitted today and with a top accommodation of 110 beds, it is apparent that our plan of two days sedation and three days rehabilitation will not be practicable…. As we are now discharging patients, psychotherapeutic talks to groups about to be discharged have now been instituted. These consist of simple explanations of psychogenic symptoms "exhaustion versus shell shock" etc…. Many of the men understand the mechanism of their trouble alright, and most are ready to admit that the origin is emotional rather than physical but many are without any incentive to carry on further.

16 July 1944: Twenty-three patients have been admitted today and our bed strength is now eighty-four.

17 July 1944: Hope of adequate care and rehabilitation will have to be abandoned…. The treatment cases are without pyjamas and the convalescents have to wear their dirty and tattered clothes.

18 July 1944: We were awakened this morning by a terrific roar of gunfire…. rumour is that "This is it" and that the show should soon be over. So far our admissions have not exceeded the usual level: about twenty-two today…. We face a serious shortage of sedative.

21 July 1944: Yesterday fifty-nine patients were admitted. Today has been heavy. We have admitted over eighty patients and they are still coming in. Our routine sedative, Sodium Amytal, is exhausted and most of a bottle of Medinal we borrowed is gone. However, the day has been saved by the arrival of 2000 capsules of Sod. Amytal.

22 July 1944: One hundred and one cases of exhaustion were admitted … our convalescent ward and the "morgues" are filled. Those in the morgue have had to sleep on blankets spread on the ground. The rain has been pouring down and the majority of the men are wet and muddy.

23 July 1944: Total bed state 175 … treatment will have to be limited to a one or two day period. Today has been spent in sorting and evacuating as many as possible.

corps. The Royal Canadian Army Medical Corps, especially, was committed to policies that placed the welfare of the individual soldier above considerations of manpower shortages, and Guy Simonds, among others, criticized the army's policy. The RCAMC, with the support of the General Officer Commanding, First Canadian Army, Harry Crerar, maintained its approach throughout the war, evacuating thousands of Canadian soldiers, most of whom were judged unable to return to combat.

Caen, or at least the part of the urban area north of the Orne River, fell to Canadian and British troops on July 9 after an intense and costly battle for the surrounding villages, which the Germans had fortified. The Regina Rifles captured the Abbaye d'Ardenne, the headquarters used by Kurt Meyer of the 12th SS. Here on June 7 Meyer's men had systematically executed nineteen Canadian soldiers, shooting each one through the head while the others waited, comforting each other. Similar executions on an even larger scale occurred at the Château d'Audrieu. In both cases the murders were committed in cold blood under the supervision of officers of the 12th SS.

During battle both sides committed war crimes,

Left to right: Standartenführer Kurt Meyer, Oberführer Fritz Witt, Obergruppenführer Sepp Deitrich, Sturmbannführer Hubert Meyer, Field Marshal Gerd von Rundstedt.

shooting prisoners who had surrendered. The motive was almost always revenge for some incident that had enraged the perpetrator, but in war as in civil life no one can control a psychopath, and some crimes were committed by individuals who clearly fit this description. The executions at the Abbaye and Château fell into the very different category of systematic premeditated murder, which is why Meyer was tried and convicted by a military tribunal at the end of the war.

No longer a man...

By early evening we had secured Anisy. After digging a slit trench for myself, I moved out to do my job....
About five yards in front of where a sergeant was still digging in, a German soldier was staggering back and forth, ten yards one way, ten yards back, eyes wild, breathing hard, tripping on his turns. The sergeant's Sten gun was lying at the edge of his trench. If the German slowed to a walk, the sergeant aimed a burst in the ground near his feet, and went back to digging.

The anger was like rock. "This bastard" had come in with his hands up, then threw a grenade that killed one of his kids. The "son of a bitch" was a dead man the minute he did it, but this platoon wasn't going to make it that easy. In response to my question, he told me the platoon commander was looking after a

burial detail, and had left the German to him.

I went on my way, doing my job. On my way back to Company HQ, I stopped for a moment to see what was happening. The German was still on his feet. His path back and forth was worn bare. His pants and his boots were off, his jacket open. He was flailing with every step, his long underwear stained brown to his ankles with the diarrhea of dying. He slobbered, grey as death, no longer a man....

I was told later that he had been shot where he fell, finally, one limb at a time.

I had seen the face of anger, in Anisy, on my first day of war. But the shock that ended the days of my youth and the days of my innocence forever, was seeing how easily the civilized pretence of humanity slips off.

Rifleman J.L. Wagar, Canadian 3rd Division

FALAISE

The capture of Cherbourg on June 26 and of Caen on July 9 did not alter the basic pattern of the Battle of Normandy. To the west the American army was bogged down in the *bocage* country of small fields enclosed by hedgerows. South of Caen, in the Anglo-Canadian sector, the country was open, with a succession of low ridges rising to around three hundred metres near Falaise. German anti-tank guns and mortars controlled movement in this area, particularly in daylight. Mortar fragments accounted for 75 per cent of all Allied casualties, and whatever else the Germans were short of, it wasn't mortar rounds.

All across the front, American, British and Canadian divisions, joined in August by a French and a Polish armoured division, sought to develop ways of breaking through the German defensive perimeter. There has been much debate about Allied generalship and strategy in Normandy, most of it based on hindsight, but on the battlefield generals mattered little. No one knew any shortcuts; the Allies simply had to keep hammering away until the Germans broke. The breakthrough, and more remarkably a break-out into the heart of France, occurred in the American sector during the last week of July, but the success of Operation "Cobra" was only possible because of the relentless pressure exerted by the Allies since D-Day.

Second Canadian Corps played an important role in these actions, capturing the industrial suburbs of Caen, July 18–20, and assaulting a strong German position on Verrières Ridge on the very eve of "Cobra." This operation, code-named "Spring," was to prove one of the costliest single-day actions of the war for Canadians and has inevitably called forth much second-guessing. Verrières Ridge was the key to the defences south of Caen and was held by elements of three German divisions. Simonds believed that a repetition of

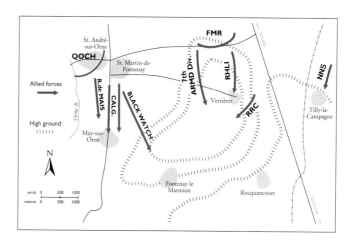

Operation Spring. Verrières Ridge is the first of a series of low ridges between Caen and Falaise. It was heavily defended on July 25 by elements of five German divisions. The higher ground on the west bank of the Orne provided the Germans with a clear view of the Canadian advance.

the daylight attack of July 19 had little chance of success so he decided to overcome the first line of resistance in full darkness. "Artificial moonlight," created by searchlights, and other aids to night movement helped the assault battalion to get to its objectives, but two of the three village strong-points, Tilly-la-Campagne and May-sur-Orne, could not be captured before dawn. With Panzer battle groups reinforcing the defenders, further attacks were unlikely to succeed, but Simonds and his divisional commanders, hampered by the fog of war, allowed the second phase to proceed. The Black Watch, a regiment from Montreal, was virtually destroyed in a daylight advance on the right flank, and other attempts to move forward were repulsed with heavy losses.

The third strong-point, the hamlet of Verrières, was taken in a brilliantly managed night action. The Royal Hamilton Light Infantry, commanded by J.L. "Rocky" Rockingham, cleared the village and dug in with well-positioned anti-tank defences. For the next three days the Rileys withstood repeated counterattacks, which surged around and beyond their positions.

The German response to "Spring"

Footsore personnel of the South Saskatchewan Regiment take a break at Rocquancourt, August 11.

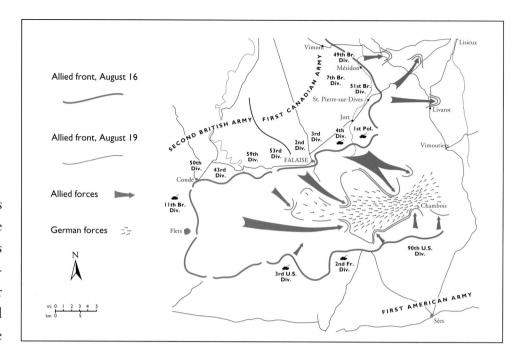

The Falaise Gap. Between August 16 and 21, tens of thousands of German soldiers escaped through the Falaise "Gap" north of Chambois, where 2 SS Panzer Corps held open the road to Vimoutiers and Rouen.

was all that Allied strategists could have hoped for. The battle cost the Germans precious men and equipment and distracted their high command. Several crucial days passed before their armoured divisions were available to respond to the American break-out.

Montgomery now made a fateful decision, ordering Second British Army, with its three experienced armoured divisions, to move west in support of the American advance. General Harry Crerar and First Canadian Army were left in the Caen sector with three exhausted infantry divisions and two armoured divisions, 4th Canadian and 1st Polish. In time both of these formations would become effective, battle-proven units, but in early August, within days of their arrival in Normandy, they were not fully ready to carry out a major offensive on narrow fronts.

Operation "Totalize," the first of two armoured thrusts towards Falaise, was originally intended to complement the American and British efforts to push the Germans back to the River Seine. But on August 6, two days before "Totalize" began, Hitler ordered his Panzer divisions to counterattack in the west, isolating Patton's Third U.S. Army from the rest of the bridgehead. Ultra warned of this impending attack at Mortain, and the Americans, assisted by RAF Typhoons, stopped the Germans cold. It now seemed possible to encircle the German armies in Normandy, and Patton turned his XV Corps north to meet the Canadians near Falaise.

The Canadians again attacked at night, making use of

Simond's "invention," an improvised armoured personnel carrier nicknamed a "Kangaroo." Verrières Ridge was captured, but the next day the two armoured divisions were unable to exploit their initial success. Ironically, the one armoured battle group to break through the second line of German defences lost its way and ended up several miles from its objective. The tanks of the British Columbia Regiment and the infantry from the Algonquins were destroyed in an unequal duel between Sherman tanks and the far more powerful Panthers of the 12th SS.

Soldiers of the Fusiliers Mont-Royal carrying a wounded comrade during a sniper hunt, Falaise, August 17.

The task of capturing Falaise fell to the 6th Canadian Infantry Brigade supported by tanks of the Sherbrooke Fusiliers. The South Sasks and the Camerons fought their way into the town and the Fusiliers Mont-Royal overcame the last defenders, a group of twelve SS grenadiers who fought to the end.

"Totalize" ended well short of Falaise but Montgomery chose to wait until the Canadians could mount a second attack. He decided not to reinforce Crerar's army and left the Americans waiting at Argentan for orders to move north. "Tractable," the second Canadian operation, brought Canadian troops to the town of Falaise, but the Germans were now fleeing through the Falaise "gap," harassed, but not stopped, by the tactical air forces. By the time Montgomery ordered the Americans to advance to meet the Canadians it was too late to encircle all of the German forces, though thousands were killed, wounded or taken prisoner in the last week of the battle of the Falaise pocket.

On August 18 Simonds was told he must make a supreme effort to close the gap. The long-delayed American thrust was finally underway, and the two armies were to meet at Chambois. Simonds issued his orders quickly. He knew, through Ultra intelligence, that the German retreat had only begun in earnest two days before and that it still might be possible to trap several hundred thousand men. With so much at stake every exertion had to be made. The

The best blood of Canada

Three miles or so south of Caen the present-day tourist, driving down the arrow-straight road that leads to Falaise, sees immediately to his right a rounded hill crowned by farm buildings. If the traveller be Canadian, he would do well to stay the wheels at this point and cast his mind back to the events of 1944; for this apparently insignificant eminence is the Verrières Ridge. Well may the wheat and sugar-beet grow green and lush upon its gentle slopes, for in that now half-forgotten summer the best blood of Canada was freely poured upon them.

C. P. Stacey, *The Victory Campaign*

Tactical Air Force would do its best, flying up to three thousand sorties a day, but only the army could seal the gap. The Polish Armoured Division reached the outskirts of Chambois that night, but not in sufficient strength to block the escape route. Polish units were now scattered over ten miles of hilly countryside; their key positions on the twin hills they called the "Maczuga," or mace, were the scene of intense combat as the Germans mounted an attack from outside the pocket to assist those fighting their way to safety.

The best that 4th Armoured Division could do to carry out Simonds' orders was to send a squadron of the South Alberta Regiment and a company of infantry from the Argyll and Sutherland Highlanders towards Chambois. The remaining armoured regiments were committed north of Trun, establishing firm control of other highways to the northeast.

The battle group assigned to close the gap consisted of 175 men, 16 tanks and 4 MIOs from 5th Anti-Tank Regiment. Major David Currie of the South Alberta Regiment was in command. Currie was a veteran of ten days of combat and two years of training as an armoured corps officer. A quiet, unassuming man, he had learned to lead by example, encouragement and the appearance of calm certainty. His resolve and personal courage were quickly tested. The village of St. Lambert-sur-Dives lies halfway between Trun and Chambois. Several secondary roads converge on a small bridge that spans the river and from there two lanes, little better than farmers' tracks, link up with minor roads that twist through the hills towards Vimoutiers. St. Lambert-sur-Dives controlled one of the few clear routes out of the pocket and the enemy would not give it up without a struggle.

The lead SAR troop entered the village moving slowly forward. Two sharp cracklike sounds and two of its tanks were disabled. Despite mortar fire, Currie organized the

Major David Currie who won the Victoria Cross at St. Lambert-sur-Dives.

rescue of the tank crews and then posted his men for all-around defence. It was evident that the village was full of German troops protecting the bridge and crossroads.

Infantry reinforcements arrived that night: two half-companies, one from the Argylls and one from the Lincoln and Welland Regiment. At 0800 on August 20, the Germans mounted the first of a series of massive escapes, which included counterattacks at St. Lambert and Chambois. A Polish officer describing the struggle wrote,

A German "Nebelwerfer" six-barrelled mortar. German mortars and Nebelwerfers inflicted more than 70 per cent of all Allied casualties in Normandy.

"It reminded one of the mediaeval days when the defence of a battlefield was organized by placing camps in a tight quadrangle … the Maczuga and Chambois were practically cut off…. Our wounded had to remain with our fighting soldiers…."

In St. Lambert Currie's men fought on. Four Argylls stalked and destroyed a Panther. Currie used his command tank to knock out a Tiger and a rifle to deal with snipers who had infiltrated close to his headquarters. On the hill north of St. Lambert, "B" Squadron and the 15th Field Regiment joined in the battle. "Long lines of enemy trucks, tanks, wagons, carts and vehicles of all kinds could be seen approaching down the roads from the west … the tank gunners would pick off the lead and tail vehicles and then systematically shoot up the whole convoy." One artillery officer wrote, "It was as if the Americans and British were huge brooms sweeping the

Mortars were deadly and easy to conceal but radar could locate them by plotting the trajectory. 1st Canadian and 100th British Radar Batteries were created in response to the mortar crisis in Normandy and functioned effectively in 1945.

BOTH: LCMSDS/WILFRID LAURIER UNIVERSITY

Germans into the dustpan which at that moment was the Canadian Army." Currie, according to one of his NCOs, remained in control: "We knew at one stage it was going to be a fight to the finish but he was so cool about it, it was impossible for us to get excited." One last large attack was broken up by artillery at dusk on the 20th. The remaining German troops lacked the will to continue and thousands surrendered.

The Canadians had played a major role in achieving victory in Normandy. Placed at the sharpest end of the Allied order of battle in July and early August, II Canadian Corps was then called upon to become the main instrument in the attempt to close the Falaise pocket. In the last stages of the battle there had been much confusion; there had also been incredible heroism, dedication and the courage to endure.

CANLOAN

By 1944 Britain was desperately short of qualified infantry officers while the Canadian army's delayed entry into battle had allowed a large number to be trained. Canadian officers, waiting for a posting to First Canadian Army, were offered the chance to volunteer for service with British regiments, and 623 infantry officers plus 50 from the ordnance corps responded.

The infantry officers wore the badges of their adopted regiment with an added Canada flash on their shoulder. Most quickly adapted to life in their new regimental families, though many found the greater class distinctions in the British army difficult to deal with. Originally Canadians had been requested as reinforcements, but the volunteers were an impressive group and most joined their battalions before D-Day. At both "Sword" and "Gold" beach "Canloan" officers were part of the first wave, and they continued to play a key role at the sharp end. The British seemed to believe that all Canadians were adventurous and skilled at night-patrolling. As one "Jock" in 51st Highland Division put it, "Ye're a Canadian an ye like this sort of thing." When the officer protested, he was told, "Well, Sur-rr, ye volunteered, did ye no?"

Inevitably, casualties to Canloan officers were high. Most served as platoon and company commanders constantly exposed to danger, and of the 500 who served in Normandy 208 were wounded, 77 killed, 11 missing and 3 taken prisoner. By VE day, 75 per cent were battle casualties.

U.S. AIR FORCE PHOTO

A disabled Panther tank, August 16. The sloping frontal armour of the Panther deflected hits from anti-tank guns and crews quickly learned to hold their fire until the sides or back of the tank could be targetted.

60033

A V1 flying bomb dives upon London. Those below knew the danger was greatest when they heard the engine stop. The V1 at right landed intact in France and did not explode. A bomb disposal unit disassembled it and took it to the U.S. for study.

FLYING BOMBS AND MISSILES

The German army and air force had begun work on long-range rockets and missiles in the 1930s, but these programs were given few resources until Hitler insisted on the highest priority for weapons he could employ to retaliate against London for the bombing of German cities. The V1 "buzz bomb," essentially a small, pilotless jet plane, carried one ton of high explosive and could be launched from the air or from specially designed launching platforms that resembled ski jumps. The V1 flew at a speed of 375 mph and could be launched on a direct line to a large area such as London, where, out of fuel, it would fall to the ground in a slanting crash-dive.

The V2 was a liquid-fuel rocket, a guided missile not an airplane, and was originally intended to carry poison gas. Converted to carry the same explosive power as the V1, the missile was an extraordinarily expensive way of striking at London. It would have taken 18,000 of them to equal the weight of attack during the Blitz, but despite massive efforts just over 3,000 were launched.

The British learned of the new priority given to the

Squadron Leader Russ Bannock, DSO, DFC and Bar, and his observer, Flying Officer R.R. Bruce, DFC and Bar, of 418 RCAF Squadron pictured in front of their "Mossie."

V1 and V2 in 1943 and identified the development complex located on the Baltic coast at Peenemünde. In August 1943, Bomber Command carried out Operation "Hydra," a precision low-level attack using techniques developed by the Dam Busters. No. 405 RCAF Path-

finder squadron under Wing Commander John Fauquier was one of the squadrons employed to mark the target, in cooperation with a master bomber who circled the target correcting marking errors. The raid set back V1 and V2 production by four to six months, but the cost of forty bombers, or 7 per cent, was frighteningly high.

The air force continued to devote large resources to countering these weapons, particularly after large numbers of "ski" sites were located along the coast of France. Operation "Crossbow" committed medium and fighter-bombers of the tactical air forces as well as the heavies to bombing raids on these small targets, which were protected by anti-aircraft guns. It may be small comfort to the pilots who were lost on these costly "Crossbow" missions, but such operations further delayed the V1 launch date and forced the Germans to devote time, energy, manpower and materiel to a scheme which could not possibly affect the outcome of the war.

The first V1 struck London on June 12, 1944. Of the 22,000 fired, approximately half were aimed at London. About one-third of these malfunctioned or were destroyed by anti-aircraft fire or fighter-interceptors. An RCAF Mosquito pilot, Squadron Leader Russ Bannock,

shot down no less than nineteen V1s. On the night of July 3, Bannock and his observer, Flying Officer R.R. Bruce, RAF, attacked five buzz bombs, destroying three at ranges of less than two hundred yards. Their last V1 kill in August was the most memorable. The V1, hit by cannon shell from close range, slowed down, "dipped its right wing and headed back to France." Bannock followed it, using his machine guns to shoot it down as it approached the French coast at Boulogne.

Neither bombing nor air defences could prevent large numbers of these flying bombs from reaching London. More than 2,400 struck the metropolitan area and another 3,400 fell in areas around the city. The only final answer to the V1 was to overrun the launching sites in the Pas de Calais region, and it was to this task that First Canadian Army turned after Normandy.

CINDERELLA ARMY

The delay in closing the Falaise pocket allowed several hundred thousand German soldiers to escape, but the Germans had nevertheless lost 400,000 men, including 200,000 taken prisoner. Despite Hitler's orders to defend a new line at the Somme, they had little choice except to flee north to Holland and Germany.

Patton's army had liberated Paris on August 25 and was still heading east when strategic and personality conflicts erupted in the Allied command. Montgomery wanted Patton halted and all resources devoted to a "single thrust" to the Rhine and Berlin, preferably under his command. Eisenhower could not accept this proposal, which made slight logistical, military or political sense, but with his focus on the V1 launching sites, the Channel ports and Antwerp, "Ike" gave Montgomery priority and offered his strategic reserve, First Airborne Army, to the British field marshal.

On September 5, Antwerp, the largest port in Europe, was liberated with the help of the Belgian Resistance. Unfortunately Antwerp is sixty-five miles from the sea, and the banks of the long, narrow Scheldt estuary were controlled by elements of the German Fifteenth Army. This army, including the coastal garrisons and six divi-

sions that had not been drawn into the battle for Normandy, was ordered to defend the Channel ports of Boulogne, Calais and Dunkirk and to create two "fortresses" at the mouth of the Scheldt estuary.

Eisenhower and Montgomery knew through Ultra that Hitler had demanded a fight to the death to prevent the Allies from gaining control of the ports. They also knew that their supply situation, still dependent on the Normandy beaches, was critical; but the apparent col-

lapse of the German army led them to approve Operation "Market Garden," an assault across the Rhine that it was hoped would end the war in 1944.

"Market Garden" began on September 17 when three divisions struck from the sky. The 101st U.S. Airborne Division captured Eindhoven and the canal crossings, while 82nd U.S. Airborne seized the bridges at Nijmegen, but 1st British Airborne, dropping across the Rhine at Arnhem, had been asked to win "a bridge too

(Facing page) Sherman tanks of the 4th Canadian Armoured Division cross the pontoon bridge over the Seine at Elbeuf, August 28, 1944. While 3rd and 4th divisions advanced east of Rouen, 2nd Division was caught up in the bloody struggle for the Forêt de la Londe south of the city.

(Below and right) Re-entering Dieppe held special significance for the Canadians. A formal parade was held to mark the occasion, with General Harry Crerar taking the salute.

(FACING) D.I. GRANT/DND/NATIONAL ARCHIVES OF CANADA/PA113660 (BELOW) LCMSDS/WLU

NATIONAL ARCHIVES OF CANADA/PA136020

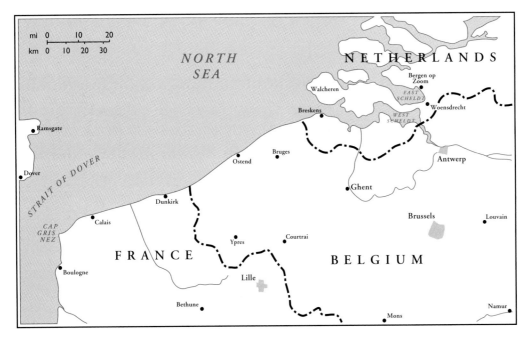

The Channel ports to the Scheldt estuary. Third Division was given the task of liberating Boulogne, Calais and the coastal gun batteries near Cap Gris Nez, while 2nd Division advanced to Dunkirk. Montgomery then decided to "mask" Dunkirk, which remained in German hands until May 1945.

This air photo of Cap Gris Nez, dated September 12, 1944, illustrates attempts by Bomber Command to destroy the large coastal guns. Bombs were ineffective against concrete casements and 9th Brigade captured the area on September 29, capturing 1,600 prisoners.

far," and despite heroic efforts were overwhelmed. Canadian engineers played a vital and dramatic role using storm boats to rescue the survivors, but for the rest of the Canadian army "Market Garden" and the Arnhem salient were the reasons they coined the phrase "Cinderella Army" to describe their role.

First Canadian Army crossed the Seine on August 30 and the next day 2nd Division was welcomed to Dieppe by cheering crowds. Once across the Somme the Canadians faced a well-organized withdrawal by Fifteenth Army, unlike the scattered remains of German divisions they had dealt with in Normandy. I British Corps, which had fought under Crerar in August, had been grounded to save on supplies, and Montgomery had "borrowed" 1st Polish Armoured Division, so Crerar was left with just the three Canadian divisions and 2nd Armoured Brigade. By mid-September, 4th Canadian Armoured Division was instructed to limit operations to masking Scheldt Fortress South, the "Breskens Pocket," while the infantry divisions captured the Channel ports.

By then most of the German Fifteenth Army had escaped across the Scheldt and joined in counterattacks on the exposed Arnhem salient. Second Division was ordered to Antwerp to defend the city, while 3rd Division was left alone to lay siege to Boulogne, Calais and the cross-Channel guns at Cap Gris Nez. These operations, which began on the same day as "Market Garden," took more than two gruelling weeks to complete, and when the job was done 3rd Division was rushed forward to join in the battle to free the approaches to Antwerp.

A funeral service for men of the Black Watch killed on Black Friday, October 13, 1944.

THE BATTLE OF THE SCHELDT

First Canadian Army's "Cinderella" role did not end with the capture of Calais and Cap Gris Nez. On September 27 Montgomery issued a new directive that called for destroying all enemy forces "preventing us from capturing the Ruhr and opening the port of Antwerp." The Ruhr battle was to be fought by twenty Allied divisions, while the Canadians were to clear the Scheldt with just two infantry divisions.

Guy Simonds, who replaced an ailing Harry Crerar for the Scheldt operations, accepted Montgomery's allocation of resources without complaint. He devised a complex plan to attack the Breskens Pocket using "Buffalo" amphibious vehicles to land a brigade behind the German defences. While 9th Brigade prepared to deliver this right hook, 7th Brigade attacked directly across the Leopold Canal, drawing enemy reserves into a fierce battle for a narrow stretch of land that rose above the surrounding fields, flooded by the defenders.

While 3rd Division fought its battle in the polders,

Decisive for the further conduct of the war

The defence of the approaches to Antwerp represents a task which is decisive for the further conduct of the war. After overrunning the Scheldt fortresses, the English would finally be in a position to land great masses of material in a large and completely protected harbour. With this material they might deliver a death blow to the North German plateau and to Berlin before the onset of winter ... and for this reason we must hold the Scheldt fortresses to the end. The German people are watching us.

Major-General Gustav von Zangen

Deliberate flooding of large areas along the Scheldt estuary was possible because much of the land was below sea-level. Combat in this "polder country" was particularly difficult because slit trenches filled with water. Battle exhaustion casualties quickly became a major problem.

The waterlogged ground of the Breskens Pocket made it difficult even for universal carriers to operate off road.

Wear out the garrison by attrition

Strongly defended Walcheren Island presented a formidable objective. General Simonds decided to flood Walcheren.

Bombing operations should be undertaken to break the dikes and completely flood all parts of the island below high water level. Those parts of the island which remain above water should then be systematically attacked, day and night, to destroy defences and wear out the garrison by attrition.

Lieutenant-General Guy Simonds

Fall from his bicycle...

On October 3, the RAF bombed the Westkapelle Dam at the westernmost point of Walcheren.

As I circled over the target area I was at such a low altitude that I saw a frightened civilian fall from his bicycle after seeing our plane heading towards him. On return to base, we discovered that a number of German telephone wires were wrapped around the Lancaster.

Pilot Officer Sidney Aldridge, Bomber Command

2nd Division moved north from Antwerp to seize the entry to the Beveland Peninsula and advance to Walcheren Island, "Scheldt Fortress North." Simonds believed that Walcheren would be the toughest part of the struggle and he convinced Bomber Command to flood the island by breaching the surrounding dykes. This was accomplished on October 3 and most of the saucer-shaped island disappeared under seawater.

Simonds had underestimated Hitler's resolve to deny the Allies the use of Antwerp. Still convinced that V1 and V2 attacks would weaken British morale, Hitler was determined to slow the Allied advance and prolong the war. The Breskens Pocket was defended by an entire division with limitless supplies of ammunition left behind as Fifteenth Army withdrew. Major-General Dan Spry's 3rd Division took on a force of roughly equal strength and his men had to keep attacking. The fighter-bombers of 84 Group RAF, which supported the Canadian army, helped out by flying hundreds of sorties in close support on days when cloud and rain lifted. But neither air power

wooded area was a key defensive feature. The paratroops also fortified the railway embankment that carried the line to Walcheren, effectively controlling access to the island.

The 6th Parachute Regiment, not content simply to hold the Canadians at bay, mounted a series of counter-attacks which cost many lives on both sides. The first attack began with intermittent mortaring and shelling that seemed designed to cover the infiltration of patrols. The Black Watch captured one group of twenty-four young soldiers. Their war diary notes that they belonged to parachute battalions, ranged in age from twenty to twenty-six, and were "fine physical specimens, keen to fight and with excellent morale." Their high morale had not prevented them from advancing into a trap, suggesting that inexperience and overconfidence were also characteristics of the parachutists.

A young Dutch girl offers the crew of a South Alberta Regiment tank a precious cup of coffee, and children wave orange flags symbolizing the Dutch monarchy as Canadian tanks enter Bergen op Zoom.

By mid-day on October 10, the German counterattack seemed to be spent. Von der Heydte's regiment had suffered heavy casualties, estimated at 480 men, in addition to more than fifty prisoners of war. Much is made in the secondary literature of the prowess of the German officer corps and the fighting power of the German infantry. Yet the battle for Hoogerheide demonstrated major deficiencies in German strategy and tactics which were not uncommon in northwest Europe. Von der Heydte had launched a frontal attack against forces which had gone over to the defensive and persisted in pressing forward despite heavy losses. To attack in this manner, when reconnaissance would have shown the weakness of the Canadian right flank, suggests overconfidence and doctrinal rigidity. The texture of the battle also indicates that both in their defensive positions and in their tactical counterattacks the Canadians were more than a match for the enemy.

nor artillery could occupy and hold ground, and Operation "Switchback" continued until November 2 when General Eberding surrendered at his bunker on the golf course of Knocke-Heist. Third Division casualties numbered more than two thousand, and one quarter of these lie buried in the Canadian cemetery at Adegem, Belgium.

Second Division found its task even more demanding. The advance to Hoogerheide went quickly but the Germans reacted to the threat by rushing reinforcements in the form of the 6th "Von der Heydte" Parachute Regiment and an armoured assault battalion. This formidable battle group occupied the village of Woensdrecht and the sandy ridge behind it. The "ridge" was all of ten metres high, but in the flat polder country this elevated and

Allied generals could be as stubborn as their German

185

An enthusiastic reception: Canadians of 2nd Division with Dutch girls after the liberation of Beveland. The soldiers are Sergeants R. Y. Williams, J. J. Coghill and W. Anaka of the Fort Garry Horse.

DND/NATIONAL ARCHIVES OF CANADA/PA137920

On October 16 the war diarist at 5th Brigade headquarters recorded a view shared by everyone in 2nd Division: "Cannot understand why they do not put more troops in the area and finish the job once and for all instead of playing about, shifting first one battalion and then the other. This is beginning to look like a winter campaign unless something breaks soon." Help was in fact on the way, for as the battle for Woensdrecht raged, Montgomery agreed to assign "complete priority" to operations to open Antwerp.

As C.P. Stacey noted, "As soon as the new orders took effect the situation north of Antwerp was transformed. The 4th Canadian Armoured Division … was to be used as a hammer to loosen the German formations confronting 2nd Division." Fourth Division was to clear the country northeast of Woensdrecht and free 2nd Division's flank. It in turn would be supported by 49th West Riding, 1st Polish Armoured and 104th U.S. "Timberwolf" Division in an operation certain to force a rapid German retreat to the Maas.

counterparts. Montgomery was reluctant to give up his thrust to the Ruhr and only agreed to give priority to Antwerp after Admiral Bertram Ramsay, the only senior commander who really understood the situation, prodded Eisenhower to overrule "Monty."

Unfortunately, 2nd Division was not permitted to wait until reinforcements arrived. On October 13, "Black Friday" for the Black Watch Regiment, an attempt to seize the railway embankment while Woensdrecht and the ridge were still in German hands cost 145 casualties of whom 56 were killed. Two days later, the Royal Hamilton Light Infantry captured Woensdrecht and skilfully defended it against repeated counterattacks. This four-day battle cost the Rileys 167 casualties but the ridge and railway were still in German hands.

(Facing page) A flail tank comes ashore at Westkapelle, Walcheren Island, in support of Commandos of 4th Special Service Brigade, and (below) a view of the flooded land in the vicinity of St. Phillipsland and Tholen Island where the Lake Superior Regiment operated. The aerial view was taken November 17, 1944.

Never knowing what you'd be running into...

You'd have two or three farm buildings together, and then up to maybe a half-mile of open fields surrounded by deep water. There was no cover. It was what we called a section job. Each section – a corporal and a rifleman usually – would leapfrog forward, advancing past the lead section. These attacks would take us from farmhouse to farmhouse. We'd do this five or six times a day – tense, stressful, never knowing what you'd be running into, or what they might suddenly start to send your way.

Company Sergeant-Major Charlie Martin, Queen's Own Rifles

Not flattered

Dear Dad,

Had quite a time on the Scheldt.... The Jerries had all fought in Russia for years and one lad I was talking to told me he had been wounded three times and was only twenty-one years old. They claim we Canadians are the British SS troops. Can't say we are flattered, although there is no doubt their SS get all the dirty jobs.

Everybody always says what a wonderful soldier Jerry is, it's born in him, etc., but when it comes to pure cussed fighting, I don't think the Canadian can be beaten.

Captain James Stewart,
19th Army Field Regiment

Second Division staff now turned their attention to Beveland and the approaches to Walcheren Island. Operation "Vitality I" was launched on the morning of October 24. In the early hours of "a rainy, pitch-black morning, two 'Jock Columns' of Essex Reg't Infantry, 8 Recce Armoured Cars, and Fort Garry tanks" set out for the Beveland Canal. Progress was slow, and when three recce cars and three tanks were knocked out the armoured thrust ended. The next day, a conventional infantry attack with the artillery pouring fire on two crossroads brought complete success. That night "Vitality II," an amphibious assault across the Scheldt, carried out by a brigade of the 52nd (Lowland) Scottish Division, forced the enemy to abandon their new defensive line at the Beveland Canal and conduct a hasty retreat to Walcheren.

One last great effort was demanded of 2nd Division. The Royal Navy was waiting to launch a major amphibious assault on Walcheren and had assembled a large task force to land the 4th Special Service Brigade at Westkappele and Flushing. Surprise was essential, and 2nd Division was ordered to attack across the causeway to Walcheren Island on the eve of the landings. The hope was to focus

German attention to the east while the assault craft moved in. The Calgary Highlanders and later the Régiment de Maisonneuve got men onto the island, but German counterattacks prevented any advance. The Canadians were finally relieved by Scottish troops after the landings had succeeded. Both infantry divisions were now sent to rest areas in Belgium where the citizens of Ghent and other cities waited to take the Canadians into their homes.

Field Marshal Montgomery, who had belatedly recognized the extraordinary sacrifices he had demanded of the Canadians, wrote a letter to Simonds, which was as close to an apology as he could offer:

I think everything you are doing is excellent and your troops are doing wonders under appalling conditions of ground and weather. I doubt if any other troops would do it so well and I am very glad the Canadians are on the business. Please tell your chaps how pleased I am with their good work.

General Guy Simonds with Montgomery (above) and Defence Minister J.L. Ralston (left). Ralston visited Canadian units to obtain firsthand information about the shortage of reinforcements. He returned to Canada convinced that conscripts would have to be sent overseas.

NATIONAL ARCHIVES OF CANADA/PA129125

NATIONAL ARCHIVES OF CANADA/PA138415

CONSCRIPTION

From the plebiscite of 1942 to the summer of 1944, the issue of conscription faded into the background. At home Canadians were fully employed building the weapons and growing the food essential to an Allied victory. The navy and air force were involved in constant action, but there was never a shortage of volunteers for either service, or for the merchant marine, which carried the vital supplies to England. Nor was there any shortfall of army volunteers. By 1944 almost 500,000, including 42,000 NRMA men who decided to volunteer for "General Service," had enlisted. The casualties suffered at Dieppe and in Italy were replaced from the reinforcement pool and there seemed no reason to worry about another conscription crisis.

Unfortunately, the Canadian army had adopted British estimates of casualty rates based on experience in North Africa. In the desert, overall battle casualties had been low and were not concentrated in infantry units. British and Canadian planning for Italy and for Operation "Overlord" severely underestimated the proportion of losses that would occur in the infantry. They also ignored the phenomenon of battle exhaustion, of which most casualties were in the infantry.

After the brilliant successes of D-Day, the fighting in Normandy, like the struggle in Italy, became a battle of attrition. The Allied infantry were required to attack, occupy and hold small parcels of ground under circumstances that fully paralleled the agonies of combat in the First World War. Modern memory has a firm image of "suicide battalions" and long casualty lists in the Great War, but we are not accustomed to thinking of Italy or

NATIONAL ARCHIVES OF CANADA/C87133

1944 was the "decisive year" and a supreme effort was required of everyone especially the men at the "sharp end."

Normandy in these terms. For the infantry, who made up just 15 per cent of the army and suffered 70 per cent of the casualties, the Second World War was much like the western front in 1916.

British and Canadian planners, despite the early lessons of Italy, did not change their manpower allocations for Normandy. The British knew that if the fighting in France was heavy they would have to disband at least two infantry divisions for lack of reinforcements, but they preferred to hope the war would end quickly. By early August 1944 the crisis was at hand and 59 (Staffordshire) Division, which had fought beside the Canadians at Caen, was cannibalized. The Canadians, for whom infantry casualties were running at 76 per cent of the total, were short 2,000 riflemen (the equivalent of four battalions) at the beginning of August and more than 4,000 by the end of the month. Half-strength infantry companies were common.

With only three divisions in northwest Europe, the Canadians could not disband anything. The short-term solution was to remuster artillery, service corps, armoured and engineer troops to infantry. Throughout the late summer of 1944 thousands of these men were given crash courses in infantry weapons and tactics. The new riflemen and some hastily dispatched reinforcements from Canada patched up the holes for September and early October, but the struggle to clear the approaches to Antwerp and the assault on the Gothic Line in Italy quickly exhausted this supply. By mid-October men were stretched to the breaking point. Battle exhaustion casualties were again looming as a serious problem as men recognized that there was "no rest, no leave, no escape." Bitter feelings towards the government and the conscript

Not separatists

We are not Separatists, but let us not be forced to become Separatists. We wish, indeed, to dwell in the same house, but the house must be habitable for all, and I fear that those who agitate in favour of conscription are about to forge the nails which will seal the coffin of National Unity, and perhaps, Confederation.

Maxime Raymond, in the House of Commons

I care more than ever about my country

It is only after having lived abroad for two years that one can feel a national sentiment which I had always considered to be simply vain words. I care now more

than ever about my country, and would like to see it evolve toward greatness. I am neither a nationalist or an imperialist. I know their excesses only too well. In my opinion, Canadians are divided into two large categories: those who think too much of France, and those who think too much of the British Empire. No one ever thinks about the Canadian Dominion any more....

Over the last few days, a single event in Canada has eclipsed all the fury of the war in Europe, at least in the eyes of the Canadian Army. I'm talking about the latest government decision on conscription. It just burns me to read in the press how tragic this event might be for our country. Could it be that we have voluntarily suffered until now, only to have our country fall victim to an issueless, ideological war?... There's only one issue in the spirit of Canadian soldiers, and that is to finish this damned war so we can live in peace. The brotherhood at the front is real, and not at all affected as it is in the press. All races and religions have joined together for a single cause – to obtain peace as soon as possible. These political quarrels will achieve nothing of value.

Lieutenant Jacques Gouin, Royal Canadian Artillery

Second-class citizens

Even when joining the army, French Canadians know that their chances for advancement are slight unless they are English-speaking. Almost all the Canadian High

Command and senior staff officers are English. In war, as in peace, a French Canadian cannot escape the feeling that he is a second-class citizen in his own country.

Editorial, *Le Canada*

A blow to the stomach

General McNaughton said he had quite serious news. That the headquarters staff had advised him that he couldn't get the men. He said it was like a blow to the stomach. He said he had the resignation of the commander in Winnipeg, and that if the commanders across the country began to resign, one by one, the whole military chain of command would run down.

W.L. Mackenzie King

A symbol of domination

Chubby Power, Minister of Defence for Air, resigned because he had campaigned in his Quebec City constituency on the pledge that there would be no conscription.

Conscription is a long way from being necessary at this stage. It is certainly convenient to send the Zombies, but convenience should give way to the national interest. I envisage the prospect of one-third of our population uncooperative, with a deep sense of injury, and being prey to the worst elements among them. And worst of all, hating all other Canadians. Conscription is considered, among French-Canadians, to be a symbol of British domination. To them it means being forced to fight for the "maudit Anglais."

C.G. "Chubby" Power, Minister of Defence for Air

I feel that I am right...

Mackenzie King addressed the House of Commons on the non-confidence vote brought against his government.

If there is anything to which I have devoted my political life, it is to try to promote unity, harmony and amity between the diverse elements of this country. My friends can desert me; they can remove their confidence from me; they can withdraw the trust they have placed in my hands; but never shall I deviate from that line of policy. Whatever may be the consequences, whether loss of prestige, of popularity, of power, I feel that I am right and that a time will come when every man will render me full justice on that score....

W.L. Mackenzie King

army at home were inevitable in this situation and when the Minister of National Defence visited combat units he got an earful of straight talk.

J.L. Ralston had been a much-loved battalion commander in the Great War and his commitment to the well-being of the ordinary soldier never wavered. Back in Ottawa he told the cabinet 15,000 additional trained infantry were needed overseas. The only possible source was the NRMA army. The Prime Minister, fearful of the country again dividing on French-English lines, looked for other solutions. He isolated Ralston from other pro-conscriptionist ministers, then announced that General A.L.G. McNaughton would replace Ralston as Minister of National Defence. McNaughton, "Andy" to many Canadians, tried to use his prestige as Canada's most famous soldier to persuade conscripts to volunteer. He quickly discovered that while the NRMA men would obey orders to serve overseas, no significant number would volunteer. McNaughton was strongly criticized from all sides. Public opinion in English-speaking Canada swung against him. On the morning of November 22 he telephoned the Prime Minister to advise him that the voluntary system would not produce enough men. There was no other solution; the conscripts would have to go overseas.

The Conscription Crisis of 1944 again divided the country along linguistic lines, but since most French Canadians believed that Mackenzie King had done his best to maintain a volunteer system, the attempt to create a new Quebec nationalist party failed. As for the conscripts, they turned out to be well-trained, effective soldiers who helped to win the battles of 1945.

Survivors of U-boat U-744 coming aboard HMCS *St. Catharines*, March 6, 1944.

THE WAR AT SEA

The withdrawal of the wolf-packs from the North Atlantic had been forced on the German navy by the success of Allied escorts and aircraft, but the Germans still possessed hundreds of U-boats. As well, they were building a new type of submarine that was twice the size of the standard U-boat and could reach a speed of eighteen knots even when submerged. A new torpedo with an acoustic homing device was also rushed into production for 1944. The U-boat threat was far from over.

There were important developments on the Allied side as well. The Admiralty changed its convoy cypher, which the Germans had been reading since 1939, and the new system proved to be secure, while Ultra continued to supply details of U-boat movements, often in "real time." On the ocean the biggest change was the gradual replacement of corvettes by the new River-class frigates equipped with modern radar, sonar, High Frequency Direction Finding (HF/DF or Huff Duff) and the Hedgehog, an anti-submarine mortar. RCN frigates also carried twin four-inch guns.

Marc Milner, the Canadian naval historian, suggests that the whole concept of anti-submarine warfare

R. REED/DND/NATIONAL ARCHIVES OF CANADA/PA157782

HMCS *Clayoquot*: Survivors are rescued by HMCS *Fennel* after the *Clayoquot* was sunk by a U-boat off Halifax, December 24, 1944.

changed in 1944. Instead of convoy battles, operations "centred around a response to the movement of U-boat concentrations" reported by Ultra. While close escort groups would continue to shepherd convoys, support groups moved to the battle area to hunt U-boats for as long as was necessary. This helps to account for the fact that of the eighteen U-boats sunk by the RCN in 1944–45, none were caught in North American waters. The Germans concentrated their resources on the approaches to the United Kingdom and made only occasional forays to the western Atlantic.

The Allies continued to sink U-boats while maintaining the security of convoys, and the German navy was crushed when it tried to interfere with the Normandy landings, losing 28 U-boats for just 10 ship sinkings. The only option left to Admiral Dönitz was to operate against merchant shipping in coastal areas where the shallow and wreck-strewn waters might prevent detection. U-boats were re-equipped with *Schnorchel*s which allowed batteries to be recharged under water, limiting the danger of discovery by radar. U-boat captains were told to be patient. Instead of fleeing to deep waters when attacked, they were to "bottom" and wait until the search moved on.

The primary target area was the coast of Great Britain, but the temptation to try the waters off Halifax proved irresistible. U-806 made the first trip, arriving in mid-December. The captain spent a week studying the pattern of traffic before attacking an American Liberty ship on the 21st. Three days later U-806 positioned itself to attack two convoys converging on Halifax. This careful plan was sabotaged by the sudden appearance of three RCN escorts, the frigate HMCS *Kirkland Lake* and the Bangor-class minesweepers *Clayoquot* and *Transcona*. They were conducting a normal anti-submarine patrol in the harbour approaches, but the U-boat believed it had been discovered. A torpedo lashed out at the nearest vessel and *Clayoquot* went down in a matter of minutes. The hunt was quickly organized but U-806 slipped away. It returned to Germany after a four-month cruise, having damaged one merchant ship and sunk a minesweeper. A trivial return for such a sustained effort.

U-806 was barely gone when U-1232 began operations. On January 4 two small merchant ships moving from Sydney to Halifax were sunk. Escort Group 16, composed of the frigates *Antigonish*, *Charlottetown*, *Springhill*, *Stettler* and *Toronto*, was assigned to the hunt while EG 27 reinforced the convoy's escorts.

Escort Group 27 had been formed in October 1944 in anticipation of a renewal of the German U-boat offensive. It was one of seven Royal Canadian Navy "support groups" organized to assist the "close support groups" that actually shepherded the convoys across the Atlantic. The Senior Officer, Acting/Commander St. Clair Balfour, DSC, was typical of the young RCNVR officers so vital to RCN operations. Commissioned in 1939, Balfour served aboard HMCS *St. Laurent* and commanded *Lethbridge*, a Flower-class corvette, before his

appointment as captain of HMCS *Meon*. Assigned to Escort Group 9, *Meon* supported the Normandy invasion and then hunted U-boats in the English Channel, providing experience badly needed at home. By late 1944 all signs pointed to the return of German U-boats to North American coastal waters in the new year.

On January 14, Convoy BC 141 arrived from Boston with a close escort of two minesweepers, *Westmount* and *Nipigon*. EG 27, now consisting of just three ships, *Meon*, *Ettrick* and *Coaticook*, closed with the convoy, which formed a single file to enter Halifax harbour. Torpedoes struck two merchant ships, and the U-boat remained in the area hitting a third ship. *Meon* ordered "adopt scare tactics," which meant all escorts were to fire depth charges. HMCS *Ettrick* dropped shallow-set charges along the wake of a torpedo. As the third depth charge exploded, *Ettrick* crashed into Dobratz's conning tower destroying the attack periscope and electronic gear. U-1232 was now out of action and fled the area to begin the long voyage home. No merchant ships were ever sunk off Halifax again, though HMS *Esquimalt*, a minesweeper, was sunk in April 1945.

The professionalism demonstrated by EG 27 was typical of the performance of the Royal Canadian Navy in the last years of the war. Escort Group 9 (*Saint John*, *Monnow*, *Nene*, *Loch Alvie* and *Port Colborne*) was transferred from Londonderry to northern Scotland in late January 1945 and achieved outstanding results in the new area, including the sinking of U-309 by HMCS *Saint John*. Escort Group 25 added another U-boat kill in February, and EG 26 got one in March. The Royal Canadian Navy had come a long way since 1939.

A standard of life

Admiral Leonard Murray addressing the graduating class at Dalhousie University, Halifax:

The seaman, in his life at sea, has learned three things. First, how to get along with his fellow man; second, the value of teamwork as opposed to backbiting competition; and third, to work with all his might to achieve something worthwhile without consideration for personal reward. I advise you follow his example. Do not struggle for a "standard of living" – empty success – but for a "standard of life" which provides comfort for the soul.

Admiral Leonard Murray, RCN

Afraid of what the future holds

William "Pat" Patterson joined the RCAF as a navigator.

Dear Pat,

I'm growing more and more afraid of what the future holds, both for you and me as individuals, and for others.

Jean Partridge

Dear Jean,

I dreamt that we had a son and he was with me. In my dream he was about three or four years old, and I can remember just how he looked and just how strong were my feelings for him. When I woke I felt that something I wanted very much had been taken from me. In waking, I can build  my defences and keep my subconscious longings from hurting me too much. But at night, they have their way. Some blessed day, my lover, defences will no longer be necessary and we can live again.

Pat

December 6, 1944

We are no longer a virgin crew, sweet, for we got one in yesterday. Someday I'll tell you all about it. I'll tell you all about everything connected with the Air Force once and then hope to forget it. I can see that the life here isn't going to consist of much but flying and sleeping, with the hours irregular to say the least. I'm lucky to have Brownie as a pal because he's just the company I need, and we get on perfectly rooming together.

December 8, 1944

We got our second one today, Paddy froze his face very badly and has gone into hospital for a couple of weeks and they seem doubtful whether he will fly again. It's fine and warm in the cabin, but the boys in the turrets are exposed to the cold, which of course is severe at operational heights....

December 19, 1944

It looks like another early call tomorrow, so this little chicken is going to be in his bed very early. The news of the Germans' Ardennes new offensive makes it look as though we might be busy for quite a while....

December 22, 1944

My Dearest Pet,

We have four trips in now, and but for the winter weather would be a good bit farther on than that. We had a good crack at Jerry yesterday, giving GI Joe a helping hand. There is very little Christmas atmosphere here and it doesn't worry me.... I lie awake at night thinking about a happy life with you and a lifetime of work and happiness to look forward to. Still, I know I'm doing something useful and necessary now, and when it's over I can say I've done my share....

On December 23, 1944, the Lancaster in which "Pat" Patterson was navigator was shot down over the North Sea. All on board were killed.

Every time a gun went off...

I had to march at the rear of a section because I kept falling, tripping up anyone behind me. Our way took us through our gun areas. Every time a gun went off, I fell. If it was some distance away, I stumbled to my knees; if it was close, I fell flat on my face. I had no control over the reaction. Over the next week, I continued to do my job, but continued to fall all over myself when the guns went off.

Rifleman J.L. Wagar, Canadian 3rd Division

Jumpy as a cat

The first time I went in I didn't actually realize how a shell could cut a bunch of fellows up and so on – but I do now. Some of the fellows I know that have been on the wrong end of a terrific shelling are now as jumpy as cats even at our own guns firing. It is only natural that a soldier is one hell of a lot more nervous when he comes out of a shelling than when he went into it.

Lieutenant Reg Roy, Cape Breton Highlanders

It is my painful duty...

CANADIAN PACIFIC
TELEGRAPHS
World Wide Communications

W.D.NEIL, GENERAL MANAGER OF COMMUNICATIONS

WAA21 34/33 2EX GB REPORT DELIVERY

RCAF OTTAWA ONT 24 314A

MISTER H J MORRISON   2609

26 GALLEY AVE TORONTO ONT

M9949 REGRET TO ADVISE THAT YOUR SON R'ONE SIX ONE TWO FOUR FOUR

SERGEANT BRUCE RALPH MORRISON IS REPORTED MISSING AFTER AIR

OPERATIONS OVERSEAS JANUARY TWENTY SECOND STOP LETTER FOLLOWS

RCAF CASUALTIES OFFICER

January 22, 1944
File No. 405S/408/116/P.1
Dear Mrs. Morrison,

Before you receive this letter, you will have had a telegram informing you that your son, Sergeant B.R. Morrison, has been reported missing as a result of air operations.

On the night of 21/22nd January 1944, your son, along with his crew and other members of this Squadron, were engaged in action over enemy territory. Unfortunately his aircraft did not return from this operation. It is the sincere wish of all of us here that he is safe.

Your son was popular with this Squadron, and was an excellent air gunner. He is greatly missed by his comrades and his loss is regretted by all....

R.J. Lane, Wing Commander,
Commanding No. 405 Squadron, RCAF

January 26, 1944
Dear Mr. Morrison,

It is my painful duty to confirm the telegram recently received which informed you that your son, Sergeant Bruce Ralph Morrison, is reported missing on active service....

Advice has been received from the Royal Canadian Air Force Casualties Officer, Overseas, that your son was a member of the crew of an aircraft which failed to return to its base after a bombing raid over Magdeburg, Germany....There were two other members of the Royal Canadian Air Force in the crew and they also have been reported missing. Since you may wish to know their names and next of kin, we are listing them below:...

W.R. Gunn, Squadron Leader,
RCAF Casualties Officer for Chief of the Air Staff

February 9, 1944
Dear Mother,

I've just got back from leave and found your letter ... also an air letter from Hazel written on the 24th in which she said that Bruce had been reported missing. It was one of the worst shocks I've had for a long time and I hardly know what to say – it will be very hard on you and everyone at home – the best thing is just to keep hoping that he has landed safely and is in enemy hands or trying to get back. There's a very good chance that he is alright and you'll get word through the Red Cross....

Please don't worry about me. I have every confidence in the rest of the crew and we are flying in the best machines with the best of equipment, and I'm sure of coming through this....

Write again soon and give me all the news. I won't say don't worry about Bruce – you will – but keep chins up and hope for the best.

Love, Ossie

March 6, 1944
Dear Mr. Morrison,

It is my painful duty to confirm the telegram recently received by you which informed you that your son, Warrant Officer Second Class Oscar Langdon Morrison is reported missing on Active Service.

Advice has been received from the Royal Canadian Air Force Casualties Officer. Overseas, that your son was a member of the crew of an aircraft which failed to return to its base after a bombing raid over Leipzig, Germany, on the night of February 19th....

There were five other members of the Royal Canadian Air Force in the crew and they also have been reported missing. Since you may wish to know their names and next of kin we are listing them below:...

W.R. Gunn, Squadron Leader

March 27, 1944
Dear Mr. Morrison,

Confirming my telegram of recent date, I regret to inform you that the Royal Canadian Air Force Casualties Officer, Overseas, has advised me that a report has been received from the International Red

ADDRESS REPLY TO:
The Secretary,
Department of National Defence for Air,
OTTAWA,   Canada.

OUR FILE 1040-K-2
REF. YOUR:
DATED:

ROYAL CANADIAN AIR FORCE

OTTAWA, Canada, 27th March,

Mr. H.J. Morrison,
26 Galley Avenue,
Toronto, Ontario.

Cross Society concerning your son, Sergeant Bruce Ralph Morrison, previously reported missing on Active Service.

Oscar (left) and Bruce Morrison.

The report quotes German information which states that your son lost his life on January 21st, 1944, but does not contain any further particulars. The International Red Cross Society is making every effort to obtain the location of your son's grave. However, I feel sure you will appreciate the difficulties attendant upon securing additional details....

W.R. Gunn, Squadron Leader

April 22, 1944
Dear Mr. Morrison,
Further to my letter of March 27, I wish to inform you that although no additional news has been received regarding your son, Sergeant Bruce Ralph Morrison, a report regarding certain occupants of the aircraft has been received from the International Red Cross Committee.

This report, quoting German Information, states Flying Officer Speyer, Royal Canadian Air Force, and Sergeant Stevens of the Royal Air Force, lost their lives on January 21st, 1944. As they were members of your son's crew, it was felt that you would wish to know of this report.

In conveying this information to you, please accept my sympathy with you in your continued anxiety, and you may rest assured that any further news received will be at once forwarded.

L.J. Gratton-Smith, RCAF Casualty
Officer for Chief of the Air Staff

September 8, 1944
Dear Mr. Morrison,
I have heard with deep regret that your son, Sergeant Bruce Ralph Morrison, is now for official purposes presumed to have died on Active Service Overseas on Janu-

ary 21st, 1944. I wish to offer you and the members of your family my sincere and heartfelt sympathy.

It is most lamentable that a promising career should be thus terminated and I would like you to know that his loss is greatly deplored by all those with whom your son was serving.

Robert Leckie, Air Marshal, Chief of the Air Staff

February 6, 1945
Dear Mrs. Morrison,
Thank you for the completion and return of our form P.64.

We have on file your son's will dated the 17th of April, 1942, wherein you are named sole beneficiary and appointed sole executrix of his estate....

G.S. Gilroy, Flight Lieutenant, Director of Estates

Dear Mrs. Morrison,
Prior to this time you will have received from the Treasury Office a cheque payable to your order in the amount of $17.19.

This was the total held at credit to your son's Service estate, being made up as shown in the following statement:

Cash in effects	$1.77
Balance in pay account	3.04
Balance withdrawn from Canadian Bank of Commerce, Wright & Roncesvalles Branch, Toronto	12.38
	$17.19

You are entitled to this money as the sole beneficiary named in your son's Will....

G.S. Gilroy for L.M. Firth, Colonel, Director of Estates

October 2, 1945
Dear Mrs. Morrison,
You are advised to forward the War Savings Certificates to the Registrar of War Savings Certificates ... with your instructions as to whether you wish them to be redeemed or transferred to your name.

Your son's personal effects have now been received from overseas and will go forward to you within the next few days in a carton by express prepaid....

C.Y. Swanton, Director of Accounts

PART VI

VICTORY

Celebrating liberation at Harderwijk in the Netherlands,
April 18, 1945.

THE YEAR OF VICTORY, 1945, DID NOT BEGIN auspiciously for the Allies in northwest Europe. Today we know that the total defeat of the Nazi war machine was only four months away, but matters seemed very different at the time. The German army's Ardennes offensive, the famous Battle of the Bulge, was still raging as 1944 came to a close and on New Year's Eve the enemy launched yet another offensive, Operation "Norwind." Aimed at the extended southern flank of the Allied line, "Norwind" was designed to recapture Strasbourg and force Patton's Third U.S. Army to turn away from the Bulge.

On New Year's Day the Luftwaffe, without warning, launched more than a thousand sorties against ground targets, particularly airfields. More than three hundred aircraft, including a number from RCAF squadrons, were destroyed. With hindsight it is clear that German losses in all of these battles squandered reserves that were badly needed for the defence of Germany, but as the deadline for the renewal of the Allied offensive approached, no end to the war in Europe could be foreseen.

Such a prospect, if it included the kind of casualties the Allies had sustained in the last months of 1944, was truly frightening. The manpower crisis, which had forced the Canadians to draw upon 16,000 men conscripted for service in Canada only, was equally serious in the American and British armies. On January 12 the British war cabinet suggested for the first time that the war might not end in 1945, and a new program to find 250,000 more men for the army was set in motion. Eisenhower was combing U.S. Army service and communication units and transferring men from the air force to reinforce ground combat units. There were no more trained divisions back in the United States, so "Ike" would continue to improvise.

One partial solution to the man-

power problem was to transfer more troops from Italy to northwest Europe. When the Joint Chiefs of Staff met at Malta in early February they agreed to send five divisions, including 1st and 5th Canadian, to strengthen Montgomery's army group. The move north began in February, and by the end of the month I Canadian Corps was reunited with First Canadian Army.

Flight-Lieutenant Richard Audet shot down five German aircraft on a single day, December 29, 1944. He was killed in action on March 3, 1945, shot down by enemy flak.

Allied plans for 1945 called for the elimination of German forces west of the Rhine in a series of converging attacks. These operations were seen as a prelude to the main assault on Fortress Germany, the crossing of the Rhine. The first major offensive of the new year, Operation "Veritable," was to be carried out by Lieutenant-General Harry Crerar's First Canadian Army. Montgomery was no admirer of the quiet, nationalistic Canadian commander, but he did not question the competence of Crerar's staff officers, engineers and support

The aftermath of the "Hangover Raids," January 1, 1945. No. 2 TAF lost 127 aircraft destroyed and 133 damaged, but Luftwaffe losses of more than 300 aircraft and 241 pilots were far more serious.

Stalin, Roosevelt and Churchill pictured at their first meeting in Teheran, November 1944.

troops. First Canadian Army Headquarters was well able to manage the 340,00 men and 10,000 tons of supplies a day required to sustain them.

The human costs of "Veritable" would be lowered if the Soviet army mounted a winter offensive in the east. On January 6, 1945, Churchill asked Stalin "whether we count on a major Russian offensive on the Vistula front or elsewhere during January." On January 12 the Red Army launched a massive attack striking at exactly the point Hitler insisted was the least likely. By February 2 Soviet spearheads were within sixty miles of Berlin and more than one million German soldiers had been killed, wounded or taken prisoner.

These tremendous Soviet victories eased the burden on the Allied armies while greatly increasing the pressure on Churchill and Roosevelt to accept Soviet plans for re-shaping Eastern and Central Europe. When the "Big Three" leaders met at Yalta in the Crimea for the conference which was to determine the fate of Poland, Operation "Veritable" was less than a week old and was not going very well. The contrast between the spectacular Soviet victories and Allied military reverses helped to create an atmosphere in which Soviet demands required Allied concessions.

The growing rift between the Soviet Union and the western democracies was unfortunately not the only problem confronting the Allies. Anglo-American relations were increasingly marred by conflict among the generals as the British continued to press for a single offensive in the north to be commanded by Montgomery. The British and Canadians were not strong enough to carry this out by themselves so Montgomery sought control of large American forces. Eisenhower, ever anxious to find a workable compromise, had agreed to "loan" Montgomery General Bill Simpson's U.S. Ninth Army and to give operations in the north priority, but he refused to call off a secondary offensive by American troops south of the Ruhr.

As with most compromises no one was satisfied. Generals Bradley and Patton accused Eisenhower of giving in to the British while Montgomery raged against Eisenhower's failure to accept his plan in its entirety. The endless disputes were doing enormous damage to British–U.S. relations and may have influenced Roosevelt's growing interest in direct discussions with the Soviet Union. Churchill's ability to influence the direction of the war and the character of the peace were undermined by his failure to recognize that the Americans were no longer willing to accept British strategic direction of the war.

"VERITABLE"

The plan for "Veritable" had originally called for rapid penetration of the Siegfried Line. It was hoped that the ground would still be frozen, allowing armoured units to be deployed in the early stages. A second assumption was that U.S. Ninth Army, a powerful force of twelve divisions under General Simpson, would begin its part in the Rhineland battle, Operation "Grenade," within forty-eight hours of "Veritable." When the offensive began on February 8 the ground had thawed and the Rhine dikes had been cut, flooding the northern flank. To the south the Germans had released the waters of the Roer dams, turning the river the Americans had to cross into a raging torrent. "Grenade" was postponed for nearly two weeks!

"Veritable" began as a primarily British battle with English, Scottish and Welsh divisions attacking through

199

the Reichswald forest while 3rd Canadian Division, now known as the "Water Rats," cleared the flooded Rhine flank in Buffalo amphibious vehicles. Second Canadian Division captured Wyler to open a supply route for the British, but II Canadian Corps did not take the lead until the exhausted divisions of British XXX Corps had lost momentum.

"Veritable" became a bitter, costly struggle against a well-entrenched enemy assisted by enormous fire power, including artillery firing from the east side of the Rhine. The weather was consistently awful and the tactical air force was frequently grounded. Tanks quickly bogged down in the saturated ground and everyone was cold and wet. Inevitably, combat stress again became a serious problem. The 53rd Welsh Division suffered 3,000 casualties in the Reichswald and more than 500 were due to battle exhaustion. The Canadian divisions soon faced a similar crisis. The Corps psychiatrists explained that many veterans were now "emotionally depleted," and large numbers who had been previously wounded or treated for battle exhaustion could not, under any circumstances, be returned to their unit.

The Allied armies demanded a great deal of their combat troops. Their battle doctrine called for systematic attacks well supported by artillery, and while it was usually possible to suppress enemy fire during the advance, once on

NATIONAL ARCHIVES OF CANADA/C12934

The Reichswald or State Forest begins close to the German–Dutch border. In 1945 a system of fixed defences extended across the northern edge, but the forest itself was the main barrier.

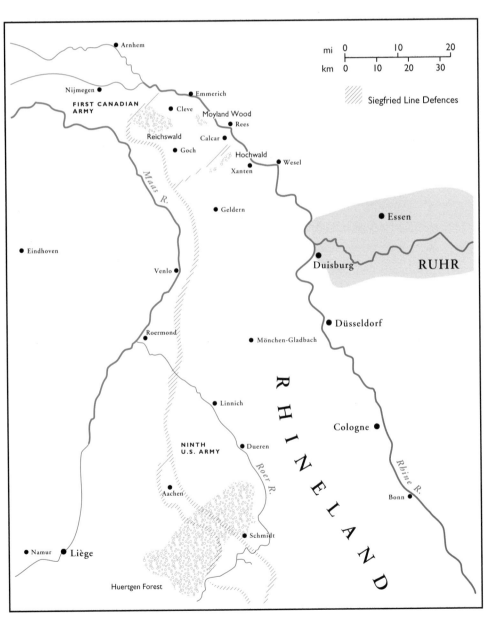

The Rhineland Campaign.
February–March 1945.

200

Cleve battlefront area showing trench system and craters in Siegfried Line defences. Middelaar vicinity February 14, 1945. The Siegfried Line, built before the outbreak of war, was dismantled to create the "Atlantic Wall" in 1943–44. These anti-tank ditches were hastily dug in the winter of 1944–45, linking some of the remaining fortifications.

the objective the real trouble began. The enemy invariably hit back with accurate preregistered fire, striking the Allied troops as they mopped up. Then came the first counterattacks, small groups of German infantry led by powerful tanks or self-propelled guns.

In theory, infantry battalions were to have their own six-pounder anti-tank guns in position with the heavier guns of the divisional anti-tank regiment tied in to the defence. Tanks of the supporting armoured squadron were to help out in the initial stages, but their Shermans were highly vulnerable and usually

> Harry Crerar was always informed, because he made constant flights over the battlefield in a small observation aircraft. Those flights were dangerous. But Crerar, knowing he was sending men to their death, did not hesitate to expose himself to enemy fire.
>
> Lieutenant-General Brian Horrocks

withdrew as soon as anti-tank defences were organized. From then on it was up to riflemen in slit trenches, the mortar platoon, and above all the FOO, or Forward Observation Officer, from the artillery field regiment to defend the battalion fortress.

The enemy's most lethal weapons, the mortar and the Nebelwerfer, continued to account for 70 per cent of all Allied casualties, but German technical superiority in the design of light machine guns, armoured fighting vehicles, and anti-tank guns, including the fearsome "88," had a profound effect on the battle-

The Germans breached dikes and dams to impede the Allied advance. The photos on the facing page show (top) Buffaloes loaded with men of the North Shore Regiment, near Nijmegen, February 8, 1945, and 20th Field Company troops of the Royal Canadian Engineers operating a ferry service near Cleve, February 23. Third Infantry Division, the "Water Rats," had employed Buffaloes in the Scheldt. Now these amphibious vehicles were used to reach enemy strong-points surrounded by flood waters.

field. The Allies' numerical superiority and dominance of the air could not compensate for marked inferiority in the weaponry of close combat.

The British and Canadian armies recognized this problem in 1942, and by early 1943 operational research teams were examining all aspects of the land battle. Operational research (OR) began as the scientific study of tactics and weaponry in RAF Fighter Command. OR also played a crucial role in improving Britain's anti-aircraft defences and in the offensive against the U-boat. The army, always at the bottom of priority lists, finally began to expand its involvement in OR to maximize the effect of new weapons such as the PIAT (Projector Infantry Anti-Tank), the 6- and 17-pounder anti-tank guns, and the new generation of tanks. Work on armoured fighting vehicles and anti-tank guns was begun by a remarkable Canadian physiologist, Omand Solandt. Solandt, who had been at Cambridge when war broke out, initially joined the Medical Research Council's blood transfusion unit. Reports from North Africa about excessive crew fatigue in British tanks led the Royal Armoured Corps to seek scientific help, and Solandt established a physiological lab to study the human factor in armoured warfare. He also played a key role in the development of the 17-pounder anti-tank gun and its use in "Firefly" Sherman tanks.

The work of army operational research touched on dozens of battlefield problems. These were not the men who designed new weapons; their job was to get the most out of what was available. Work on improving gun accuracy had been OR's priority before Operation "Overlord," but once the troops were ashore the most urgent

problem became locating and destroying enemy mortars. Army scientists had long been interested in the uses of radar, and two new units, 1st Canadian and 100th British Radar batteries, were formed. For "Veritable" both were used with great success to locate German mortar positions.

Experiments with radar did not end there. The Operational Research section attached to Montgomery's 21st Army Group had studied the problem of employing bombers close to the front lines in Normandy. The Rhineland battle would be fought in winter under cloudy skies, so a new method of improving bombing accuracy was needed. OR officers supervised the use of Mobile Radar Control Posts which permitted medium bombers to fix their position in relation to fluid battle lines. The battles of February and March were not marred by the "short bombings" which had been a problem during the Normandy campaign.

Operational research made a significant contribution to solving some battlefield problems, but German technical superiority in weaponry was never overcome. Scientists could help to make the soldier's job a little easier, but the essential task was still to occupy and hold ground and ultimately no one but infantry could accomplish that goal.

The Canadians re-entered combat on February 15 when 3rd Division took over the flank from 15th Scottish Division. Their first task was to clear towards Louisendorf and occupy the wooded area west of the village of Moyland. The Scots had suffered dreadful casualties near Moyland in what they described as their "worst experiences since the campaign began." Seventh Canadian Brigade, which took over the task, soon agreed. The enemy held the Moyland–Calcar sector in strength and were supported by artillery firing from the east bank of the Rhine.

The Regina Rifles made several attempts to occupy the woods, taking more than a hundred casualties. However, the enemy was able to reinforce the area and there was no way one battalion could rout well-dug-in paratroops supported by unlimited artillery. The Canadian Scottish also received rough handling and the interven-

Canadians drive through the flooded streets of Kranenburg, near Cleve. Supplying II Canadian Corps in the last stage of "Veritable" was a major challenge to the Royal Canadian Army Service Corps.

tion of the Fort Garry Horse could not prevent further heavy losses, including fifty-three men taken prisoner. General Simonds was unhappy with the way Major-General Dan Spry handled the battle, but for the moment it was Brigadier Jock Spragge who was replaced. Lieutenant-Colonel A.S. Gregory, the calm, tireless CO of the Reginas, took over the brigade and mounted a carefully coordinated attack using divisional mortars and artillery to blast the area sector by sector. The Camerons of Ottawa hosed the woods with their heavy machine guns, before the Royal Winnipeg Rifles, with Sherbrooke tanks and "Wasp" flamethrowers, used real fire and movement to clear the woods.

KEN BELL/DND/NATIONAL ARCHIVES OF CANADA/PA145762

Seventh Canadian Brigade suffered 485 casualties in its six-day encounter with 6 Para Division.

While the battle for Moyland raged, 2nd Division took over the Louisendorf sector and started an advance towards Calcar Ridge. Fourth Brigade led off, reaching the Goch–Calcar road. Battle groups from Panzer Lehr and 116th Panzer divisions mounted immediate counterattacks, and another bitterly fought struggle erupted. The Essex Scottish and Royal Hamilton Light Infantry dug in and their FOOs called down defensive fire,

Lance Corporal R.B. Wrightman of the Provost Corps looking at signs, Calcar, Germany, February 26, 1945.

but with nightfall the Essex were overrun, as was "C" Company of the Rileys. Lieutenant-Colonel Denis Whitaker of the RHLI organized his own counterattack and Brigadier Cabeldu sent the Royal Regiment and two companies of the Queen's Own Cameron Highlanders to restore the Essex position. The next day further attacks were beaten off at heavy cost to the enemy. Canadian losses were also high with the casualty toll reaching four hundred men.

The battle for the Goch–Calcar road provides a good case study of both Allied and German battle doctrines in 1945. Second Division used a rolling barrage of 450 guns to get 4th Brigade onto its objectives. The assault companies were brought forward in Kangaroo armoured personnel carriers. The reserve companies moved up quickly to help form battalion fortresses. A limited objective was taken at relatively light cost. German doctrine called for immediate counterattacks, and battle groups composed of tanks or self-propelled guns supported by infantry rushed to overwhelm the defenders. As darkness fell, Canadian armour, rigidly following a doctrine practised throughout 21st Army Group, withdrew; anti-tank defence now depended on battalion 6-pounders and the 2nd Anti-Tank Regiment RCA. Fortunately, 18th Battery was equipped with 17-pounders, which were highly effective against all German armour. This battery alone destroyed seven German Panthers. Allied methods, however costly to the infantry, were successful because the enemy's mobile reserves were used up in costly counterattacks. The German doctrine "to strike the enemy before he can improve his position" may have been sensible when the Wehrmacht was winning, but in 1945 it was a disastrous policy.

"Veritable" came to an end on February 22 but the next night General Simpson gambled on an assault crossing of the Roer before the flood waters had fully receded. The attack was made without a preliminary artillery barrage. Within twenty-four hours Ninth Army had twenty-eight battalions across the river. There were only two German divisions left in the south and both were quickly destroyed. On the 25th Simpson reported that "there was not much in front of Ninth Army." Montgomery urged

Simpson to strike for the Rhine and then turn north to Wesel, trapping the enemy on the west bank. Rapid success would depend upon a renewal of the Canadian and British offensive to prevent the Germans from shifting resources to check the American advance.

"BLOCKBUSTER"

The Canadians launched Operation "Blockbuster" on February 26 in a series of well-executed attacks that secured the Calcar ridge. Sixth Brigade led off. The Fusiliers Mont-Royal, in the centre, leaned into the barrage and were quickly on their objective, "taking a heavy toll of the enemy." The South Sasks, on the left, attacked the "pimple" at the peak of the ridge and with the support of Sherbrooke tanks crushed an enemy counterattack; "all who survived were taken prisoner." The Camerons encountered soft ground and mines before finding an indirect route to their objective. Here a ferocious battle erupted as successive counterattacks were turned back. Fifth Brigade had been equally successful, with the Black Watch, fully recovered from the effects of the Scheldt, especially effective.

In 3rd Division's sector the countryside was open and flat with each village and farmstead turned into a

Churchill, on a visit to the Canadians in March 1945, is seen with (left to right) General Crerar, Field Marshal Alan Brooke, General Simonds and Field Marshal Montgomery. Churchill had insisted on being present for the assault across the Rhine and took the opportunity to meet with British and Canadian troops.

miniature fortress by the Germans. The artillery could suppress enemy fire during the advance, but good infantry–tank cooperation was required to clear the strongpoints. Sergeant Aubrey Cosens of the Queen's Own Rifles won the Victoria Cross for his courage and skill at Mooshof and there were many other heroes that day. At Keppeln the North Shores encountered especially strong resistance, which required a new set-piece attack. The delay jeopardized the advance of the Chaudières, who described the fighting south of Keppeln as among the most difficult encountered in the war. Tanks of the 1st Hussars were crucial to the success of these small battles. Military historians who criticize the Allies for failing to develop good infantry–tank cooperation would do well to examine the role played by 2nd Canadian Armoured Brigade in the Rhineland.

Fourth Canadian Armoured Division entered the bat-

tle in the late afternoon. Brigadier Robert Moncel's "Tiger Force" captured the high ground at Todtenhügel. "Smith Force" took the next bound, reaching Katzen-Berg despite darkness and scattered opposition. It had been a superb day for 4th Division, and 9th Brigade was equally effective in the fight for Üdem. The 116th Panzer Division was forced to give up vital ground and five hundred prisoners.

The same night, 4th Division's "Lion Group" (South Alberta Regiment, Algonquins) set out for the rounded hill, Point 73, which dominates the western end of the "Hochwald Gap." Simonds and 4th Division's GOC, Major-General Chris Vokes, must have believed German resistance had been broken, for they overruled the CO of the South Albertas, who thought a night advance deep into enemy territory was unwise. At first all went well as one part of "Lion Group" reached the Goch–Xanten rail-

WESTERN CANADA PICTORIAL INDEX/UNIVERSITY OF WINNIPEG

After the Germans withdrew to the "Wesel Pocket," the Canadians were ordered to capture Xanten and Veen. Fourth Armoured Division attacked Veen, "a miniature fortress," in a four-day battle.

J.S. SMITH/DND/NATIONAL ARCHIVES OF CANADA/PA113677

The South Alberta Regiment, 4th Armoured Division's armoured reconnaissance regiment, provided close support to the infantry battalions. At Veen the SAR and the Argylls began the attack, but tanks of the British Columbia Regiment and additional infantry from the "Lincs" were required to finish the job.

way line, but the Germans quickly concentrated all available resources against this isolated spearhead, and thus began the bloody struggle for the Hochwald Gap.

To the senior commanders, these actions, which lasted from February 28 to March 3, may have been viewed as part of a coordinated offensive, but this was not apparent to anyone at the sharp end. The reality is that no armoured unit, least of all a Sherman-equipped armoured brigade, could lead advances unless enemy anti-tank guns had been overcome. In the Hochwald Gap 4th Armoured Division was asked to attack an enemy which was being steadily reinforced and supported by numerous artillery and anti-tank gun batteries. The Argylls and Lincs were quickly pinned down by fire of "unbelievable intensity." Shortly before midnight

KEN BELL/DND/NATIONAL ARCHIVES OF CANADA/PA138399

Major-General Bruce Matthews, a militia "gunner" who never took a staff course, became CRA (Commander Royal Artillery) of 1st Division and then II Corps. A brilliant soldier, he took command of 2nd Canadian Infantry Division in November 1944 and led it for the rest of the war.

the Grenadier Guards and British Columbia Regiment were sent forward. Fourth Armoured Brigade's war diary reported "the enemy guns took such a heavy toll, movement became impossible."

To the north, 2nd Division had begun a second advance into the Hochwald. The Calgaries broke through the Schlieffen Line, but once in the forest the brigade was struck by the same heavy artillery fire that had stopped "Lion Group." Simonds now committed everything he had. Fourth Brigade advanced into the northern part of the forest led by the Essex Scottish. It was here that Major Fred Tilston won his Victoria Cross.

South of the Gap the Chaudières led 8th Brigade into the Tuschen Wald while 4th Division and 6th Brigade made a new attempt to advance. On the morning of March 2 three Canadian

and three British divisions were inching forward, taking and inflicting heavy casualties. The impact of the American advance was first felt on the British front where 3rd British Division and the 6th Guards Tank Brigade had been fighting for every foot of ground. Suddenly they found the enemy gone. The Germans had withdrawn to a new and hastily improvised position called "the Wesel Pocket."

The Canadian role in the reduction of this last position west of the Rhine was centred on the capture of Xanten. Major-General Bruce Matthews was determined to control the Xanten battle and to this end he planned an all-arms operation built around an elaborate fire plan. Xanten, already heavily bombed, was blasted by corps and divisional artillery before 4th Brigade advanced on either side of the main road. Fifth Brigade delivered the final blow, advancing to Birten before the retreating enemy blew the last bridge at Wesel.

Hitler had devoted enormous resources to the defence of the Rhineland because defeat would expose Germany's industrial heartland, the Ruhr, to direct attack. The month-long battle had resulted in a major Allied victory but at an enormous cost in human suffering.

DRESDEN

From November 1943 to March 1944 Bomber Command fought its longest and most difficult battle of the war. After Hamburg, Air Marshal Harris was given complete freedom to send his force to attack Berlin and other important German cities. He mounted thirty-two major raids, sixteen on Berlin, in this four-month period. Harris had told Churchill that "we can wreck Berlin from end to end if the U.S.A.A.F. will come into it. It will cost, between us, 400–500 aircraft. It will cost Germany the war." Churchill was not persuaded the war could be won

From the summer of 1944 to the end of the war, Bomber Command flew a number of daylight raids on oil and other specific targets. Daylight raids proved no more precise than night operations despite the myths about American "precision" bombing.

by bombing but with "Overlord" still months away the bomber remained the only weapon available to carry the war to Germany.

Official approval for this phase of the area-bombing offensive was given without reservation but the air ministry's public relations officers and government spokesmen were reluctant to acknowledge that the purpose of Bomber Command was, in the words of Sir Arthur Harris, "the destruction of German cities, the killing of German workers and the disruption of civilized community life throughout Germany."

Official hypocrisy about the consequences of bombing greatly disturbed Harris, who told the air ministry, "Our crews know what the real aim of the attack is. When they read what the public are told about it, they are bound to think (and do think) that the authorities are ashamed of area bombing." Harris greatly underestimated the public's ability to understand both the reality and necessity of targeting German cities. In Canada the Gallup Poll reported that between 60 and 70 per cent of English-speaking Canadians approved of bombing Germany's civilian population, and there was equally strong support in the United States and the United Kingdom.

The winter offensive against Berlin and other cities ended in March when Bomber Command was placed under General Eisenhower to provide direct support for the invasion. Losses to bomber crews had been heavy, but the Luftwaffe had been virtually destroyed, enormous resources had been diverted to home defence and Berlin was in ruins.

The heavy bombers played a major role in blasting through German defences in Normandy and provided direct support to the Canadians at the Channel ports and Walcheren, but after August 1944 the RAF again turned its energies towards the German war economy. Both Bomber Command and the U.S. 8th Air Force were ordered to concentrate "on the enemy petroleum industry and oil supplies," but attacks continued to be made "on the industrial production of large cities and the spirit of their inhabitants," when conditions were not suitable for oil targets.

Nuremburg, the scene of prewar Nazi rallies, was successfully bombed in early January, and 645 Lancasters, including those of 6 Group, RCAF, struck a heavy blow at Munich a week later. Stuttgart was attacked by 608 aircraft at the end of the month. With German resistance stiffening everywhere, nightly attacks on German transportation and supply centres were ordered.

With hindsight it is clear that the ferocious German defence of the west bank of the Rhine, in response to Operations "Veritable" and "Grenade," was a last-ditch stand. This was not at all evident to Churchill, Eisenhower or Harris in January or February 1944. Churchill believed Bomber Command could play a crucial role in forcing the final collapse of German resistance, and he pressed for the implementation of Operation "Thunderclap," a series of heavy raids on Berlin, Dresden, Leipzig and Chemnitz, cities that were vital supply centres for the German armies on the eastern front.

"Thunderclap" began on the night of February 13, 1945, hours before the Canadian army began the desperate battle for Moyland Wood and the Calcar ridge. To the men in the Rhineland the war seemed far from over. They knew nothing of the horrible firestorm created in the city of Dresden that night, but if they had known, the question they would have asked was not, "Why was Dresden bombed?" but "Why does the German soldier

The badly damaged Zweinger Art Galleries in Dresden, photographed just after the war. Much of Dresden was destroyed and there were heavy civilian casualties.

> ### *No block escaped damage*
>
> *Stories picked up by* The Times *from the Swedish press describe Berlin in the late days of the war.*
>
> There is no longer any block of buildings in Berlin that has escaped damage, says the Berlin correspondent of *Dagens Nyhter* ... after three days virtual suspension of communications....
>
> Fires so large and numerous that it takes several days to put them out, and many persons are buried in cellars; but life still goes on, although in a very primitive form....
>
> Describing his walk home [the Berlin correspondent of *Allehandra*] says he spent a full hour wandering past blocks where the fires were still burning and through streets where the pavements were encumbered with mountains of furniture and household goods.... Even for those who lived through the catastrophic Berlin days around November 23rd, the impressions of the bomb-storm then pale before what we have experienced in these days.

fight with such fury in a hopeless cause while his country is being destroyed?"

After Dresden, Bomber Command continued to strike at urban targets in Germany as part of the overall battle. On March 28, six weeks after the raid on Dresden, Churchill decided "the moment had come" to halt the bombing of towns because Germany was in a state of collapse and it was not a good idea "to come into control of a completely ruined land." This sensible decision, based on the situation that existed at the end of March, included a gratuitous comment questioning the destruction of Dresden which he had urged two months before. Historians are not the only ones who employ hindsight.

The Nazi war machine had built an army on a scale that the British Commonwealth and the United States could not match. If the Allies were to carry the war to Germany before 1945 only their air forces could do it. They were not always successful and casualties were high but it is difficult to imagine how the war could have been won without them.

CROSSING THE RHINE

Field Marshal Montgomery's operation to cross the Rhine began on the night of March 23, 1945. Operation "Plunder" – a classic set-piece attack – opened with heavy air strikes and a crushing artillery bombardment.

While it was still dark, elements of four British and American divisions, plus a commando brigade, crossed five hundred yards of swift water. Three bridgeheads were established and duplex-drive amphibious tanks were probing enemy positions by first light. The second phase of the Rhine crossing – known as Operation "Varsity" – was under way.

By employing heavy artillery fire, the German army had turned the Anglo-Canadian offensive on the west bank of the Rhine into a battle of attrition. Much of that fire came from positions in the forested hills overlooking the valley. Montgomery proposed to avoid a similar encounter on the east bank by using two airborne divisions to capture enemy artillery before it could harass the landings. The tactical use of airborne forces meant that parachute battalions would jump in daylight from low altitudes and move immediately into action from their drop zone. Glider-borne troops would also land close to enemy gun positions. First Canadian Parachute Battalion played a vital role in the enterprise and in destroying enemy forces in a wooded area along the Wesel–Emmerich road.

A vast armada of 10,000 aircraft stretched for hundreds of miles across the sky and reached the Rhine in

KEN BELL/DND/NATIONAL ARCHIVES OF CANADA/PA145730

Patrol of the Queen's Own Cameron Highlanders of Canada entering a house near the south bank of the Rhine River,

DND/PL42765

Operation "Varsity," the airborne landing across the Rhine, involved 1,589 aircraft and 1,337 gliders.

waves. The American C-47 Dakotas that carried the Canadians faced intense flak and machine-gun fire and the men were widely scattered. "C" Company was the first to jump and it lost all of its officers. Two non-commissioned officers took charge of the small group that hit the drop zone and a subsequent attack on enemy machine-gun crews at the edge of the forest secured the area.

Another company landed a mile to the east, but reached the drop zone in thirty minutes. Its objective – a group of houses that would become battalion headquarters – was taken after Company Sergeant-Major George Green led a house-to-house assault. A second CSM, John Kemp, led a company against a fortified farm. His men formed up at the edge of the farm and moved forward under Bren gun fire. They fired as they went and overran the bunkers and buildings.

Gliders approaching the drop zone drew mortar and artillery fire that inflicted heavy casualties. Men of the field ambulance section, who had dropped with the first wave, rescued

(ABOVE) B.J. GLOSTER/DND/NATIONAL ARCHIVES OF CANADA/PA113687 (BELOW) D.I. GRANT/DND/NATIONAL ARCHIVES OF CANADA/PA134435

glider pilots and tended to the wounded. Corporal George Topham, a medical orderly, saw two of his comrades fall as they tried to save another soldier. He ran to one of the wounded men and administered first aid. "As he worked on the wounded man, he was himself shot through the nose," notes his Victoria Cross citation. "In spite of severe bleeding and intense pain he never faltered in his task. Having completed immediate first aid, he carried the wounded man steadily and slowly back through continuous fire to the shelter of the woods." Corporal

Guardsman D.F. Napier of the 22nd Canadian Armoured Regiment (Canadian Grenadier Guards) writing home in a dug-out under his tank, near Emmerich. His cap badge and shoulder flash have been obliterated by the censor.

The security of my tank

Foot soldiers and tank crews differed on the relative advantages of their occupations. Some infantry men did not relish the idea of being trapped in a blazing tank with exploding ammunition, but tank men often regarded their machines with affection and named them after their wives or girlfriends.

I was glad of the security of my tank. In the Hochwald, in a minefield, there were a lot of wounded foot soldiers lying on the ground. Even with my earphones on I could hear them shouting, "Stretcher-bearer! Stretcher-bearer!" These guys screaming... you don't forget that.

Trooper Al LaRose, Sherbrooke Fusiliers

Platoon of the Cameron Highlanders of Ottawa, Rhine crossing, March 26, 1945. The Camerons of Ottawa, 3rd Division's machine gun battalion, fought the war dispersed in platoons supporting the infantry.

Topham continued to seek out and rescue the wounded. After a carrier transporting casualties was hit and ablaze, he risked his life again by bringing injured men to safety. His actions earned him the VC, and the eternal gratitude of the battalion.

By late afternoon the leading elements on the 15th Scottish Division reached the embattled paratroops. The Germans counterattacked the airborne bridgehead all day, but the link-up went according to plan because the

landings were within range of Allied artillery and ground troops were close by.

The bridgehead expanded rapidly and Montgomery was ready to move east. He had already exhorted his troops with the message, "Having crossed the Rhine we will crack about in the plains of northern Germany, chasing the enemy from pillar to post." The soldiers and airmen had overcome the last natural defensive barrier shielding Hitler's Reich. It could only be a matter of weeks before the war in Europe ended.

(Facing page) Blackfriars Bridge, the pontoon bridge across the Rhine at Rees, Germany, and (below) the Rhine town of Emmerich under mortar and Typhoon fire. Both photos were taken March 30, 1945.

Belsen, May 1945.

LCMSDS/WILFRID LAURIER UNIVERSITY

UNCOVERING THE HOLOCAUST

For Hitler the Second World War had a dual purpose, the conquest of "living space" for his "Thousand Year Reich" and the destruction of European Jewry. Long after the first goal had to be abandoned the Nazis continued to pursue their "final solution," the mass murder of all Jews who could be rounded up and transported to death camps. Even as the Soviet and Allied armies closed on the heart of Germany, the trains continued to bring men, women and children to the death camps.

Very little of what happened to the Jews was understood outside the small circle of diplomats and politicians who began to receive detailed reports in 1942. The Nazis had begun construction of new death camps in Poland and the mass deportations to Chelmno and Belzec could not be totally hidden. Reports appeared in the international media, including an August 1942 story in

Concentration camp survivors.

NATIONAL ARCHIVES, WASHINGTON

the *Montreal Star* headlined "Nazi Slaughterhouse – Germans Massacre Million Jews in Extermination Drive." Hearing or reading about such atrocities did not necessarily mean believing in them. As one student of the Holocaust, Yehuda Bauen, put it: "Knowing usually came in a number of stages: first the information had to be disseminated; then, it had to be believed; then, it had to be internalized, that is some connection had to be established between the new reality and a possible course of action...."

When news of the mass killings at Auschwitz reached London and Washington in the summer of 1944 the new reality was quickly understood and an intense debate about possible courses of action, including bombing the railways and the gas chambers, was considered. In the end, no such bombing missions were ordered, largely

Tonight I am a different man...

April 24, 1945

Tonight I am a different man. I have spent the last two days in Belsen concentration camp, the most horrible festering scab there has ever been on the face of humanity.... It makes me sick to my stomach even to imagine the smell, and I want to weep and go out in the streets and kill every Nazi I see when I think of what they have done....

You have seen pictures in the paper but they cannot tell the story. You have to smell it and feel it and keep a stern look on your face while your heart tears itself into pieces and the tears of compassion drench your soul....

I have seen hundreds of people dying before my eyes. I have seen filthy green corpses used as pillows for the living. I have seen forty thousand people living and dying amongst their own fetid offal. They are dying faster than they can be buried. For most of them food is absolutely of no use. Their stomachs will not take it – they vomit or they have dysentery and it goes right through them....

I do wish this letter wasn't like this darling, but you are the only one I can tell my thoughts to. I couldn't help thinking of your mother and father. If they were living in Europe they would have been in such a place....

King Whyte, PR Officer,
Department of Psychological Warfare, Canadian First Army

"This picture was taken from the inside of one of the 'lagers' looking out onto the main road which you see in [the picture below]. In the foreground are just a few of the thousands and thousands of dead lying about the place."

"I took this from the steps of one of the watch towers in Belsen and it shows part of the main road through the camp. Most of the bodies have been taken away from the main road but if you look closely you can still see some lying around. The fire hoses brought the first pure water into the camp that these people have had for many months...."

"These are German SS troops hauling away the people they killed. These men were the guards at the camp and were taken when we liberated it. They are, of course, just a few of the several hundred. You will recognize me standing there. This sort of thing was so usual that none of the prisoners paid any attention to it whatsoever. Only when some of the guards were getting beat up did they stop and look. A few moments later the SS man on the left caved in. He was beaten up and then thrown on top of the corpses in the truck until he came to. At this time they were dying much faster than they could be picked up and carted to the pits."

"A small portion of the women's quarter. Imagine what it must have been like in winter...."

"The girl [in the bottom photo] is suffering from typhus and malnutrition. She was too weak to walk and is being helped by her sister on the left and her friend. The drill was that the typhus people were taken out of the huts, stripped of their clothing because it was diseased too, wrapped in a blanket and taken away in an ambulance.... It is difficult to see but on the left of the picture you will notice a chap with a parka affair and one chap bent over. The one bent over is just about to put a blanket around the girl. They are just buck privates in the Medical Corps and are wearing special anti-disease suits. These fellows did a most superb job and it was one of the nastiest jobs any man could tackle. They were gentle but firm and worked like slaves. The girl, incidentally, is just nineteen and she had spent five years of her life in concentration camps. She was one of those whom they believed they could save, so you can imagine what the majority of those who had typhus looked like...."

216

JERZY TOMASZEWSKI, COURTESY OF THE UNITED STATES HOLOCAUST MEMORIAL MUSEUM

A German soldier takes aim at a Jewish mother during an "aktion" against the Jewish population of Ivangorod. The photo was enclosed in a letter from a German soldier on the eastern front, which was intercepted in the Warsaw post office by members of the Polish Home Army.

MAIN COMMISSION FOR THE INVESTIGATION OF NAZI WAR CRIMES, WARSAW, POLAND, COURTESY UNITED STATES HOLOCAUST MEMORIAL MUSEUM

An execution in Krakow, Poland, in which seven people were hanged in revenge for railway sabotage.

because airmen doubted that a sufficient degree of accuracy could be achieved.

When British forces reached Bergen-Belsen on April 19, 1945, the western world finally knew and understood what the Nazis had done. Belsen had been transformed into a concentration camp in late 1944, and throughout the last winter of the war streams of men and women from other camps overrun by Soviet forces were sent to Belsen, where the former commander of Birkenau implemented the techniques of mass murder. In March and April tens of thousands of camp inmates were brought to Belsen on foot and by railcar, 28,000 in the week of

April 4 alone. The food supply was cut off, though there was abundant food in the area, typhus raged unchecked, and when British troops entered the camp there were 10,000 unburied bodies. Photographs, films and news stories about what was found at Belsen finally broke through the barrier of knowing without understanding. The Holocaust had been all too real.

LIBERATING HOLLAND

On March 28, 1945, Field Marshal Bernard Montgomery declared: "We have won the battle of the Rhine." Confident the war would soon end, he urged his commanders to exploit the new situation as quickly as possible. First Canadian Army was not to be part of the advance towards Berlin, but its tasks – to clear northern Holland and the adjacent coastal area of Germany while liberating western Holland – were of vital importance, at least to the Dutch.

In military terms April was a month of anti-climax. Fourth Armoured Division was involved in a difficult fight at the Twente Canal near Delden on April 2, but twelve days later armoured spearheads reached the Kusten Canal one hundred miles inside Germany. By April 13, 2nd Division was on the outskirts of Groningen, and three days later 3rd Division reached the North Sea. In western Holland, I Canadian Corps, which had arrived from the Mediterranean via Marseilles, began operations on April 11. The veterans of the Italian campaign fought some tough minor engagements, but famine conditions in occupied Holland necessitated a truce, and the halt order was issued on April 19.

If the story of Canadian actions in April contains no

great decisive battles, it does include a potent mixture of triumph and tragedy. Canadian and Dutch memories of April are usually of that "Sweetest of Springs," the spring of liberation. Canadian soldiers were embraced by a population that knew all too well what the war had been fought for. They showered their liberators with kisses, flowers and love. But April was also the cruellest month; while the war had been won, the killing did not stop.

Fatal casualties are often the best measure of the intensity of combat. For Canadian soldiers in northwest Europe the worst days during the last year of the war had been June 6, 1944, with 359 fatalities; July 8, 262; July 25, 344; August 8, 290; August 14, 261; and February 26, 1945, 214. On sixteen other days, many of them in October 1944, fatalities exceeded 100 men. The last such 100-

fatality day was March 10, 1945, at Xanten and Veen. In April 1945 more than 50 soldiers were killed on each of seven days; 114 more were killed between May 1 and the surrender on May 5, including 12 on the last day of fighting in Europe.

The Allied air forces also suffered grievous losses. Bomber Command attacked oil targets, U-boat construction and the German navy, while providing direct support to the army. Casualties were not large as a percentage, but each loss was deeply felt. The valour and endurance of bomber crews never ceases to amaze. As an example, Flying Officer D.M. Payne was hit in the legs and an arm while flying over Kiel. His Lancaster was struck by heavy flak, but he piloted the plane away from danger and crash-landed in the North Sea. The survivors

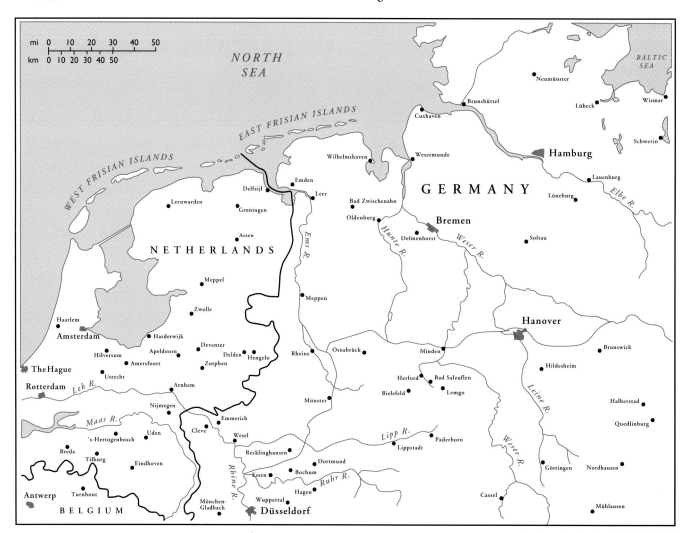

I Canadian Corps was assigned to liberate the old provinces of Holland, advancing beyond Apeldoorn before an armistice was declared. II Canadian Corps was engaged in heavy fighting in northern Holland and Germany.

Happy crowds celebrated the liberation of Delden, Netherlands, by personnel of the 3rd Canadian Division, April 13, 1945.

The town went mad

At present I am on the shores of the Zuider Zee and thus we have cut off the Jerries in Holland. Two days ago we liberated our first big town and it was an experience I shan't forget for a very long time.

I entered the town in a small armoured car about 2:00 a.m. This was the first time the Dutch had seen Allied soldiers. What a welcome we got. The town went mad, completely mad, with joy. People thronged the streets and with foolish cheering, waving, kissing and crying. Flags and streamers appeared in every house as if by magic. Girls dressed themselves in red, white and blue dresses and everyone had a bit of orange on them (for the royal family).

Huge bands of men and women marched through the streets, arms linked and ten to fourteen abreast, singing their national anthem over and over. People everywhere were laughing, singing, shouting for joy. We were mobbed with kindness. They couldn't do enough for us. I'd give the world if you could have seen it and experienced it. You can't imagine how good it makes you feel to bring such happiness to so many.

Lieutenant Reg Roy, Cape Breton Highlanders

huddled in a raft for twelve days before reaching land in Germany, where they were taken prisoner during the last days of the war in Europe.

Tactical air force pilots flew close support missions from airfields in Germany. Attacks against enemy transport and gun positions helped ease the army's path, but flak was intense and losses continued to the last day of fighting. U-boats continued to seek out targets and HMCS *Esquimalt* was torpedoed and sunk in the approaches to Halifax on April 16. Most of the crew escaped, but thirty-nine men perished from exposure before help arrived. Even the German surrender did not end the losses. One of the new type XXIII subs failed to hear the cease-fire signal and sank two merchant ships off Newcastle on May 7. Men of the merchant marine who had contributed so much to the Allied victory were among the first and last casualties of the war in Europe. This

Infantrymen of the Queen's Own Cameron Highlanders going up under smoke cloud, covered by Fort Garry Tank, south of Oldenburg, Germany, April 22.

tragic toll of young lives took place against a background of a triumphant victory over that "most monstrous of tyrannies never surpassed in the dark, lamentable catalogue of human crime."

The Allied armies had developed a battle doctrine that called for the expenditure of massive amounts of artillery shells and, if possible, bombs instead of lives. In the final stages of the war, this doctrine could not be applied to Holland, so the battles of April were fought using field artillery regiments and mortars as the main firepower. When 2nd Division reached Holten, not far from the site where the last Canadian military cemetery in Europe would be built, the enemy was dug in along a railway line and in the town centre. Aimed fire from battalion anti-tank guns and two-inch mortars was used to overcome resistance and limit casualties among a population that rushed out onto the street "dancing jubilantly near the burning buildings."

When the enemy prepared to

German children displaying the surrender flag, April 10, 1945.

fight for Apeldoorn, a city swollen with thousands of refugees, 1st Division's plan of attack called for isolating the city and infiltrating infantry without employing artillery. The garrison abandoned Apeldoorn once 5th Armoured Division and 2nd Brigade had pushed beyond the city, and the soldiers were greeted by wildly rejoicing citizens instead of bullets. The war diary of the Hastings and Prince Edward Regiment notes that the battalion's entry in the city was "tough going due to the cheering and crowding of the thousands of liberated Dutch people who showered bouquets of flowers on the troops. A good-looking soldier had to use his weapon to beat off the girls, and many a fair maiden's kiss was forced on the boys."

A very different pattern was evident in Groningen, where a Dutch SS battalion with little to lose joined miscellaneous German units in determined defence of the city. The Essex Scottish used Kangaroos to rush a bridge and penetrate the city's southern edge. The Royal Hamilton Light Infantry then fought a fierce hand-to-hand engagement to gain the railway station. Machine guns covered the streets, and snipers, including SS men in civilian clothes, harassed the Canadians.

Major-General Bruce Matthews sent 6th Brigade into the main battle while using 5th Brigade to attack from the west. The Dutch resistance helped where it could, lashing barges together to make a bridge. The Black Watch, directed to clear the houses around a park, fought a pitched battle using PIATS and Brens against an entrenched enemy. Finally the two-inch mortars and a burst from a Wasp flamethrower forced an enemy withdrawal. The division suffered 209 casualties.

WESTERN CANADA PICTORIAL INDEX/UNIVERSITY OF WINNIPEG

Prisoners of war. In the photo at top, members of the Canadian Provost Corps are searching the belongings of German soldiers for stolen goods. In the lower photo, prisoners taken by Canadian soldiers in France are marched along toward the rear. Despite Hitler's threat to punish the families of prisoners of war, hundreds of thousands of German soldiers surrendered to Allied forces.

and Canadian divisions fighting for Hamburg, Bremen, Oldenburg, Leer and Emden, Delfzijl could not be simply masked.

Major-General Bert Hoffmeister's 5th Armoured Division was given the task on April 21 and the prospect was not pleasant. The ground was flat, waterlogged and criss-crossed by canals and drainage ditches. The coastal guns at Emden and on the Island of Borkum could support the heavy batteries around Delfzijl. And here, as elsewhere in the Netherlands, the plan was to use the minimum amount of artillery. Hoffmeister first discussed this with battalion and company commanders and all agreed to limit the use of heavy and medium artillery to a counter-battery role.

The 11th Infantry Brigade began a careful process of squeezing the perimeter on April 25. The Perths, the Irish Regiment and the Westminsters, with the tanks of the British Columbia Dragoons, were able to advance steadily with occasional assists from Spitfires of 84 Group. The Perths had the roughest time, suffering seventy-eight casualties before the Cape Breton Highlanders relieved them. The final attack began on April 30, and the next day infantry of the Cape Breton Highlanders and the Irish Regiment dealt with the last die-hards who had not surrendered or escaped across the Ems River.

Across the border in Germany no restrictions applied and resistance was more intense. Young boys, with only an armband for a uniform, were among the civilians found with weapons. One of the most poignant photographs taken in the last phase shows two young lads in

H.G AIKMAN/DND/NATIONAL ARCHIVES OF CANADA/PA113654

Historians, including the author, have questioned the necessity of Operation "Canada," the siege of Delfzijl, but close examination of the record suggests there was little choice. The town was part of the heavily defended Ems estuary that led to the German port of Emden, a base for E-boats and midget submarines. With British

A group of generals of First Canadian Army. Left to right, seated: S. Maczek, 1st Polish Armoured Division; Guy Simonds, II Canadian Corps; H.D.G. Crerar, First Canadian Army; Charles Foulkes, I Canadian Corps; B.M. Hoffmeister, 5th Armoured Division. Standing: R.H. Keefler, 3rd Division; A.B. Matthews, 2nd Division; H.W. Foster, 1st Division; R.W. Moncel, 4th Armoured Division; S.B. Rawlins, 49th (West Riding) Division.

Liberated

For prisoners of war in Germany, the knowledge that the Allies would soon bring liberation was often all that kept them alive. With the Russians advancing on the eastern front, POWs were often force-marched to camps further west by captors determined to stay one step ahead of the Russians. Having marched 824 kilometres in thirty-nine days to arrive at his new camp in Ziegenhain, Lorne T. Goat writes of his last days as a prisoner of war.

Leading Aircraftman Lorne T. Goat (left) and his brother, Sergeant James Goat, photographed in 1941.

There are hundreds of trucks going by on the road and they are all filled with American soldiers.... God, it's good to see a uniform on a soldier that is not green.... These Yanks could not stop, but they waved and yelled at us, throwing cigarettes and candy as fast as they could. Del got a box of rations and passed out a little meat and biscuits. I got the wrapper. Hell's Bells! WE HAVE BEEN LIBERATED!...

Well, this closes one of the greatest days of my life. March 30, 1945. Betty's birthday! Good Friday! The day of my liberation! Due to all the excitement, I did not get to bed until after ten o'clock. Bill Ralston got over 120 fags from the Yanks and he never even offered me one.

Leading Aircraftman Lorne T. Goat

Sogel, Germany, with raised hands and pockets turned out to prove they are unarmed.

The German defence of ports was especially well organized. Third Canadian Division called its attack on Leer Operation "Duck" because once again the "Water Rats" mounted an amphibious assault. The attack went well, but there were seventy casualties.

These last days of the war in Germany were a miserable period for everyone. Resistance was spotty and prisoners were taken in droves, but the enemy seemed to have plenty of mortar rounds and enough determination to use them. It rained steadily and the tired, soaked men, who were asked to maintain pressure without taking too many chances, collapsed into deep sleep when they were rotated out of action. But pressure had to be maintained to bring the war to an end. When the German capitulation was announced there were few celebrations; the predominant emotion was relief at having survived.

Back in western Holland it was all very different. The truce was extended to allow heavy bombers to drop food supplies to the hostage populations of Amsterdam and Rotterdam. Operation "Manna" delivered tens of thousands of ration packs but the population, verging on starvation, needed much more. On May 3, convoys, one every thirty minutes, began crossing the truce line. Three days later 1st Division began its triumphal march to Amsterdam.

General Harry Crerar's message to all ranks summed up the achievement of the nation-in-arms: "From Sicily to the River Senio, from the beaches of Dieppe, to those of Normandy and from thence to Northern France, Belgium, Holland and North West Germany, the Canadians and their Allied comrades in this army have carried out

To die when you are young...

It is awful to die when you are young and have fought a long time....And when you know that the war is won anyhow. It is awful and you would have to be a liar or a fool not to see this and not feel a misery, so that these days every man dead is a greater sorrow because the end of this tragic dying is so near.

Martha Gellhorn

The wife of Ernest Hemingway was writing about the swift advance after Canadians broke through the Gothic Line.

Last Communion

Sergeant Art Charette was an Essex Scottish lad, who came over to the Royal Hamilton Light Infantry lines during confession and told me his platoon couldn't attend Mass, as they had orders to fire anytime. "Can you bring Communion to our gun positions?" He was wet and so was I. It was dark, and we had some distance to travel, so I consecrated some extra Hosts and started off

K. BELL/NATIONAL ARCHIVES OF CANADA/PA175799

Dead German soldier, Beveland Canal, Netherlands.

The will of God

Yes, luck, sure. But my mother attributed my continued survival to the Will of God. Was this the same God who reigned over the dead German soldier in a Normandy wheatfield, for whom I said a silent prayer while standing over his bloated, stinking corpse in the hot August sun? His wallet lay on the ground, family pictures scattered, looted by friends or victors. Flies buzzed at every exposed orifice: eyes, ears, nostrils. And was this the same God who decided that so many of my friends, including my three closest, should die?

Despite such questions, we were not cynical about religion. When I canvassed my platoon to see who wanted a Bible, every single man carried one in his left pocket, over his heart, including me.

And they did not go unread. Nor was prayer a stranger to us. When in the hospital at Bramshot I learned of Earl Stoll's death and realized that our four had tragically been reduced to me, I fell to my knees – not a Jewish practice – in the hospital chapel, mumbling in heartbreak and loss prayers from my childhood. Tears coursed down twenty-three-year-old cheeks.

KEN BELL/DND/NATIONAL ARCHIVES OF CANADA/PA175799

Wounded Sergeant W.G. Grant awaiting first aid, Bayeux, France.

on foot, as Brigade might stop me if they saw a truck. As we arrived, their guns appeared in the moonlight, still covered from the rain that had just stopped. I stood to hear their confessions. It was a tense moment as they recited the *"Confiteor"* then *"Domine Non Sum Dignus,"* the prayer of a Roman centurion to Our Lord. Among those whose faces I recognized, reflected in an oil lamp, were Jim Caba, Moriarity, and Art Charette who'd come for me. That was Art's last Communion. Next morning, only a few hours later, he fell in honoured glory. Rest in Peace.

Padre Michael Dalton, Essex Scots Regiment

Perhaps there were no answers. Perhaps God could not be understood. But we lived with His constant presence, our lifeline to sanity in the midst of insanity.

Lieutenant Barney Danson, Queen's Own Rifles

B.J. GLOSTER/DND/NATIONAL ARCHIVES OF CANADA/PA137038

Body of Sergeant H.A. Barnett, No. 2 Film and Photo Unit, is carried to the burial ground, Xanten.

The ensign of the Royal Canadian Navy flies over German submarine U-889, which surrendered off Shelburne, Nova Scotia. Overhead flies a Canso, the Montreal-built amphibious version of the PBY Catalina. PBYs served in Allied air forces as naval patrol and convoy escort aircraft, sinking a number of submarines. From a PBY the battleship *Bismarck* was found, leading to its destruction, and Squadron Leader Len Birchall was flying one when he spotted the Japanese fleet approaching Ceylon.

their responsibilities in the high traditions which they inherited…. Crushing and complete victory over the German army has been secured. In rejoicing at this supreme accomplishment we shall remember the friends who have paid the full price for the belief they also held that no sacrifice in the interests of the principles for which we fought could be too great."

This was the official view. The ordinary soldier, in a reflective moment, would simply say: "It was a job that had to be done."

VE DAY AND AFTER

On May 7, 1945, General Dwight Eisenhower informed the Combined Chiefs of Staff that "the mission of this Allied force was fulfilled at 0241 local time."

Finally, the war in Europe was over. The fires died slowly, the smoke cleared and millions of hungry and tired people dug themselves out of the rubble. Victory-in-Europe Day was celebrated, but the noise from those celebrations was muted because there was still another enemy to beat. And if the war in the Far East continued for much longer, the soldiers in Europe would have to move to another battlefield.

The victory of May 1945 could not bring everything that was expected or hoped for. The alliance with the Soviet Union

One of the huge flak towers built to defend German cities stands amid the ruins of Hamburg, May 1945. The strategic bombing offensive forced Hitler to devote large resources to the "Second Front" over Germany.

did not survive Hitler's defeat. The Cold War came to dominate international relations and the threat of nuclear war overshadowed the achievement of peace. The Allied victory did not bring an end to human greed or lust for power or cruelty, but it did turn back a new form of barbarism and provide the western world with the opportunity to build a new society.

On the battlefield the sudden collapse of German resistance and the announcement of a cease-fire took most people by surprise. The war had been part of everyone's lives for so long that no other context seemed possible. For Canadians the war had been the best of times as well as the worst of times. The casualty tolls were dreadful and the news of what had happened in Nazi concentration and death camps might make people despair for the future of the human race, but the men and women who served in the Canadian forces had other memories too.

Canadians had played an important part in a great struggle to preserve humanity from the horrors of Nazi tyranny. They had forged deep and lasting friendships with those who shared their experience of war. Many had arrived overseas little more than teenagers. They had grown up together, laughing, crying, praying and relaxing. They had become comrades and now it was over; the brave battalions would soon be just memories.

Some, more than enough, volunteered for the Pacific theatre and it was these adventuresome souls who got home to Canada first. The rest faced the prospect of occupation duties or long periods of waiting for their turn to be sent home. The professionals, and those who hoped to make a career in the postwar army, navy or air force, spent time analysing the lessons learned and developing grandiose plans for new equipment and doctrine. The vast majority wanted little more than a quick return to civilian life and said so, loudly and often.

Repatriation was organized on a point system that initially emphasized a first-in, first-out principle, giving priority to married men. There was a steady exodus from

NATIONAL ARCHIVES OF CANADA/PA150931

The victory issue of the *Maple Leaf*, the newspaper published for Canadian troops, arrives at 12th Field Regiment. (Below) Triumphant headlines in the Vancouver papers.

(Overleaf) Huge crowds gathered in London's squares to celebrate the end of the war in Europe. Here thousands of civilians and servicemen jam Trafalgar Square.

DND/PL145008

Riots in Halifax

With the announcement of victory in Europe, spontaneous celebrations occurred across Canada. In Halifax, the Canadian city most affected by the war, the mayor invited citizens and members of the forces to a celebration, but liquor stores, theatres, shops and most restaurants were closed. The decision to close the liquor stores was the government's, but the stores and restaurants were closed by their owners. For six years they had dealt with servicemen and merchant seamen out on the town blowing off tensions, and they were worried.

The crowd filled the streets and the looting and destruction began. Before the riots ended, 55,000 bottles of hard liquor would be "liberated," along with 18,000 bottles of beer and 15,000 bottles of wine; few stores escaped having windows smashed and goods looted. The mayor blamed the navy. Admiral Murray defended it:

During the rioting, several liquor stores were broken into and the bootlegging trade is now in possession of considerable stocks. I am satisfied that in almost all cases, and particularly at the looting of liquor stores, at the entry of Keith's Brewery, and at the breaking of windows, civilians led the assault and encouraged service personnel to take part. I am also satisfied that the participation of service personnel, though no doubt reprehensible, was dictated more by drunkenness and excitement than by any desire to loot, and that the major portion of the looting that did take place was perpetrated by the civilian population. I need refer you only to the proportion of civilians to servicemen in the pictures in today's *Halifax Daily Star* and *Halifax Mail.* It should also be realized that the maintenance of law and order is a function of the civil government.

Rear Admiral Leonard Murray, RCN

With a federal election campaign underway, the reaction to Admiral Murray's defence of his men was swift. On May 12, the only Canadian to command a theatre of war was dismissed as Commander-In-Chief of Canadian North-west Atlantic and made titular head of HMCS Stadacona, *the Halifax shore establishment. Three months later, the government fired him.*

Deepest and truest feelings...

Caraquet was tied up in Plymouth, but with no shore leave. The mood of the ship's crew was ugly. Our tight-knit little society was steadily deteriorating, revealing its deepest and truest feelings about the war and all its rottenness, that each day was taking away forever, more and more of our lives.... Someone broke into the canteen, took all of our precious store of duty-free Canadian cigarettes, and very deliberately, scattered them through a porthole on the harbour's surface. Next morning, in the dim light of dawn, our ship was surrounded by a white mass of tens of thousands of cigarettes, floating and bobbing in the gentle swell. They seemed to capture, once and for all time, the total emptiness and destruction of our young lives. And the final act of all, came over the radio that, in the fine old naval port of Halifax, on VE-Day, the navy, and others, went berserk and took the town apart in rioting and destruction. Although we in the *Caraquet* were far away, perhaps we could understand just a little what was behind it all, though we felt keenly for all our close friends and families in Halifax, who'd taken us into their homes and their hearts. War is rotten.

Frank Curry

NATIONAL ARCHIVES OF CANADA/PA116725

units throughout the summer of 1945. Those who remained learned about their future options through the Rehabilitation Training Program and went on weekend leaves in friendly Dutch or British towns and cities. They also tried to make sense of what they had been through, expressing simple, even naive hopes for a better future in a world without war.

Many of them brought wives home with them. Between August 1941 and January 1947, the Department of National Defence moved 61,334 dependants from Great Britain and northwest Europe, 41,351 of whom were servicemen's wives and 19,737 their children. Together with the 1,867 persons transported before August 1944 and others still waiting to go, the final number would exceed 70,000.

The men and women who returned to Canada in the

summer of 1945 discovered a nation transformed by the experience of total war. First Division veterans who crossed to England in 1939 left a country deep in the throes of the Great Depression, the Dirty Thirties. Twenty per cent of the population was on relief and many young people had never held a permanent job. For older workers unemployment was a chronic condition; tens of thousands had been out of work for more than five years. For the majority who still had jobs, life was darkened by the threat of unemployment and fear for the future of their children.

The welfare state, which would offer a safety net to future generations, barely existed. There was a small, means-tested old age pension available to the destitute at age seventy, and a mother's allowance for widows with children. Beyond these token measures, ordinary Cana-

The 1st Battalion, the Black Watch, the Royal Highland Regiment, parades down St. James Street in Montreal for the last time.

LCMSDS/WILFRID LAURIER UNIVERSITY

229

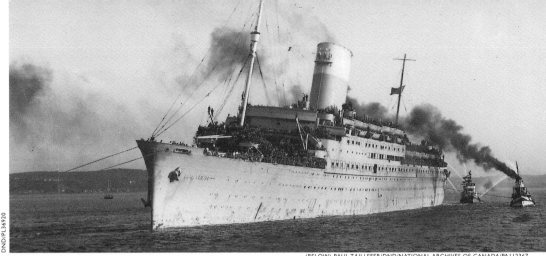

The SS *Pasteur* carried thousands of "repats" home. The group below is arriving at Halifax on June 30, 1945, complete with trophies.

Thousands of war brides followed their husbands to Canada, the majority from the United Kingdom, but also a large contingent from the Netherlands. In the photo above, brides embark at Greenock in Scotland. At left, wives of Canadian servicemen on the railway platform in London on their way to board the **SS** *Mauretania* at Liverpool. They were part of the first large group of war brides to go to Canada, in February 1946.

dians in trouble had to rely on municipal relief or private charity.

The government had no plans for altering this situation, but in 1944 Canadians finally persuaded reluctant politicians to think about the shape of things to come. In 1942, William Beveridge had published his famous report on postwar social security for Britain, and almost overnight public debate had begun about a new society "when the war is over." Canadians heard about proposals for health insurance and other reforms in more detail when news of a report on social security for Canada reached the public in 1943. Leonard Marsh, a social work professor at McGill University who had supervised detailed studies of prewar Canadian society, advocated compulsory health insurance, better old-age pensions and a family allowance system.

Professors could easily be ignored, but no politician

could afford to overlook evidence of widespread dissatisfaction with the *status quo*. The two most important signs of change were the rise of trade union militancy and growing support for the Co-operative Commonwealth Federation. Organized labour was signing up tens of thousands of new members and pressing for a Canadian version of the Wagner Act, the American "New Deal" legislation that required recognition of unions and good-faith collective bargaining. Labour was also after a new minimum wage of fifty cents an hours.

The CCF had lost ground in the 1940 election because of its half-hearted support of the war, but by 1944 the party had become one to contend with. The new Gallup Poll tracked the rise of the socialists in British Columbia, Saskatchewan and Ontario. In August 1943 the CCF won 32 per cent of the popular vote in the Ontario election, with just four fewer seats than George

RIVETING DEPT. CURTISS S.B.W. COMPONENTS
ST. LAURENT PLANT (UPPER FLOOR)
8.11.44.

A scene that would not be common again in Canada for forty years: women and men on the shop floor in the rivetting department of Canadian Car and Foundry's St. Laurent plant.

Drew's Conservatives. Then Tommy Douglas was elected premier of Saskatchewan. Clearly, the Liberal government in Ottawa would have to respond to public pressure for major reforms in Canadian society.

The first breakthrough came with the announcement that a family allowance would be paid to 1.4 million Canadian mothers. The monthly payments – six to nine dollars per child – would be especially helpful to poorer families and would also help to stimulate the postwar economy. Organized labour, which preferred its fifty-cent-an-hour minimum wage plan to "baby bonuses," was offered its own prize in the form of an order-in-council imposing compulsory collective bargaining and union certification on reluctant employers.

Plans were also announced for a Department of Vet-

erans Affairs to administer the Veterans Charter with its wide range of educational and financial benefits. A new Department of Health and Welfare was created as a sign of the government's intent to improve health care. C.D. Howe, the czar of Canadian war industry, received a mandate to manage the Department of Reconstruction and guaranteed "work for all" when peace returned. The National Housing Act held out promise of home ownership to families who had never imagined such a thing was possible.

There were also prospects of a new world order. The Charter of the United Nations, with its ringing declaration "to save succeeding generations from the scourge of war" while advancing "human rights and social progress," seemed full of promise for a better future.

In one important area government, with broad public support, took a step backwards. During the war the economy had relied upon women workers, including married women, and an elaborate network of plant-based day nurseries had been created with the cooperation of industry and government. With the end of the war federal participation in daycare was abandoned and the program quickly collapsed. By 1945 the authorities were determined to get married women out of the labour force, particularly out of "men's jobs" needed for veterans. Once victory was achieved, "Rosie the riveter" and her sisters either returned home to look after children or found a job in traditional women's occupations.

HIROSHIMA

The announcement of the Japanese surrender, broadcast to Canadians on the evening of August 14, set off celebrations across the country. Prime Minister Mackenzie King declared VJ-Day a national holiday and he then went for a drive to watch the celebrations. It was, he wrote, "a pretty sight to see the crowds, all looking so cheerful, girls without hats, all looking so young."

The simple joy expressed by young and old alike on that day seems strange to many modern observers. The end of the war with Japan is now remembered in terms of the tragedy of Hiroshima and Nagasaki: the beginning of the nuclear age, not the end of a long and bloody war.

This approach to August 1945 is entirely understandable.

A plane attacks the new cruiser **HMCS** *Uganda*, Ryukyu Islands, Japan, April 4, 1945. *Uganda* was serving as a picket ship, using anti-aircraft fire against kamikazes attacking the U.S. fleet at Okinawa. After VE Day the crew of *Uganda* were told they had to revolunteer for the Pacific and the majority voted to return to Canada.

An aircraft carrier of the British Pacific Fleet burning after it was hit by a Japanese kamikaze aircraft off the Sakashima Islands, May 9, 1945.

G.M. MOSES/DND/NATIONAL ARCHIVES OF CANADA/PA115792

No use for prisoners

The Canadian and British soldiers captured in the fall of Hong Kong had passed long miserable years in Japanese labour and prison camps, both in the conquered lands and in Japan itself. Many had died of sickness or starvation by war's end

Also at Moaspetty ... also working as labourers, were some Jap marines. Their cruiser was sunk in the Battle of the Java Sea. In their navy, army and so forth, if you lose anything, you are punished, and they got nine months of hard labour for losing their cruiser. That is unbelievable in our forces but that is the way they ran it.... Also, a soldier ... who became sick, such as catching malaria, or dysentery, or anything like that, went on half rations. If he got wounded fighting, he retained his full rations. But their theory was, if you got wounded in battle it was honourable; if you just got plain sick, you were no good for the Emperor, so you didn't deserve to be fed. This, of course, accounted for some of the outlook they had for their prisoners. They had absolutely no use for prisoners....

Oss Luce, RCAF mechanic

Self-inflicted wounds

I had heard stories of Jap brutality but was ill-prepared for what I was to see. A young lieutenant led the way. I guess I looked shocked – his face was wired on. Honest-to-God, those bastard Japs had practically separated his face from the skull. A second man was helping a third who was wearing a towel. I offered him a pair of slacks. He said, "Thanks, Jock, but I won't be wearing slacks for a while," then he pulled the towel away. His penis had eight or ten large cupid thorns through it. They are arrow-headed thorns two to three inches long. His buddy said they were self-inflicted. I said, What!? He laughed and told me the soldier was having a leak when a Jap guard passed. He gave a flick and splashed the guard, and anybody who peed on a Jap guard was asking for trouble.

John Lynch

Leaving this camp for ever

January 3, 1942
A Middlesex team beat us 4-0 at football. They must be eating better than we are.

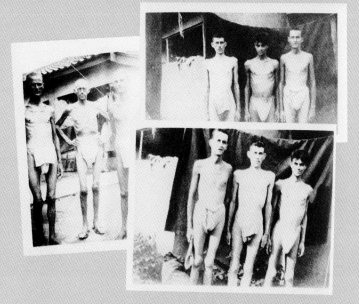

These photographs of emaciated prisoners of war were taken by Japanese officers. Glen Mann, a prisoner, took them from the officers when the camp was liberated.

January 4, 1942
A shivery night, the main topic of conversation that was food. Jenkins suddenly declaimed:
> You may live without books, what is knowledge but grieving;
> You may live without hope – what is hope but deceiving;
> You may live without love – what is passion but pining;
> But where is the man who can live without dining?

October 4, 1942
The Japs took Halbert's pet monkey. He has made an electric toaster and water heater, must keep them hidden at all times as the Japs confiscate on sight. Another Rifle died.

October 5, 1942
Nine Canadians have died since moving here. Old Paddy Armstrong today. Clear and hot.

October 7, 1942
Marcel Robideaux and Herb Mabb died of diphtheria. I knew them well, more likable fellows would be hard to find anywhere. We shall miss them.

October 15, 1942
A Rifle sergeant died. A spoonful of peanut oil on rice once a day now.

August 14, 1943
I am one of 380 Canadians picked for the draft to Japan, plus twenty-five Dutch Navy and seventy-five Imperials.

January, 1944, Japan
I woke up and the building seemed to be sinking beneath me. Then I heard the awful screams of men being crushed. I felt the ceiling settling over me. I was in an upper bunk, but not all the deaths were in the lower ones. Sampson died on my left and Harold Jones on my right, while in the lower bunk, little Joe Furey, one of the brightest boys that ever enlisted, and one of the most cheerful, and one of the most helpful, kind-hearted friends a man ever had, lay lifeless beneath a heavy timber. Seven men were dead. And eight died later in that earthquake that demolished our building because it was nuthin' but a shack. … The only human beings in Japan who showed me any kindness were some of the old ladies who worked on the docks. They were fifty or sixty years old. If none of our foremen were watching, they might slip us a sweet potato or a handful of … soy beans…. One morning walking down the track, we came across the body of a large black cat lying on the rail. It had been cut in two by the train. We immediately exclaimed, "Here's something for the soup." Joe Falcon skinned it and Tommy Wilson cooked it in the soup. If you didn't know what it was, you might have thought it was rabbit….

September 5, 1945
Nugata, Japan: Tonight we are leaving this camp for ever…. So much food was dropped from the air the ground is littered with tins (empty, of course), boxes, cardboard, paper, rubbish scattered about. Men shouting, singing and staggering about. For once, for the first time, the Jap guard is very quiet, modest and self-effacing. No more strutting or swaggering. At eight o'clock tonight, clad in our new raiment dropped from the air, we climbed into buses and drove to the nearest railway track — no station, not even a siding, just a lonely stretch of

"As a prisoner of war in Hong Kong. I am trying to look cheerful."

track. Before the last truck left, our bugler played the Last Post. We waited by the track for a good hour. We are carrying dry K rations and a can of fruit juice, all dropped from the air. We rode all night, very cramped, never slept a wink. As dawn broke we neared the vast area of ruins that was once Tokyo…. Many men in an exuberant mood threw gum and bars at every pretty face they saw near the track….

October 8, 1945
It was dark when we pulled into Union Station in Winnipeg. I said goodbye to Austin Roberts and Jimmy Webb, and the other Rifles I knew so well. It was all in the papers the next morning — the wildest, most exciting mass of humanity I ever saw — the thrill, the joy, the heartfelt gratitude of being spared to meet my loved ones, my own family, my own friends, my own neighbours. "Kiss all the girls you can while you can," was the sage advice of my brother, Jim.
Private Tom Forsyth, Winnipeg Grenadiers

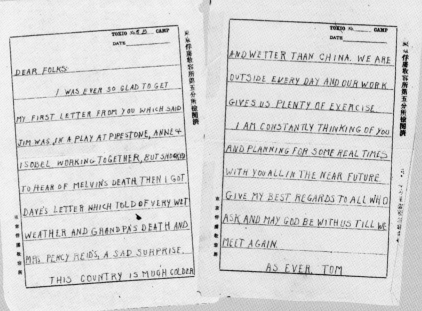

```
TOKIO No. 4 B  CAMP
DATE _____

DEAR FOLKS:
    I WAS EVER SO GLAD TO GET
MY FIRST LETTER FROM YOU WHICH SAID
JIM WAS IN A PLAY AT PIPESTONE, ANNE &
ISOBEL WORKING TOGETHER, BUT SHOCKED
TO HEAR OF MELVIN'S DEATH. THEN I GOT
DAVE'S LETTER WHICH TOLD OF VERY WET
WEATHER AND GRANDPA'S DEATH AND
MRS. PERCY REID'S, A SAD SURPRISE.
    THIS COUNTRY IS MUCH COLDER
```

```
TOKIO No. ____  CAMP
DATE _____

AND WETTER THAN CHINA. WE ARE
OUTSIDE EVERY DAY AND OUR WORK
GIVES US PLENTY OF EXERCISE.
    I AM CONSTANTLY THINKING OF YOU
AND PLANNING FOR SOME REAL TIMES
WITH YOU ALL IN THE NEAR FUTURE.
GIVE MY BEST REGARDS TO ALL WHO
ASK, AND MAY GOD BE WITH US TILL WE
MEET AGAIN.
            AS EVER, TOM
```

"It often took months for a letter to get home, sometimes years. The Japs would censor every word and hand your note back and tell you to write it over again till there was almost nothing left."

Canadian and British prisoners await liberation by a landing party from **HMCS** *Prince Robert*, Hong Kong, August 30, 1945. Canadian prisoners of war were quickly repatriated and sent to various military hospitals for treatment, examination for pensionable disabilities, and discharge. The Department of National Defence refused to award "campaign pay" or to cash Japanese military yen. The Hong Kong Veterans Association of Canada was forced to lobby for fair treatment for many years, until 1971 when most outstanding grievances were resolved.

The generations that grew up with the threat of nuclear war tried to understand how that reality happened and what might happen in the future. Japan, once defeated, was a minor player in east-west confrontations, and the struggle to subdue its military power was of marginal interest. Individuals who knew, and cared to know, nothing about the war in the Pacific developed firm opinions about the decision to drop the A-bombs. Military thinkers assumed that warfare had been revolutionized and placed their faith in nuclear deterrence. Critics of American foreign policy insisted that the bombs had been used in atomic diplomacy, a first step in the Cold War. Few were interested in the actual events of the summer of 1945.

The first responsibility of historians is to establish, as best they can, what actually happened. To achieve this they must ask clear questions and search for information from the best sources. Answers will always be incomplete and imperfect but they can be true in the sense that they accurately reflect the available evidence. Historians have little difficulty in reaching agreement on the answers to clearly stated questions; what they quarrel about is which questions are important. For the men and women involved in the struggles of 1945, the most important question is what caused Japan to surrender.

Close examination of events in August 1945 reveals that Japanese military and political elites were sharply divided. A majority, even in the army, was prepared to end the war but sought terms well short of the unconditional surrender demanded by the Allies. The Potsdam Declaration of July 26, 1945, had allowed for retaining the Emperor, if that was the freely expressed will of the Japanese people. However, this concession was regarded as insufficient in Japan.

The moderates were trying to use the Soviet Union, still neutral in the Pacific war, as a mediator. Joseph Stalin, who intended to attack Japan as soon as it was militarily possible, was uncooperative. The Japanese moderates persisted in assuming that the ongoing sacrifice of Japanese and American lives was a small price to pay if they could avoid foreign occupation of the home islands, the trial of war criminals by the Allies, and the humiliation of the armed forces.

Japanese decision-makers ignored the fire-bombing of Tokyo, which took 130,000 lives, and the subsequent unopposed air attacks on Japanese cities. They considered the loss of civilian lives regrettable, but their army was still powerful, and thousands of aircraft, including kamikaze suicide bombers, were available for a last stand. A compromise peace allowing the military to remain in power was thought possible; it was believed the Americans would not want to risk the horrendous casualties they had suffered on Iwo Jima and Okinawa.

A few of the ones that weren't so lucky. These medical record ID cards of Winnipeg Grenadiers who died in Japanese POW camps state that they died of pellagra, chronic enteritis and "melancholic psychosis."

These attitudes began to change only after the news that "Hiroshima was destroyed instantly by a single bomb" reached Tokyo. Even then the cabinet was split on whether to accept the Potsdam Declaration. The Emperor finally insisted on capitulation after the second atomic bomb destroyed Nagasaki on August 9. It was feared Tokyo and Kyoto would be next. Despite last-minute attempts to organize a military coup and continue the war, the Emperor announced the surrender August 15. The A-bombs ended the war in the Pacific.

Few would disagree with this summary, but many would argue that we have considered the wrong question. Rather, they would ask, was it necessary to use the A-bombs to end the war? This is the kind of approach to the past that encourages controversy. The question can't be answered because it is about events that didn't happen. Any number of counter-factual arguments may be presented with some plausibility.

Most historians would have no trouble agreeing that Japan had lost the war and would have been forced to surrender sometime in the fall of 1945 or early 1946 without the A-bombs. But there is no agreement on how or when this might have taken place. Some would argue that the Soviet conquest of Manchuria, completed by August 20, would have forced a surrender. This is unconvincing, because it was the occupation of the sacred home islands, not Manchuria, that was at issue. However, it is more important to point out that the Japanese army in Manchuria collapsed after the A-bombs were used, so we can't possibly determine the outcome of the battle in the absence of the bombs.

What can be said is that American plans for ending the war without the A-bomb included conventional bombing of Japanese cities. Indeed, it was expected that all significant urban targets would be destroyed by November 1945. The naval blockade, which had already cut off all shipping with Japan, was slowly starving the population. U.S. battleships were shelling coastal cities while naval aviators attacked the pitiful remnants of the Japanese fleet. Operation "Olympic," the invasion of the southern island of Kyushu, was scheduled for November, with the assault on Honshu, the main island, set for early 1946.

Canadians would have been affected had the war continued. The desperate plight of the surviving prisoners of war from Hong Kong would have worsened and many more would have died. Elements of the Royal Canadian Navy and the Royal Canadian Air Force would have been drawn into the action, including HMCS *Uganda,* slated to return to the Pacific with an all-volunteer crew. Canada's expeditionary force, an infantry division under Major-General Bert Hoffmeister, was to be part of the follow-up force, landing after the planned assault on Honshu. If the war had lasted that long casualties would have been numerous. We can never know what might have happened, but it is clear that the alternative to dropping the A-bombs was not peace but a continuation of a terrible war.

After all this is said there remains the horrific reality of Hiroshima. When the Smithsonian Institution developed its controversial exhibit to mark the fiftieth anniversary of the bombing, the image of the mushroom cloud and what it meant for the future of humanity led the designers to underplay the harsh realities of 1945. They might have understood the position of the veterans who protested the planned display if they had had direct experience in the Pacific war or had read a book such as George Macdonald Fraser's memoirs, *Quartered Safe Out Here: A Recollection of the War in Burma.*

Fraser, known to many as the creator of the Flashman series, was a nineteen-year-old volunteer in the Border Regiment when the war ended. His memoirs capture the

> ### Under an obligation
>
> All my life, I will be under the obligation of accomplishing something as a result of having lived through the war. Something tells me I must work hard, as if ... atoning for not being killed. I will doubtless outlive this feeling. But that will be because I have lost touch with the soldier's truth. Not to have been killed is unfashionable among those who are still dying. Not to have been wounded is something to do penance for.... I think of the splendid ones who have died; how splendid ... few will know. They have made it seem as if anything short of intense labour is trifling, or shameful. I suppose their smiling eyes, perpetually young and soldierly in memory now, will be the strict judges of my leisure forever. You cannot stare them out, or turn them aside with a sleepy look. They can exact anything.... Tonight I have the feeling they will make me work. It is owing.
>
> Lieutenant Donald Pearce, *Journal of a War*

flavour of life and death in the infantry with an authenticity few authors have achieved. He recalls that the news of Hiroshima evoked "no moralizing and no feeling at all of the guilt which some thinkers nowadays seem to want to attach to the bombing." The use of the A-bombs, he acknowledges, was barbaric but the alternative, the death of more Allied soldiers, in a war which was already won, against an enemy who would not quit, was simply unacceptable. So the bombing was right. Or was it?

Fraser reveals the complexity and ambiguity of counter-factual arguments in a passage that challenges all our assumptions. He writes, "I have a feeling that if ... Nine section had known all that we know about Hiroshima ... and if some voice from on high had said, 'There – that can end the war for you if you want ... the alternative is that the war, as you've known it, goes on ... and some of you won't reach the end of the road ... it's up to you,' I think I know what would have happened. They would have cried 'Aw fook that' with one voice ... and then they would have been moving south. Because that is the kind of men they were."

Perhaps not every Allied soldier, sailor or airman, and certainly not every prisoner of war suffering in Japanese hands, would have been as self-sacrificing as Fraser's comrades. But we should not underestimate the basic decency and humanity of the men and women who went to war on our behalf fifty years ago. At the least we should resist the temptation to offer easy judgements about events that took place somewhere we have never been, among people we can never fully understand.

A French veteran of the First World War salutes a column of
Canadians moving up for their part in Operation "Goodwood,"
south of Caen.

NOTES

The author especially wishes to thank the many individuals who contributed their own or friends' or relatives' personal papers, including journals, letters, unpublished memoirs and photographs.

PART I: FOLLY

p. 18: The Toronto *Globe*, Saturday, July 25, 1936, p. 1.

p. 20: The Montreal *Gazette*, Saturday, March 12, 1938, p. 1.

p. 23: "Hitler outlines his plans…" from *Documents on Nazism, 1919–1945*, Jeremy Noakes and Geoffrey Pridham, eds., London: Cape, 1974, p. 521.

— "Bonnet tells the Czechoslovakian convoy…" from *Defense de la Paix, Vol. I*, Paris, 1946, p. 129.

— House of Common speeches are from *Debates of the House of Commons*, United Kingdom, October 1938.

p. 24: Mackenzie King's diaries, National Archives of Canada (NAC), MG 26 J 13.

P. 25: "What's the Cheering For?", *The Winnipeg Free Press*, editorial, September 30, 1938.

p. 27: "Jews Sob in Sorrow, 20,000 Torontonians Protest Persecution", *Toronto Daily Star*, November 21, 1938, p. 1.

p. 29: "A Huge Army in Canada", text from interview and photograph courtesy Barney Danson, Toronto.

p. 30: "Successes can no longer be won…", Hitler, "Minutes of the Conference of May 23, 1939 – The Führer on the Present Situation and Political Objectives", Noakes, *Documents on Nazism*, p. 538.

p. 34: Text and photo courtesy Dr. Reginald H. Roy, Victoria, B.C.

p. 37: The Ottawa *Citizen*, Tuesday, April 9, 1949, p. 1.

p. 39: "It's a War of Ideas…" translation, from Claude Châtillon, *Carnets de Guerre: Ottawa–Casa Berardi, 1941–1944*, Ottawa, Éditions du Vermillon, 1987, p. 12.

p. 40: "A Second Expeditionary Force", unpublished notes, courtesy John Ellis, Simcoe, Ontario.

p. 41–42: Betty Scott diaries, Canadian War Museum, 58A1.28.5. Photograph courtesy Betty Scott of Wales, no relation, who served in the British Red Cross.

p. 43: Correspondence between William "Pat" Patterson and Jean Partridge and photographs appear courtesy of Jean (Partridge) Crowe.

— "I Was Sure My Number Would Come Up…", text and photo from J. Ralph Wood, *My Lucky Number Was 77: WWII Memoirs of J. Ralph Wood, D.F.C., C.D.*, privately published, Moncton [1985?].

p. 44: Diary entries and photo, NAC, MG 31 D230, appear courtesy G. Hamilton Southam, Grignan, France.

— Churchill's speech, *Debates of the House of Commons*.

PART II: LIFELINE

p. 46: Churchill, *Debates of the House of Commons*.

p. 48: "It Happened by Mistake…", William L. McKnight, found in NAC, MG 30 E 527.

p. 49: "A Sky Full of Planes" is from Ernie McNab's article for *Rockcliffe Air Review*, May 1941, as quoted in *High Blue Battle: The War Diary of No. 1 (401) Fighter Squadron, RCAF*, Dave McIntosh, ed., Toronto: Stoddart, 1990.

— Letters from William Sprenger located in Canadian War Museum, 58A1 43.2-3.

p. 52: Photographs by King Whyte appear courtesy of his daughter, Maureen Whyte Ivans, Toronto.

p. 55: Text courtesy Carl Christie, Ottawa.

p. 58: "Unnatural and unhealthy…" Wolfgang Luth, quoted in *The Tools of War*, Westmount: Reader's Digest Association (Canada) Ltd., 1969, p. 16.

p. 60: John Mara's letter appears courtesy Mrs. K. Mary Mara, Victoria, B.C.

p. 62: Laura Bradbury's letter appears courtesy of her brother, Ralph Bradbury, Surrey, B.C., and Frank Mercer, Bay Roberts, Newfoundland.

— *The Globe and Mail*, Metropolitan Edition, Toronto, Monday, June 23, 1941, p. 1.

p. 64: Nano Pennefather's text and photo appear courtesy Nano Pennefather-McConnell, Aylmer, Quebec.

p. 65: Wilson Duff papers, Directorate of History (DHist), J43890, Ottawa.

— "Trinity to Wellington in a Year" and photos courtesy Robert G. Dale, D.S.O., D.F.C., C.D., Toronto.

p. 68: Jimmie Agrios's correspondence appears courtesy Mary Agrios, Nanaimo, B.C.

p. 71: Churchill quoted in C.P. Stacey, *Six Years of War*, Ottawa: Queen's Printer, 1957, p. 438.

— *The Globe and Mail*, Toronto, Metropolitan Edition, Monday, December 8, 1941.

p. 72: Ismay quoted in Stacey, *Six Years of War*, p. 440.

— Ralston quoted in *Six Years of War*, p. 442.

— Crerar quoted in *Six Years of War*, p. 441.

p. 75: Photo and text (here translated from the French) appear courtesy of the publisher of Georges' memoirs, Éditions du Septentrion, and his brother, Michel Verreault. From *Journal d'un prisonnier de guerre au Japon, 1941–1945*, by Georges Verreault, Éditions du Septentrion, Sillery, Quebec, 1993, pp. 23, 30, 34, 37, 38, 40.

p. 76: Thomas Smith Forsyth text and photo can be found in NAC, MG 30 E 181. Appear courtesy Thomas Smith Forsyth, Reston, Manitoba.

— Photo and letters appear courtesy Jean (Partridge) Crowe.

PART III: THE END OF THE BEGINNING

p. 80: *The Vancouver Sun*, December 8, 1941, editorial, p. 15.

— Inset and text from *The Vancouver Sun*, Monday, August 31, 1942, editorial, p. 4.

p. 81: Text from *This Is My Own: Letters to Wes & Other Writings on Japanese Canadians, 1941–1948*; Muriel Kitagawa, Roy Miki, editor, copyright © 1985, Talon Books Ltd., Vancouver, B.C. Family photo courtesy Ed Kitagawa, Toronto.

— Newspaper insets: *The Vancouver Sun*. "Stop Selling Gasoline to Japs", December 23, 1941; "Lock Them Up", December 1941.

p. 83: "Death of Ernest Lapointe" excerpt from A. Laurendeau, *The Conscription Crisis*, quoted in Philip Stafford, ed., *André Larendeau, Witness for Quebec*, Toronto: Macmillan, 1973.

— King diaries, NAC, MG 26 J 13.

— Dorothy Seiveright's letter located in Queen's University Archives, Coll 5024, Wartime Correspondence. Courtesy Donald C. Macdonald, Toronto.

— The Montreal *Gazette*, April 7, 1942, p. 1.

p. 85: "A Flying 25-ton Bomb…" from Ralph J. Wood, *My Lucky Number Was 77*.

p. 86: From Jerrold Morris, *Canadian Artists and Airmen*, Toronto: Morris Gallery, 1975. (Quoted in Brereton Greenhous, *The Crucible of War, 1939–1945*, Toronto: University of Toronto Press, 1994, p. 552.)

pp. 86–87: Brackenbury's report drawn from his "Questionnaire for Returned Aircrew, loss of bomber aircraft 19 May 1945." National Defence, DHist 181.00 1 (D24), Folder 13. (Quoted in Greenhous, *The Crucible of War*, p. 567.)

p. 87: John Fauquier quoted in Greenhous, *The Crucible of War*, p. 559.

Airmen in the U.K. meet some of the local inhabitants.

— The Singleton Report, a public record, was quoted in Sir Charles Webster and Dr. Noble Frankland's four-volume *The Strategic Air Offensive Against Germany, 1939–1945, Volume 1*, p. 338. London: HMSO, 1961.

p. 99: Report from the German Fifteenth Army from Terry Copp and Robert Vogel, *Maple Leaf Route: Antwerp*, Alma, Ont.: Maple Leaf Route, 1986.

p. 100: Sabourin, here in translation, is quoted in Pierre Vennat, *Dieppe n'aurait pas dû avoir lieu*, Montreal: Éditions du Meridien, 1991.

— W. Denis Whitaker, from his book *Dieppe: Tragedy to Triumph*, Toronto: McGraw-Hill Ryerson, 1992, p. 242. Photo courtesy Brigadier-General W. Denis Whitaker.

pp. 100–101: H.H. Ditz quoted in Whitaker, *Dieppe: Tragedy to Triumph*, p. 254.

pp. 101–102: Dollard Ménard, here in translation, is quoted in Vennat, *Dieppe n'aurait pas dû avoir lieu*.

p. 102: Herbert Webber, quoted in Whitaker, *Dieppe: Tragedy to Triumph*, p. 248.

— Jack Dunlap, quoted in Whitaker, *Dieppe: Tragedy to Triumph*, p. 265.

— Padre John Foote's remark is paraphrased from RHLI Intelligence Officer Major Richard McLaren's recollection in Whitaker, *Dieppe: Tragedy to Triumph*, pp. 264–65.

p. 108: Leonard Murray papers located in NAC, MG 30 E207.

pp. 108–109: Photo and text from diaries and privately published memoirs by Jim Liddy appear courtesy Lillian Liddy, Saint John, N.B.

p. 110: Harry Ferns's letter courtesy Jean (Partridge) Crowe.

p. 110: Photo and Southam diaries, NAC, MG 31 D230, courtesy G. Hamilton Southam.

PART IV: FIRST STRIKE – 1943

p. 115: Public record documents found in Webster and Frankland, *Strategic Air Offensive, Volume 4*.

p. 116: "Ground Crews… a Hell of a Life" from Ron Cassels, *Ghost Squadron* (Gimli, Manitoba: Ardenlea Publishing, 1991), quoted in Greenhous, *Crucible of War*, p. 754.

p. 118: Photos and text courtesy John R. Harding, Guelph, Ontario.

p. 122: Photo courtesy Dr. Leith G. Douglas, Wellesley Hospital, Toronto.

— Harding's text from his privately published book, *The Dancin' Navigator*, courtesy John R. Harding, Guelph.

— Nano Penefather extract appears courtesy Nano Pennefather-McConnnell.

p. 128: Lieutenant Frank C. Hall's letter and photo appear courtesy Patricia (Hall) Hedley.

p. 129: "The Bullet Meant for Me" from Colonel Strome Galloway, *Sicily to the Siegfried Line* (manuscript), Ottawa.

p. 130: "Position Warfare" from Galloway, *Sicily to the Siegfried Line*.

p. 134: Family photos and Alton Kjosness papers, from Ferdy E. Baglo, ed., *WWII Letters from an Ordinary Soldier* (manuscript), appear courtesy Ferdy E. Baglo, Chilliwack, B.C.

p. 137: Charles F. Comfort papers, NAC, MG 30 DB1.

p. 143: "The Po Swamp" text courtesy Dr. Reginald H. Roy.

p. 145: Excerpt from Charles Fraser Comfort, *Artist at War*, Second Edition, 1995, by permission of Remembrance Books, an imprint of Log House Publishing Company Ltd., R.R. 1, Pender Island, B.C., Canada V0N 2M0.

— Diary entries, Claude Châtillon, *Carnets de Guerre*, pp. 55, 73–74.

p. 146: Photo and letter, Wilfred Bark Collection (990.40), Marine Museum of the Great Lakes at Kingston, Ontario. Report and inset, the Ottawa *Citizen*, Evening Edition, March 15, 1943.

p. 147: Southam letters, NAC, MG 31 D230, courtesy G. Hamilton Southam.

— Patterson and Partridge letters courtesy Jean (Partridge) Crowe.

p. 150: "Forland Interrogation Report" located in National Defence, DHist 74/250.

— Aidan Crawley is quoted in Carlton Younger, *No Flight from the Cage*, London, 1981.

p. 151–52: Photos and letters courtesy Nano Pennefather–McConnell.

PART V: LIBERATION

p. 159: Alec Flexer's letter and photos courtesy Mrs. Fay Shuster, Montreal.

p. 161: "Thin on the Ground" is excerpted by permission from Charles Martin, *Battle Diary: From D-Day and*

Normandy to the Zuider Zee and VE, Toronto: Dundurn Press, 1994.

p. 164–65: "Recollections of D-Day" from papers courtesy Joseph Lester "Les" Wagar, Red Deer, Alberta.

p. 167: "A Pistol Shot to the Temple" from Charles Martin, *Battle Diary*.

p. 168: Highland Light Infantry of Canada, Battalion War Diary, quoted in Terry Copp and Robert Vogel, *Maple Leaf Route: Caen*, Alma, Ontario: Maple Leaf Route, 1983.

p. 170: "I Don't Know What You Say…" from Les Wagar.

—Dr. John Burwell Hillsman is quoted in *The Canadians at War 1939/45, Volume 2*, p. 511. Westmount: The Reader's Digest Association (Canada) Ltd., 1969.

p. 171: Major Burdett McNeel, 1st Canadian Exhaustion Unit, War Diary, quoted in Terry Copp and Bill McAndrew, *Battle Exhaustion: Soldiers and Psychiatrists in the Canadian Army, 1939–1945*, Montreal: McGill-Queen's University Press, 1990.

p. 172: "No Longer a Man…" courtesy Les Wagar.

p. 175: C.P. Stacey, *The Victory Campaign: The Operations in North-West Europe, 1944–1945*, Ottawa: Queen's Printer, 1966.

p. 179: Photo and text by King Whyte appear courtesy Maureen Whyte Ivans.

p. 183: Major-General Gustav von Zangen quoted in Stacey, *The Victory Campaign*.

p. 184: Lieutenant-General Guy Simonds quoted in Stacey, *The Victory Campaign*.

—Pilot Officer Sidney Aldridge quoted in Stacey, *The Victory Campaign*.

p. 187: "Never Knowing What You'd Be Running Into…" from Charles Martin, *Battle Diary*.

p. 188: Letter from Captain James Stewart located in personnel files, Directorate of History.

p. 190: Photo and text by Lieutenant Jacques Gouin, here in translation, from Jacques Gouin, *Lettres de Guerre d'un Québécois, 1942–1945*, Montreal: Éditions du Jour, 1975, and appear courtesy of Michel Gouin.

—C.G. Power papers located in the C.G. Power Collection, Queen's University Archives.

p. 193: "A Standard of Life" from Convocation Address, Dalhousie University, 1943, Leonard Murray papers, NAC, MG 30 E207.

p. 194: Photo and letters courtesy Jean (Partridge) Crowe.

—"Every Time a Gun Went Off…" courtesy Les Wagar.

—"Jumpy As a Cat" courtesy Dr. Reginald H. Roy.

pp. 195–96: Personal papers courtesy Doris (Morrison) Clark, Ennismore, Ontario.

PART VI: VICTORY

p. 201: Lieutenant-General Brian Horrocks quoted in J.L. Granatstein, *The Generals: The Canadian Army's Senior Commanders in the Second World War*, Toronto: Stoddart, 1993, p. 201.

p. 210: "No Block Escaped Damage" excerpt quoted in Greenhous, *The Crucible of War*, p. 767.

p. 213: Al LaRose quoted in chapter 15 of W. Denis Whitaker's *Rhineland: The Battle to End the War*, Toronto: Stoddart, 1989.

pp. 215–16: Photos and text by King Whyte courtesy Maureen Whyte Ivans.

p. 219: "The Town Went Mad" courtesy Dr. Reginald H. Roy.

p. 222: Photo and text Lorne T. Goat, Canadian War Museum, 58A1 81.1, appear courtesy Lorne T. Goat, Calgary.

p. 223: Padre Michael Dalton papers, located in NAC, MG 30 E421, appear courtesy Michael Dalton.

—"The Will of God" from interview, Barney Danson.

p. 228: Leonard Murray papers, NAC, MG 30 E207.

—Frank Curry papers located in NAC, MG 30E 332.

p. 234: Oss Luce's text courtesy Oss Luce, Thorold, Ontario.

—John Lynch's text courtesy John Lynch, Scarborough, Ontario.

pp. 234–35: Forsyth photos and diary, located in NAC, MG 30 E 181, appear courtesy Thomas Smith Forsyth.

p. 238: "Under an Obligation" excerpted from Donald Pearce, *Journal of a War*, Toronto: Macmillan, 1965.

SUGGESTED READING

The best single-volume history of the Second World War is Gerhard L. Weinberg, *A World At Arms* (Cambridge University Press, 1994), now available in paperback. Weinberg's bibliographical essay and detailed footnotes provide a reliable guide to the best scholarly writing about the war. For the situation in Canada, C.P. Stacey, *Canada and the Age of Conflict: The Mackenzie King Era* (Toronto: Macmillan of Canada, 1981) and J. L. Granatstein, *Canada's War: The Politics of the Mackenzie King Government, 1939-45* (Toronto: Oxford University Press, 1970) are good places to start.

Canadian views of the crisis in Europe include Charles Ritchie, *The Siren Years : A Canadian Diplomat Abroad* (Macmillan of Canada, 1974) John English, *Shadows of Heaven: The Life of Lester Pearson* Vol. I (Toronto: Lester & Orpen Dennys, 1992) and James Eayrs, *In Defence of Canada, Vol. 2 Appeasement and Rearmament* (University of Toronto Press, 1965).

The home front is a very neglected subject and the serious reader has to search among more general books on labour, social and women's history to get below the surface. Robert Bothwell and William Kilbourn, *C.D. Howe, a Biography* (Toronto: McClelland & Stewart, 1979) is good on war industries, and David Zimmerman, *The Great Naval Battle of Ottawa* (University of Toronto Press, 1989) illustrates some of the problems of building a large navy. Muriel Kitagawa, *This is My Own* (Vancouver: Talon Books, 1985) and Ken Adachi, *The Enemy That Never Was: A History of the Japanese Canadians* (McClelland & Stewart, 1976) should be read with J.L. Granatstein, *Mutual Hostages: Canadians and Japanese During the Second World War* (University of Toronto Press, 1990), a book written in collaboration with Patricia Roy and two Japanese historians. Frederick W. Gibson and Barbara Robertson (eds) *Ottawa at War: The Grant Dexter Memoranda 1939-1945* (Winnipeg: Manitoba Record Society, 1995) offers an insider's view of developments in Canada.

The Royal Canadian Navy is carefully studied in Marc Milner, *The North Atlantic Run: The Royal Canadian Navy and the Battle for the Convoys* (University of Toronto Press, 1985) and *The U-Boat Hunters* (University of Toronto Press, 1994). Tony German, *The Sea is at Our Gates* (McClelland & Stewart, 1990) is a well written popular history of the RCN. The classic accounts by veterans of the battle are Hal Lawrence, *A Bloody War* (Macmillan of Canada, 1966) and Alan Easton, *50 North: An Atlantic Battleground* (Toronto: Ryerson Press, 1966). Ken Macpherson, *The Ships of Canada's Naval Forces 1910-81* (Toronto: Collins, 1981), W.H. Pugsley, *Saints, Devils and Ordinary Seamen: Life on the Royal Canadian Navy's Lower Deck* (Collins, 1945), Robert G. Halford, *The Unknown Navy: Canada's World War II Merchant Navy* (St. Catharines, Ont.: Vanwell, 1994), Mac Johnston, *Corvettes Canada* (Toronto: McGraw-Hill Ryerson, 1994) and Marc Milner and Ken Macpherson, *Corvettes of the Royal Canadian Navy* (Vanwell, 1993) are also recommended.

The third volume of the official history of the Royal Canadian Air Force, B. Greenhous et al, *The Crucible of War, 1939-1945* (University of Toronto Press in cooperation with the Department of National Defence and the Canadian Government Publishing Centre, 1994) provides a great deal of information in its more than one thousand pages. The second volume, W.A.B. Douglas, *The Creation of a National Air Force* (UTP, 1986) includes chapters on the British Commonwealth Air Training Plan, home operations and the RCAF role in the Battle of the Atlantic. Spencer Dunmore and William Carter, *Reap The Whirlwind* (McClelland & Stewart, 1991) provides a well written account of No. 6 Bomber Group, RCAF.

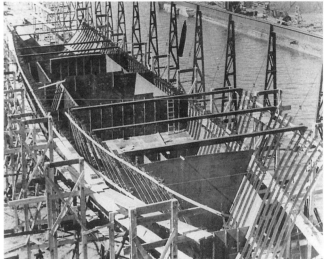

Of the large number of other air histories, Larry Milbery and Hugh Halliday, *The Royal Canadian Air Force At War 1939-1945* (Toronto: CANAV Books, 1990) is the best book to begin with. Their selected bibliography offers a guide to books on the RCAF. Carl Christie, *Ocean Bridge* (University of Toronto Press, 1995) tells the story of Ferry Command, while Arthur Bishop, *The Splendid Hundred* (Toronto: McGraw-Hill Ryerson, 1995) describes the Canadian pilots who fought in the Battle of Britain. Murray Peden's *A Thousand Shall Fall* (Stittsville, Ont.: Canada's Wings, 1979) remains the best memoir by a RCAF bomber pilot.

The army has been the subject of hundreds of books and only a few can be mentioned here. The three-volume official history, C.P. Stacey *Six Years of War* (Ottawa: Queen's Printer, 1957) (which includes good accounts of Dieppe and Hong Kong), G.W.L. Nicholson, *The Canadians in Italy 1943-45* and C.P. Stacey, *The Victory Campaign: The Operations in North-West Europe* are out of print but available in libraries. For the Italian campaign Farley Mowat, *The Regiment* (McClelland & Stewart, 1955) and his very different version of the same events

Corvette construction at Collingwood, Ontario. The top photo shows HMCS *Battleford*'s keel, October 3, 1940. In the next photo, the framing of HMCS *Barrie* is well advanced and bulkheads are in place, July 16, 1940. At the bottom, HMCs *Galt* is shown from astern, October 3, 1940, with the main deck nearly plated in and framing in place for the raised forecastle.

And No Birds Sang (McClelland & Stewart, 1979) are a good place to begin. Daniel Dancocks, *The D-Day Dodgers* (McClelland & Stewart, 1991) combines good anecdotal material with a clear narrative. Dominick Graham and Shelford Bidwell, *Tug of War: The Battle for Italy, 1943-45* (New York: St. Martin's Press, 1985) integrates the Canadian story into the overall campaign. *Canadian Military History,* the bi-annual journal, published a special issue on the fiftieth anniversary of the beginning of the campaign. Copies are still available from Wilfrid Laurier University. War artist Charles Comfort's *Artist at War* (first published 1956; second edition Pender Island, B.C.: Remembrance Books, a division of Log House Publishing Co. Ltd., 1995) and is highly recommended.

The role of the Canadian army in northwest Europe is analyzed in John A. English, *The Canadian Army in the Normandy Campaign* (London: Praeger, 1990). Another view is presented in Terry Copp and Robert Vogel, *Maple Leaf Route,* 5 Vols. (Alma, Ont: Maple Leaf Route, 1983-1988). Terry Copp, *The Brigade: The Fifth Canadian Infantry Brigade 1939-1945* (Stoney Creek, Ont.: Fortress Publications, 1992) further develops the case for the military effectiveness of the Canadian and Allied armies. *Canadian Military History* also published anniversary issues on the campaign in northwest Europe. For a complimentary copy, write to *CMH*, Wilfrid Laurier University, Waterloo, Ont. N2L 3C5.

Denis and Shelagh Whitaker's books, *Tug of War: The Canadian Victory That Opened Antwerp* (Toronto: Stoddart, 1984); *Rhineland: The Battle to End the War* (London: Leo Cooper, 1989) and *Dieppe: Tragedy to Triumph* (McGraw-Hill Ryerson, 1992) are all based on extensive research, including hundreds of interviews. Of the

books dealing with special topics, Wilfred I. Smith, *Code Word Canloan* (Toronto: Dundurn Press, 1992), Terry Copp and Bill McAndrew, *Battle Exhaustion: Soldiers and Psychiatrists in the Canadian Army 1939-1945* (McGill-Queen's University Press, 1990) and J.L. Granatstein, *The Generals: The Canadian Army's Senior Commanders in the Second World War* (Stoddart, 1994) are recommended. David Bercuson, *Battalion of Heroes* (Calgary: Calgary Highlanders Regimental Funds Foundation, 1994) tells the story of the Calgary Highlanders. Other regimental histories likely to appeal to the general reader include George Cassidy, *Warpath: The Story of the Algonquin Regiment* (1948, reprinted Cobalt, Ont.: Highway Book Shop, 1990) and Geoff Hayes, *The Lincs: The Lincoln and Welland Regiment at War* (Maple Leaf Route, 1986). Charles Martin, *Battle Diary* (Dundurn Press, 1994) is an engaging personal account of the campaign.

The Canadian Battle of Normandy Foundation and Wilfrid Laurier University have published two battlefield guides which combine history with touring information: Terry Copp, *A Canadian's Guide to the Battlefield of Normandy* (1994) and *A Canadian's Guide to the Battlefields of Northwest Europe* (1995).

Troops of the 49th (West Riding) Division, which served with First Canadian Army in northwest Europe, in a damaged factory building at Arnhem.

INDEX

About the Authors

TERRY COPP is professor of history at Wilfrid Laurier University and the author of a number of books about the Canadian military in the Second World War. He has recently published two guidebooks to the Canadian battlefields in Normandy and northwest Europe. Professor Copp is the editor of the biannual journal *Canadian Military History* and served as the historical consultant for the *No Price Too High* television series.

RICHARD NIELSEN's career in Canadian television began in 1961 when he joined the CBC as a producer–writer, and then became executive producer in Public Affairs. From 1972 to the present, he has worked as an independent producer as president of Nielsen-Ferns (1972–80), chairman of Primedia Productions (1980–85) and since 1985 as president of Norflicks Productions Ltd. His screen credits as a producer include *A Third Testament, The Newcomers/Les Arrivants* and *The Wars,* a feature film that won three Genie Awards in 1981. His credits as a writer–producer include *Canada's Sweetheart, The Saga of Hal Banks,* which won a Gemini Award for best screenplay, and the recently released feature film *Oh, What a Night.* He co-authored the script of the series *No Price Too High* with James Wallen and produced the series.